THE
ART OF
VICTORY

Strategies for
Personal Success and
Global Survival
in a Changing
World

GREGORY R. COPLEY

THRESHOLD
EDITIONS

New York   London   Toronto   Sydney

THRESHOLD EDITIONS
A Division of Simon & Schuster, Inc.
1230 Avenue of the Americas
New York, NY 10020

First Threshold Editions trade paperback edition September 2007

THRESHOLD EDITIONS and colophon are trademarks of Simon & Schuster, Inc.

Designed by William Ruoto

Manufactured in the United States of America

10 9 8 7 6 5 4 3 2 1

Library of Congress Cataloging-in-Publication Data

Copley, Gregory R.
    The art of victory : strategies for success and survival in a changing world / by Gregory R. Copley.
        p. cm.
    Includes bibliographical references.
    1. Social evolution. 2. Globalization. I. Title.

HM626.C67 2006
303.48'2—dc22

For information about special discounts for bulk purchases, please contact Simon & Schuster Special Sales at 1-800-456-6798 or business@simonandschuster.com.

ISBN-13: 978-1-4165-2470-0
ISBN-10:   1-4165-2470-3
ISBN-13: 978-1-4165-2478-6 (pbk)
ISBN-10:   1-4165-2478-9 (pbk)

This work, and the original treatise on which it is based,
was made possible by, and is dedicated to,
my dear friend and guide, the late
Stefan T. Possony,
the greatest strategic philosopher of the twentieth century,
and to the loving kindness of my family,
Brian, Marjorie, and Howard Copley, and
my beloved wife, Pamela.

CONTENTS

PROLOGUE

The Emerging Global Revolution

Turn and take one last look around at your life, at the life we humans have built over the past few thousand years. It is already gone. The granite columns of antiquity remain, though they crumble, and humanity, more vast in its numbers, remembers little of its past. This great upheaval we see today is how the epochs change.

Our ego, our strong and vital sense of self, tells us that this era of change is different from all past human experience, that the future is unchartable and unmanageable. But that is not so. We can shape the future, as we have always done, perhaps more so now than ever before. There are golden times again for us to make.

And yet we are in the eye of the hurricane, an Age of Global Transformation, a pivotal time for humanity. The pace of change has been accelerating, and not just in science and technology: Human numbers are surging, and flooding into urban, mostly coastal, populations. As with organisms at any level, increasing the population within a confined space generates activity, friction, heat. We cling to the known world, but are also fixated by the promises and fears of the future. But we have forgotten that in the past mankind was more aware of the tools of survival with which nature equipped us.

It is approaching four decades since Alvin Toffler, in *Future Shock,* noted that humanity was entering an age when the pace, scale, and embracing nature of change would be overwhelming. Add to that the impact of compounded population growth, coupled with climate change. Little wonder that much of humanity feels a deep sense of unease, and searches for answers, though futurists John Naisbitt and Patricia Aburdene, writing in *Megatrends 2000* in 1990, optimistically forecast "a period of stunning technological innovation, unprecedented economic opportunity, surprising political reforms, and great cultural rebirth."

They were not wrong, but they foresaw only part of the emerging world.

There are indeed many reasons for optimism, but the obsession with current technology and with imagined future innovations obscures the fact that human nature itself has not changed. It is only when faced with great threats to our existence—or merely to our comfort—that we contemplate who we are, and what we must do to reach that promising future. And we have largely forgotten the implicit, innate laws of survival, which remain critical to our ability to cope with the massive change we now confront.

Man, unique among species, uses technology to improve his chances for survival. These tools enable, with increasing certainty, the existence of an ever-greater number of humans in an environment once only capable of supporting far fewer people. Massive population growth coupled with vast changes in weather and the globalization of communications and the tools of human interaction, such as computing, and abstraction and "remote engagement," have created vast swaths of people disconnected from any sense of the past, motivated solely by the present and self, yet with ready access to cheap technologies. Through such changes do we now see, for example, great tools in the hands of the historically illiterate. "Knowledge" has replaced wisdom.

This maelstrom, gathering pace over two centuries—like a burgeoning hurricane over the ocean—has obliterated from our consciousness the intrinsic principles of human societal survival. But the survival of our bloodlines and societies is our victory over nature and our rivals. The reality is that we have seen great change before. Not on the same scale. Not at the same speed. Not with the same glittering technologies. There are core principles—for the moment obscured by the accumulating detritus of centuries—which can allow us to find our horizons in this new age. They can give us comfort and direction, and enable us to control our own environment, as individuals and as societies.

Society has become, perhaps inescapably, obsessed with change and the fear that permanence is illusory, and that durable items and the structures of the past are but obstacles to our access to the future. But this obscures the reality that change is only possible because it builds on an historical base, a constantly expanding base, of lessons and evolving tools. There is an acceptance that calculators and computers have replaced the need to be able to do simple arithmetic. But what if everyone forgot the principles of mathematics? Even this would not present a problem until a crisis arose, but somewhere, someone has to understand how the process works; how the tools of society and victory were—and are—built. An understanding of that context builds confidence in facing future crises.

To control our own destinies, we need to reach back and rediscover the aspects of human nature which guide our survival instinct, and then apply this understanding to our Age of Global Transformation. This book, based on a considerably larger historical study I compiled for the intelligence and strategic policy community on the concepts and origins of victory, looks at how future trends—many even more surprising than those forecast by Toffler, Naisbitt, and Aburdene—are emerging. More important, it looks at how we can cope with these changes and master our own destiny.

This is not the work of a Nostradamus. It is based solely on some four decades of intelligence work, on observation, and on managing a complex information-gathering network with hundreds of field collectors and thousands of sources. It is the result of looking always to history, of functioning daily within an existing current intelligence apparatus, and of working over these decades with governments, institutions, and leaders in attempting to solve the major problems facing societies. What has become clear during that time is that out there are the answers to most of our challenges in a rapidly transforming world. These answers are in our genes and in our historical experience.

UNDERSTANDING HOW OUR PAST RELATES TO OUR FUTURE

We know that global warming threatens coastal environments and island communities around the world and the viability of life in regions like the arid lands of China's Xinjiang Province or Africa's Sahel. But we cannot know how aware the people of the lower Indus River Valley were that their world was changing as the last Ice Age drew to an end around 10000 B.C.E. By 8000 B.C.E, the major cities of the lower Indus Valley were beneath the sea. Higher up the Indus Valley, a number of major population centers continued to thrive for several thousand years after the last Ice Age, and archaeologists began in the twentieth century to probe their ruins and runes for the secrets of their civilization. Of greater significance, however, was the work begun at the dawn of the twenty-first century into the secrets of the cities that for ten millennia had lain hidden on the bed of the Arabian Sea.

Glaciers melted and the sea rose, in history's forgotten time before Egyptian pharaohs. The changes faced by the inhabitants of these cities were gradual. The waters lapped incessantly higher over the years. Societies had time to adjust, and to drift away to higher ground.

Even earlier, the development of human language was slow, haltingly and erratically enabling the development of concepts, because concepts require the use of words and definitions of things. This enabled mankind to move from nomadic hunter-gatherer tribes and clans to fixed locations, learning how to engage in agriculture. And as agriculture ensured consistent food supplies, towns and cities became feasible, emerging in the lower Indus Valley, and at Jericho and other locations in what is now Israel, Jordan, the Palestinian Authority, Syria, Iraq, and Lebanon. The transformation and urbanization of societies through agriculture moved slowly, steadily, and irrevocably, in most places, although some clans of hunter-gatherers ignored the transformation of humanity and persisted, even into the twenty-first century, in their nomadic way of life.

Society was again transformed with the explosion of literacy following the development of movable type and printing in 1450. The portability of knowledge caused by this development created new wealth and power. Those societies with widespread literacy and easily reproduced languages became prosperous and dominant.

Civilization profoundly altered direction yet again with the agricultural revolution of the eighteenth century, and then still more with the Industrial Revolution, which agriculture and urbanization had combined to create and which the growing complexity of human society had demanded.

All this is our heritage. But—our egos tell us—these upheavals are in the past, and we do not need to learn them again. We are different. The future is different. We have tamed change.

Or so the people living today in the shadow of Mount Vesuvius believe. No volcanic eruption will again rob them of their homes and lives. Despite the patterns of history, people are more densely packed into the towns beneath Vesuvius than at any other time in history, even though the mountain has erupted violently many times in recent centuries. The famous eruption occurred nearly two thousand years ago—it was in 79 C.E. that Pompeii and Herculaneum were swamped with lava and pyroclastic flows and with scalding ash—but it has erupted again about three dozen times since then, most recently in 1944.

Life changes constantly, and we still have not absorbed many of the changes which occurred even during the twentieth century.

After World War II, in the triumphant nations of the Allied West, a "baby boom" created a population bubble in the rich, industrialized societies. This demographic trend skewed and indeed paralyzed the economic and political thinking of our present generation. This moving demographic bloc of "baby boomers," who are now approaching retirement, will also pass. Yet few are thinking about the economic consequences beyond this blip. And what if once again totally new reproductive patterns transform the shape of societies? Certainly, China's one-child policy has already dramatically skewed the balance of sexes in the world's most populous nation, with as-yet-unknown—but significant—consequences.

Still we refuse to acknowledge the gravity of change. The tectonic shifts in history—the discovery of agriculture, the end of the Ice Age, and so on—affected everything from how wars were fought to who came to power, to how societies became prosperous.

The Art of Victory lies in understanding those laws of nature which are essentially immutable, and how these constants can be adapted to meet the turmoil of the changing world. Those societies and individuals which succeed do so by recognizing familiar paths through what appears to be an alien landscape of change. The laws of nature have not changed; we have gradually, throughout human development, discovered more and more of what nature has always held in store for us. But we have also forgotten some of the tools with which we were equipped to cope with change.

We are, in fact, better prepared to face the strange new gifts of science and the chaos of mass human concentrations than were the humans who faced the onset of the last Ice Age. And yet their survival forms the very basis of the victory we share today.

THE CONTEXT OF CHANGE

Strategic reality changes as the global context changes. *And we are now coming to a confluence of various strands of profound change.* We are on the brink of *a global shift of humanity* which has aspects in common with the end of the last Ice Age, an era which brought the birth of agriculture and the rise of towns and cities. Another great shift, with the introduction of mass literacy which followed the fifteenth-century development of movable type, then led us to the industrial and information revolutions.

Some shifts are decided by nature; some by human action. We are now engaged in a shift which is the result of the works of both nature and man.

Throughout this book we will explore these emerging trends, and the tools we need to discover, and rediscover, in order to cope with them. Let us, initially, look at a few of the major emerging trends.

CLIMATE AND POPULATION

The new global shift includes climatic and environmental change: new patterns of weather, rising sea levels, transformed ocean currents (further compounding the altered weather patterns), the creation of new areas of terrestrial aridity (and of areas of revived fertility and productivity), and so on. The shift will affect agricultural and habitat viability, with ramifications for political stability in many countries. This process has already begun, and the results are evident within our generation. The time scales of these changes are accelerating.

The new global transformation—the abyss as well as the sunlit upland into which we now stare—includes dramatic and epochal changes in population patterns: the first substantive reorientation of societies since the Middle Ages (which led to the age of colonial migration which essentially created our present global geopolitical shape). The new age of transformation—the result of the impact of technologies of transportation, computing, and mass communications, along with rising but unevenly distributed wealth—has caused a fluid and natural movement of large masses of people from low-opportunity areas to high-opportunity areas. This all changes the nature of sovereignty, the role of government, and the functioning of human mechanisms of choice (democracy in its formal and informal modes).

Along with the new technologies of transportation, computing, and communications, the blurring and loosening of artificial societal constraints embodied in the new globalism has created a surge of people from rural areas to coastal urban clusters on a more profound scale than even the gradual shift from hunter-gatherer nomadic tribes to agricultural settlements. This is particularly evident already in, for example, China, and will become increasingly evident in Africa, the South Asian Subcontinent, and the Americas.

At the same time, we are witnessing the first major

and progressive population declines in Europe and Africa in hundreds of years, the result of demographic aging and birth-rate patterns on the one hand, and disease and economic challenges on the other. We are also on the edge of the era in which mankind will move into the near-space environment—including operations on the moon—almost seamlessly, with impact in the coming decade on defense and transportation, as well as on the manufacture of specialty medicines, chemicals, and other items.

But it is also clear from history—from the era of the Black Death, particularly the lice-borne bubonic plague in Europe and Asia in 1347; from the flu epidemic which killed between 20 and 40 million people in 1918–19; from the AIDS pandemic of the late twentieth and early twenty-first centuries; and from the gathering avian flu epidemic of the early twenty-first century—that globalization will likely lead to sweeping pandemics with profound strategic consequences. Quite apart from the impact on demographics, which can distort economic models, disease can strike at the heart of victory. Napoleon Bonaparte would have created a Continental trading system excluding Britain if his 1812 invasion of Russia had succeeded. The impact on history would have been profound, and French could have been the *lingua franca* of the world today instead of English.

What defeated Napoleon, however, was not only the onset of an extreme winter in his invasion of Russia but—as has now been confirmed by exhumations in the early twenty-first century of the bodies of French Grand Army troops from mass graves—relapsing fevers transmitted by body lice.

And while the health of leaders, armies, and societies has always been a key determinant in history, perhaps the most challenging and overlooked issue facing societies today is the question of population. Not only has the population growth become an issue of profound importance when considering infrastructure and human needs, but globalization has ensured that the phenomenon of population movement and loyalty has, for the first time, become something which must be considered in an entirely new light. "Population strategies" —which at their core cover the concept of building viable, committed societies operating within new hierarchical frameworks—will become the major challenge for governments in the twenty-first century.

THE CREATION OF MILITANT SOCIETIES

Change, chaos, and anomie—of which terrorism and alienation within society are but symptoms—will lead rapidly during the coming decade or two to a reactive period of increasing and near-universal militarization and militancy. Where this does not occur, civilizations will perish or erode still further. And the companion of the militarization of society will be increasing "political correctness." In both its formal sense (militarization or increasing governmental control) and its informal sense (societally dictated or "fashionable"—actually regimented and militant—attitudes about what is acceptable), this is a normal coping mechanism of society to assert control over change; to reassert balance.

Only as political, social, and security situations stabilize will the apparent threats fade, and life—as it did in the 1960s and 1970s and briefly in the 1990s—relax.

This is not a call to arms, a suggestion that such militancy should happen; that alarm has already been sounded by the chaos of change. This study is a call to understand what it means and how to survive the change, to prosper, and to emerge victorious.

THE MILITARIZATION OF SPACE . . . AND CHINA IS IN THE LEAD

The question of the militarization of space is no longer open. Space is, and will increasingly be, militarized. Not all of this activity will be offensive in nature: Apart from contributions to science, space holds the key to neutralizing offensive strategic ballistic missiles and their nuclear or other strategic payloads. Dr. Stefan Possony, the great strategist, and Ronald Reagan—even before he became president in 1981—saw the promise of such a system, which would have been controlled by a consortium of all the major powers and would have effectively neutralized strategic ballistic missiles. Few people saw far enough into the future to realize that this system could have brought benefits to all of humanity by making nuclear war less feasible.

Today, in any event, and even without the Strategic Defense Initiative (SDI) envisioned by Possony and embraced by Reagan, we are witnessing the end of the viability of nuclear weapons. They are—as has been the case with all weapons throughout history—being overtaken by other technologies. Nanotechnologies, for example, will help make *anti*-ballistic-missile technology vastly more efficient, rendering the crude, rocket-borne weapons of mass destruction impotent. Ballistic missiles will never, with certainty, arrive at their targets, and the bluff of the states which have gambled on nuclear weapons will have been called. Moving beyond that, nanotechnologies will themselves be the basis for offensive capabilities to neutralize command and control systems, perhaps to paralyze an opponent's infrastructure. But nanotechnologies will in turn create countermeasures: Within the framework of nanotechnology itself, offensive capabilities will develop and so will hardened defensive capabilities.

Apart from nanotechnologies, other sciences envisioned for SDI are now becoming feasible: space-based, energy-derived weapons—including automatically directed lasers—able to destroy nuclear-tipped ballistic weapons as they reach into space at their apogee, before they have the chance to descend on their targets. This capability, envisioned at the beginning of the 1970s, was decried by many scientists of the day as impossible, just as human flight was ridiculed, along with space travel and submarine warfare.

But even if we were merely to extend our present capabilities in a linear fashion, terrestrially based anti-ballistic-missile systems have already made problematic the success of North Korean and Iranian ballistic missiles. The greatest potency which lingers for those nuclear weapons held by "rogue states" lies in their psychological impact. Our collective minds are held captive by icons of the past. Science has already moved on, even if many scientists and politicians have not.

TRANSFORMED ENERGY, FOOD, AND WATER PRODUCTION

The emerging new technologies and scientific, chemical, and biological breakthroughs, which will radically affect all human life, include developments in nanotechnology which will transform food production and fuel efficiencies and, indeed, the very question of what constitutes fuel. New, safe nuclear energy technologies—which do not pose the same risks as current approaches in terms of waste material or the ability to produce weapons-grade by-products—are on the brink of viability. These will further transform and revitalize the human ability to harness power for industry and for the desalination and movement of clean water, as well as reducing emissions from fossil fuels.

In the late twentieth century we were contemplating the finite life of energy resources; now we need not. We were contemplating the finite availability of safe drinking and agricultural water, and of food; now we need not. The Age of Biology is also now full upon us, and once again the farmers will provide renewable fuels for motive power: not hay for horses, this time, but cornstalks and other agricultural products to transform into ethanol. Agricultural powers once again will control their own destinies, free from hostage dependency on imported oil.

This comes just in time for the United States, for example, which is now in the last great fight for domination of the fossil fuel marketplace. It is gradually losing its dominance over that arena, but no matter: The loss of dominance over world oil resources impels the United States to ensure the smooth transition to an age dominated not by fossil fuels, but by biofuels and other energies. But the energy business—possibly the biggest single economic factor in the world today—is like a supertanker; slow to change course. And it never will change course until it sights a reef and the captain gives the order. The reef is already in sight.

PRODUCTIVE SOCIETIES SURRENDERING TO UNPRODUCTIVE SOCIETIES?

We know that science and technology allow us to take control of our destiny; to avoid, for example, the entanglements the pursuit of oil has brought. But have we the strength to grasp our destiny in our own hands? Or is it possible that we could succumb, through loss of will, to a new dark age before we can actually bring these stunning scientific breakthroughs into use? We know that we are now in an age where, once again, new states will be born, and others will die. It is up to us to choose whether to be part of the rebirth of a society or part of the slow and geriatric failing and death of one.

Lenin once said that the capitalist West would one day bid to supply the rope for its own hanging. As it transpired, the communists were not around when the time came to call for bids on the rope. Today, the productive nations of the world (the ones which produce and export food surpluses, technologically value-added goods, and services) may squabble among themselves, but their challenge comes almost solely from societies in which the people produce nothing of benefit to their fellow humans. And yet these unproductive societies are using the cheaply acquired technologies of the productive societies against them.

Think of these challengers to the industrial societies: Almost all of them produce nothing of a value-added nature. Some of them may sell oil, or coca leaf, or opium and cocaine, but this is an accident of geography, not a feat of scientific or technological progress by those from whose lands the oil and narcotics flow. Yet today, all of the efforts by the industrial world are focused on the demands of people who choose not to cherish education and productivity, the tools of survival and prosperity.

In less than a century, the oil-producing states of the Middle East will have nothing of great importance to sell unless they become diversified economies. Oil, by then, will be a minor fuel. We will look back on them as we did, with bemusement, on the salt sellers of yore, or the dealers in tulip bulbs in seventeenth-century Holland. To our detriment, we still focus our attention on the price of oil. To *their* detriment, the oil-producing states of the Middle East fail to move their societies to literacy, science, and production.

AN AGE OF SAVAGE WARS AND GLOBAL CRIMINALS

Few people today are familiar with many of the countries which existed only, say, three hundred years ago, except for the major players: France, Britain, Russia, and so on. Italy did not then exist as a sovereign state; nor did the United States of America, or Germany. And more countries will appear or disappear in the next few decades. Wars of secession, and the reshaping of boundaries—largely suppressed by the Cold War—begin anew. The wars to break up Yugoslavia are still not over. And in many of the new wars we will see a resurgence of savagery as groups "rediscover" old identities and seek to capitalize on the permissive climate of change and chaos.

Many of the superficial old "man-made" rules don't apply any more. We are back to the basic yet exceptionally sophisticated rules of survival logic with which nature equipped us. But who, today, in a world made abstract by technology and man-made constructs, has given any thought to what they are?

From this turmoil we also already see the rise of new global criminal movements benefiting from the globalization of technologies and societies. The international banking constraints imposed to restrict terrorists have not hampered the new, more vicious criminal movements. In all of these, the Albanian criminals have displaced the old Sicilians, and are sweeping aside even their old partners, the Turks. If the twentieth century was the criminal age of the Sicilian mafia; the twenty-first century is the age of the Albanian mafia. Even the Russian mafia, let loose after the collapse of communism, is no match for the Albanian criminal industry, which is now operating across Europe and into the Americas, closely tied to the Islamist jihadists. In many respects, the Al Qaeda phenomenon owes its success to the financial links with the Albanian mafia, just as the Albanian criminals owe their success to the logistics and networks of Al Qaeda.

The chaos of changing borders is fertile ground for criminality. In the coming decades there will be more and more "no go" areas in the world. And this is partly the reason why some societies will react with greater militarization and rigidity. In many respects, the terror has just begun. Criminal states, such as the Kosovo Albanian "state," could profoundly change our sense of security. Kosovo was by 2006 already a semistate where international peacekeepers went in fear, and yet it petitioned for international recognition as a sovereign state. Already it is becoming like Afghanistan under the Taliban. And like the Taliban destruction of the ancient Buddhas of Bamiyan, the Albanian Islamist process of destruction of the Christian churches will be complete, and Western civilization will be gone from a large part of the Balkans.

In its place will be a criminal terrorist state, leaching into the heart of Europe. And it was made feasible by the short-term policies of many European and U.S. politicians of the 1990s, who allowed the breakup of the former Yugoslavia to be engineered without thought to how, if it was indeed necessary, it could be undertaken without the chaos, heartbreak, and enduring hatreds that ensued.

Those who think that the creation of a spreading Albanian state across what was once the Yugoslav federation will occur without major reactions from within the region are mistaken. We will all feel the reverberations over the coming decade.

Not "Clashes of Civilizations," But New Civilizations Defined

Some were also contemplating "clashes of civilizations." It becomes increasingly clear, however, that while societies still search for separate and distinct identities and horizons, we also acknowledge that all members of the species Homo sapiens are fundamentally alike and related by common ancestry. Our view of racial differences, which has been a driving force in human history, is now being changed by scientific research and population movement. This is unlikely to stop conflict over racial and cultural issues, but globalism is indeed changing how ethnic and communal nations interact.

So what divides us will continue to be the essence of conflict. Still, within the competition between societies— and by societies, I mean essentially cultural/historical amalgams—the underlying thread that mankind is competing for survival with the rest of nature will come again to the fore. In the "peace" and prosperity which followed the titanic confrontations which were the hallmark of the twentieth century, the smug, safe, secure modern states embarked upon the divisive social policy of "multiculturalism," which created, essentially, substates of communities within states.

"Multiculturalism" in its current fashionable form has created fundamental disunity in states. For the modern host nations, the policy was not to "divide and conquer" opposing societies; it was to ingest them into modern societies, to "divide and surrender." By consciously embracing multiculturalism, we deliberately rejected nation building, and nation building was seen—in the last decade of the twentieth century and first decade of the twenty-first century—as anathema to short-term economic gain. But nation building—perhaps in new forms—is what is being undertaken by those societies which seek to end the long victory of the West.

Why should we be surprised, then, when national unity—already pressured by globalization—fails? That is not to deny the cultural heritages of the many, diverse peoples composing the modern nation-state; rather, it is critical to place this rich cultural tapestry within the context of nation building.

This new era of change will affect how we must regard our processes of society, sovereignty, government, defense, intelligence, trade, science, and technology. Clearly, the short-, medium-, and long-term economic trends are directly affected by all of this. Our jobs, our security—the value of everything we pass to future generations—is intrinsically tied to this great evaluation. It is only when we confront ourselves with such introspection, at such a time as this, that we realize we must reconsider our positions on almost everything.

THE TOOLS ARE IN OUR HEARTS AND MINDS

We cannot decide *anything* without contemplating the impact of the emerging contextual changes. We will look both at the context of the changes we face and at how societies have historically either survived and prospered or failed, particularly during times of global transformation. It is no accident that some individuals, organizations, and societies triumph over nature, and over other individuals, organizations, and societies. It is the Art of Victory.

A CONTEXT OF VICTORY

We cannot fail to see that our strategic context has changed, and will change again, and more rapidly, over the coming decades. How do we cope, adapt, thrive? What is the context for victory? Clearly, it will all get down to understanding ourselves and our societies, and understanding our environment, and determining how to act upon this knowledge.

The world is divided into only two camps: one which believes we must take responsibility for defining our future, and one which clings to the hope that someone or something else will take care of our safety and welfare. Most of us have a foot in both camps, but lean more one way than the other. The first group retains a more primal comprehension of species survival; the second wants no sacrifice in the standard of living and wealth which our forebears created. The meek shall inherit the earth? Sure; inheritance is the only way they'll get it. The rest of us have to work for our survival and independence.

Even so, many of the things which affect us are beyond our control: the last Ice Age and its effects; the current exponential growth in human population; and many aspects of the current global warming pattern—akin to the end of the last Ice Age—which may (or may not) result in part from the growth in human numbers and activity. How we react to things not of our making will decide whether we survive and prosper. Those who wait for someone else—government or God—to resolve the problems will be in for an unhappy time. Nature—God, if you prefer—has already given us the tools to survive against the threats of man and the environment. We just need to use them.

Within the framework defined for us by nature, history's path and the fate of peoples turn often upon a chance—its weight unrealized at the moment—seized by a single leader. Such a vital watershed occurred on October 14, 1066. It was a day, in autumnal England, of bloody, intense blackness which was later seen to have marked the end of a long night of civilizational stasis. The decisive—though narrowly won—military triumph by Duke William of Normandy on this day was to become one of the pivotal acts in transforming Europe and in ensuring the resumption of the rise of Western civilization. It was a civilization which had its origin in the mists of the Hellenic city-states and Roman modernism and the deeper recesses of Persian philosophy. But it had fallen into five centuries of darkness, ignorance, and chaos.

It was on October 14, 1066, that the invading Normans—a mere sesquicentury removed from their own departure in 911 from the Norse regions of Denmark—conquered the English forces near Hastings, in the south of England.

It was an invasion in which the conquerors, despite their ultimate impact on the course of history, were themselves soon absorbed into the land and culture (also predominantly Norse) which they had invaded. Their French language was preserved for a time, but only in the sovereign's court, and ultimately gave way altogether to the living, expanding idiom of English, which consumed much of the French language to satisfy its voracity for exploration and expansion.

A day's battle—the chance seized—was the catalyst for the transformation of civilization. Nothing has since been the same.

Western civilization, a millennium after the events of 1066, has grown into "modern civilization," embracing and engulfing beliefs, cultures, and nations, virtually all with hitherto incompatible and conflicting needs, aspirations, and geographical realities.

And yet humanity moves—societies and individuals move—from day to day, generation to generation, without weighing the motivation for their progress, or considering the extension of their goals and imperatives into the infinite future. The survival of the human species, and its individual societies, cultures, languages, beliefs, and dominance over the landscape, is taken for granted. History tells us that no species is immune from obliteration; no culture, language, ethnic community, nation, or belief system is guaranteed its survival. Yet we fail to learn from history. We know that the Neandertals are no more. We know that the languages and beliefs of ancient Egypt are gone beneath the sands, interpreted—as the writings of the Sumerian scribes and poets of ramparted Uruk—from fragmentary scripts chiseled into weathered stone.

Still we persist in the belief in the inevitable linear progress and dominance of our own cultures, tribes, religions, and languages. But this belief is without the foundation of a structure or conscious process to ensure the survival of those things which we hold most dear, which define our existence and purpose.

The survival and dominance of a society through history is its principal victory. As with the chance triumph of Duke William of Normandy at the Battle of Hastings, the fate of civilizations turns on unexpected things. The languages we speak, the generations which may—or, in defeat, may not—follow our family line, the welfare we enjoy: all hang upon pivotal events but must be confirmed and compounded by the consciously defined processes of history.

More than two centuries after the Norman Conquest of England, the Mongol leader Khubilai Khan—the grandson of the greatest conqueror of them all, Genghis Khan—mounted his second attempt to invade Japan. The Mongols, in three generations, had already conquered much of the Eurasian landmass, including China. Had the conquest of Japan succeeded and had Khubilai Khan lived long enough to restore the unity won by his grandfather to the Mongol leaders, it is possible that a fourth generation of Genghis Khan's heirs would have ultimately expanded, once again, in the main direction open to them: westward, further into Europe. But even they, for logistical reasons, would have had to rethink the process of their spectacular victory to that point and change their strategies to adapt to different geography.

Many factors spelled an end to what had seemed an inexorable expansion of the Mongol world, but had it continued we would have been living in a history developed far differently, an Eastern victory. As it chanced, the Mongol attempt to invade Japan failed, in large part due to one variable which still eludes the control of man: the weather. Khubilai Khan died soon thereafter. The Mongol empire, which rose from nothing to become the world's greatest power under Genghis Khan—and expanded still further under his sons and grandsons—transformed, in the period following the "globalization of Genghis Khan," into new, sedentary powers which existed until the nineteenth and twentieth centuries. The shape of the modern world was created by the conquest in 1066 of England, which prospered as a result of the massive upheaval—and then the settlement of nations and societies into new patterns—begun by Genghis Khan.

So much of the destiny of humanity hangs on what we do every day. The least we can do is to understand what led us here, what ensures our societal future, and how we can ensure that this future—if it indeed is to exist—is in the image we wish it to be.

This is the Art of Victory. So let's examine twenty-eight maxims which can provide the underpinnings of victory; how they have related historically, and how—when applied practically to everyday life and government today—they gird us for tomorrow's fray. These maxims, at the head of each chapter, are meant to highlight an underlying factor in the achievement of victory, certainly on a societal level, but also with a strong applicability to the individual.

DEFINING VICTORY

ONE

Victory is the principal goal of a society and the
first responsibility of the state, because only in
victory is survival possible.

I t is when desperation is in the air that survival is gauged
day by day, hour by hour. But to ensure survival decade
by decade, generation by generation, epoch by epoch:
there is the measure of skill. Individuals, organizations, and
societies, under threat to their continued existence, will do
anything to survive in almost any form. To survive victorious, however, is a matter of planning. It's not just about life
and death on the battlefield; we can see parallels in our immediate economic and social framework. Few modern examples illustrate the case better—as a case of corporate
survival—than the fight for survival between the U.S. automaker Chrysler and the German automaker Daimler Benz.
They joined in May 1998 in a $36-billion "merger of
equals" to create a global conglomerate—with some $150
billion a year in sales—called DaimlerChrysler.

It quickly became obvious that the "merger of equals"
was nothing of the sort; it was a takeover of Chrysler by
Daimler Benz. But what has never been discussed was the
reality that it was a fight for existence by both giant corporations. Both were in difficult circumstances; both faced
the reality that, absent some transforming catalyst, their
best years were behind them and they were now fighting
for sustainability. They were, for a variety of reasons, geri-

atric corporations. Chrysler was the weaker, more desperate party in the "merger"—and subsequently lost its birthright to Daimler—but it was Chrysler which had the longer-term strengths, and could have transformed the situation to its benefit. The difference, and the reason Daimler prevailed, lay in psychological factors: In terms of leadership, will, and self-perception, it was Daimler which had dominance.

In fundamental terms, Chrysler was an aging, and in some senses sclerotic, company, operating in a vibrant, flexible home marketplace. Daimler Benz was a more vibrant and self-assured company, operating in a moribund and increasingly stifling economic system.

The post–World War II economic miracle had led both Daimler Benz and Chrysler—along with the German and U.S. economies—into great indulgences. The seemingly unending, albeit bumpy, upward spiral of well-being led companies and governments into making long-term commitments of hypothetical future wealth to pension funds and locked-in labor-management practices. While the commitments to these schemes were long term and inflexible, the market and the realities of changing technologies were anything but constant. The difference, however, was that while the situation was set in concrete in Germany, it was merely set in clay in the United States.

True, the clay around the U.S. automakers was more firm than that in much of the rest of the American economy, but Chrysler, like most U.S. corporations, had means to either rapidly or gradually change its circumstances. In Germany, with the entrenched links of the state to the economy, the concrete was seemingly indissoluble. Even in 2005, with massive economic and unemployment problems evident, the German electorate still could not bring itself to vote decisively for structural reform, preferring slumbering narcosis until the pension checks bounced.

Daimler Benz was increasingly constrained, following the end of the Cold War in 1990, by German labor laws, which limited its growth and forced its continued commitment to often unproductive labor practices. But the company's substantial wealth enabled it to act before German and European Union laws transformed it into an irrelevant relic of the past. Daimler Benz—already deeply familiar with the global market—found the right vehicle to escape the constraints of calcified German social legislation: It acquired a substantial, but seemingly weaker or more desperate, non-European automaker through merger. By absorbing Chrysler, Daimler Benz was able to operate in the more liberal U.S. economic environment and grow outside the constraints of German productivity limitations. In essence, Daimler Benz moved its financial center of gravity out of the German economic morass, and into the United States. Chrysler might have felt constrained at the time by its own problems with labor and commitments to expensive pension and health schemes, but the company had enormous flexibility and potential simply because of its more liberal operating environment.

Daimler Benz's inherent skills were able to blossom at Chrysler, and the U.S. part of the company certainly made progress in quality and vitality through the merger. But Chrysler rapidly began to lose its own corporate identity and corporate culture. It lost its ability to determine the strategic direction of its own life. The DaimlerChrysler example is not isolated; the once German government-owned Deutsche Post—the German Post Office, which also owns Postbank—acquired U.S. parcel carrier DHL in 2002 for the same reason and created a $58-billion (2004 sales) global enterprise. Deutsche Post, in 2005, noted on its website: "It's been 10 years since Deutsche Post was organized as a stock corporation. An unbelievable amount has happened since then. The then purely 'German' Post rose from being a deficit-ridden government institution to be-coming a highly profitable global player active in over 220 countries and employing more than 380,000." In September 2005, Deutsche Post spent $8.5 billion to acquire Exel, Britain's largest warehouse and delivery company.

In essence, the German economy outsourced itself to remain viable. The globalization of economic modalities has empowered this destruction of the power of "fixed governments."

U.S. companies also outsource their production to foreign workplaces to escape the labor and pension commitments they had earlier made. The difference, however, is that the U.S. companies have the ability themselves to begin changing the way they do business at home; German companies are prisoners of a legislated economic framework which removes their ability to resolve their domestic practices. And the beneficiaries of the old profligacy are unlikely to vote to change the situation, even though it spells the eventual death of their national viability.

Survival, then, must look beyond immediate gratification; it must look to future generations, because, ultimately, what drives us as humans individually or collectively is that we must ensure that our legacy endures. It's what inspires human reproduction and the whole of our striving for achievement. Moreover, we are subconsciously aware that survival is impossible without control over our own destiny. This is victory.

THE CONSTANT WARRIOR

Victory, then, is infinitely more important than war and peace. Without victory—victory over nature, victory over adversaries, victory over self, victory over ignorance—a society fades to extinction. Mankind can tolerate the uncertainties and costs of conflict, but without victory there is no lasting peace, or any real peace at all: no prosperity, no control over destiny, no guarantee of survival. Victory in its essence *is* the survival of the species.

Victory is the goal of life and therefore ultimately of the whole range of human emotions and skills; it is a genetic imperative within the essence of each individual human being: to survive, dominate, perpetuate, grow. Society's evolution into sophisticated, complex structures has made abstract some aspects of this natural life force, but all human progress derives from the visceral will to victory. Power, prosperity, justice, religion, sovereignty, and the perpetuation of the species all derive from the natural urge to victory.

Victory, therefore, is eternal; its achievement or loss directs and contours forever the destiny of every society. Victory is not just "winning." Winning—when viewed down the silent, windswept plains of history—is tactical, a phenomenon which is, by definition, explosive, transitory, and ephemeral. Victory is slow-burning, overarching, and transcendent. Victory requires, however, that goals be continually won or achieved. It is neither a permanent nor a secure phenomenon. Society too often mistakes the process of conquest for victory itself, which is the sustained delivery of a complex pattern of successes. To be victorious, then, implies the command of an epoch and the fundamental alteration of history, personal or societal. While a single success or defeat may affect history, victory—whether eventually undone or not—marks the path of a society or of mankind.

The survival instinct is written within the genetic code of all species. Darwin called it "the survival of the fittest." And we are all consciously aware of this competitive aspect of natural behavior, both in individuals and in groups. Our sense of justice and injustice is based on intellectual interpretation of our quest for survival, which is expressed in the will to victory. However, as human society has evolved, the understanding of the complexity of survival and victory has broadened beyond the narrow definitions of "survival of the fittest."

This sense of victory is expressed and believed as a right to survive. Those who are cowed physically, intellectually, and emotionally (whether as individuals or as societies) into feeling unworthy of victory are acquiescing in their own demise. Yet as we know, this is a situation which can be transformed by circumstance and motivation.

Our "right to survive"—that is, the "right to victory"— is perceived as just and inalienable. The denial of this "right" is therefore unjust. Collectively, our sense of the importance of communal survival is expressed as a "just cause," and we extend this understanding to those who we collectively feel contribute to the perpetuation of our line. Achieving it requires social interaction: the creating of family units, and the producing of progeny, which in turn require access to a large pool of strong potential mates. Thus, victory is ultimately a collective endeavor, which in turn demands teamwork.

This teamwork extends down the generations, consolidating and building, ebbing and flowing, depending for success on how well it creates powerful tools of language (communication) and dominance. This is the essence of the rise and fall of nations.

WILL CHINA'S VALUES REPLACE THOSE OF THE WEST?

China understands victory, yearns for it, and works for it. And it has embarked on the gamble to achieve it. But victory is not a matter of population numbers. For centuries, in fact, China's massive population has worked against its chances of success. Powers with relatively small populations—Rome, Britain, the Mongols, the Hejazis, and so on—dominated in their day vast tracts of humanity.

China is doing all the things it needs to do to achieve global dominance within, say, thirty to fifty years, but it nonetheless embarked on a high-risk course to achieve it after the death of Mao and Maoism. It remains a high-risk process for China, despite the remarkable achievements it has made, largely because of the challenges which nature and population shifts impose.

The next few decades will see many nations competing against nature, against and within themselves, and against each other. Hurricane Katrina, in the southern United States in August and September 2005, showed Americans how fragile is mankind's success against nature. But within human societies we can see, in the formative first decade of the twenty-first century, the races underway in China, India, and Iran, not to mention the United States and the European Union. In the case of China—one of the most dramatic examples—it is not primarily a race between China and the West. It is a race to determine whether China can succeed in controlling its own destiny or will implode politically and socially due to an exhaustion of natural resources and the ability to manage a population undergoing profound changes.

China's massive economic and strategic growth since the end of the Cold War in 1990 was based on two things: the liberalization of the marketplace, with the attendant restoration to the Chinese people of the ability to follow their fundamental and inherent democratic urge toward self-organization and the determination of their own fortunes, and the employment of the massive pool of labor to produce low value-added consumer goods for the export market. The inherent problem is that the production base demanded a massive input of raw materials—petrochemicals for plastics-based goods, wood for products and infrastructure, cement, water, and the like.

In the space of about a decade, much of the Chinese countryside was laid waste and became less productive as it was overfarmed or denuded of trees. Populations, too, began their surging move toward the cities and the coast. Global warming, coinciding with the pollution generated by strip mining and coal-fired and relatively crude energy production, saw a decline in snowfall in the Tien Shan (and other) mountain ranges of Central Asia. This snowfall had fed the aquifers and rivers of Xinjiang and other areas of the region; and some inland rivers are now dead or dying. China, in some important areas, is running out of water. Some significant parts of its arable hinterland have dissolved into Haitilike landscapes; the initial signs are that its population is becoming increasingly less controllable within huge urban groupings, in which frustrations will rise. The coastal infrastructure will be challenged by rising sea levels as global warming increases, as it seems set to do.

The Chinese leadership is aware of the challenges and of the race. It has committed to a massive program of construction of nuclear power generators, envisaging widely dispersed, new-technology, pebble-bed modular reactors which will replace some of the dependence on coal, and which will also be useable in water desalination. Indeed, China may pave the way in demonstrating that dispersed arrays of nuclear reactors will mean that the old grid of power distribution cables and towers become a thing of the past, but the new "national grid" will comprise networks of water pipelines. Even with regard to coal use, it is looking increasingly to new techniques to make coal a more viable, clean fuel.

China is also attempting to move away from a low-value-added/high-resource-content production economy and to become more balanced, with a shift to high-value-added/low-resource-content production. This, too, might help China past the current headlong rush toward environmental and human disaster and into the sunshine of an advanced and balanced economy.

India, on the other hand, had focused its economic growth during the years of the late twentieth and early twenty-first centuries on high-value-added/low-resource-content production, and achieved remarkable results. However, this move had not spread the economic wealth to a sufficient number of voters—despite the overall statistical growth of the Indian economy as a whole—and the BJP-led government was voted out of office in 2004. The Congress (I) Party which replaced the BJP recognized that it must spread the wealth if it was to remain in office.

Its answer must be to move to a low-value-added/high-resource-content production base like China's, while retaining its high-tech industries. Thus, India will become the next big consumer of oil, gas, minerals, cement, timber, and the like. The questions which face us, then, are whether India can achieve its economic and national goals without entering the same crisis which faces China, and whether China can win its own race to escape the consequences of the Pandora's Box which leader Deng Xiaoping opened in the 1980s after the death of Chairman Mao Zedong and the end of the rigidly unproductive communist centralized control.

Within all of this lies the question of how we, in our respective societies, grasp our own victory. Victory over self is the prerequisite for victory within broader human history.

What we must determine is how we step onto the path toward achieving or retaining victory.

Embarking on the Path to Victory

Victory begins with a single act, and may begin to be unraveled by a single event, but it is only built and defended through generations of separate, patient, and conscious actions.

It may be easier to embark on the path to victory than to find the path again once it has been lost, or taken for granted. Western society, in many respects, has lost the passion for a better tomorrow, the will to conquer new worlds. It is mired in the present, and much of society wishes merely to preserve the half-slumbering warmth of contentment. It is now profoundly disturbed at being forced—just when life was going so well—to deal with change and the challenges of aspirant societies.

And yet hearts beat faster, minds race, and muscles tense as we consider the future: the world unknown which we may bend to our imagination. To look forward is the driving impulse toward survival and to achievement. Those societies and individuals lost in the moment place their fate in the hands of others. Those who dwell in the past are constrained and cautious. Those who initiate or perpetuate the paths to victory embrace the past or have unconsciously accepted its lessons and conditioning, yet delight in the challenge and hope of the future while acting in the moment.

Acting in the moment, on the basis of a vision of the future, commences the path to victory; it is the seizure or creation of opportunity. Consolidation of the initial step on the path to victory, however, requires a reflection and an understanding of the origins of the process, as well as a conscious appreciation and reiteration of the goals for the future.

How, then, for example, did Cornelius Vanderbilt become the stand-out financial success of his generation—from impecunious beginnings, he rose to become the richest man in the world—and yet have his fortune dissipated within four generations? Vanderbilt himself recognized the difficulty in sustaining victory, saying to his son, William, just before he died in 1877: "Any fool can make a fortune. It takes a man of brains to hold on to it after it is made."

The "single act" which propelled to greatness Vanderbilt and many others—such as Microsoft's Bill Gates and Wal-Mart's Sam Walton—was the exploitation (not the basic invention) of a society-wide enabling technology, a system, need, or capability at an early stage in its development. Those who commence their victory in the marketplace see possibilities and seek market domination before the regulations of government or the market reduce the chances for advantage. Significantly, in the case of Wal-Mart, success was very much a result of the combination of the growing demand for consumer goods in the broad national U.S. marketplace—not just the cities—which resulted from a broadening of the national economic base, at the same time that China began its journey into capitalism and mass production, creating a vast array of low-cost consumer goods at a time when the Wal-Mart distribution and marketing network was perfectly placed to sell them. It was a confluence of interests which made China and Wal-Mart, for a time, mutual hostages and partners. Wal-Mart—with 2002 sales of $244.5 billion, making it the biggest company in the world—remains somewhat dependent on China. In 2002, nearly 10 percent ($12 billion worth) of all Chinese exports to the United States went to Wal-Mart.

What separated Cornelius Vanderbilt from his rivals was his ability to think more broadly than just the technology itself. Vanderbilt and society were unconcerned with Vanderbilt's steamships and railroads per se; they cared how they could most easily and cheaply move the public and its goods to markets. Wal-Mart customers care only about the stores' convenience, product range, and low prices, not how the company achieves these "deliverables."

If Cornelius Vanderbilt's grandchildren, or his legacy corporate structure (New York Central Railroad), had been able to understand their purpose and place in society in an evolving fashion—as Cornelius Vanderbilt did, growing from barges to sailing ships, to steamships, and then to railroads—they would have seen the Vanderbilt victory subsequently embracing telecommunications, newspapers, and then radio, television, and the internet. These became the enabling arterial links of society as it evolved in the twentieth and twenty-first centuries.

But while the Vanderbilt victory did not inure, after a half-dozen generations, to the financial benefit of the descendants of Cornelius, it *did* become an integral and vital part of the victory of the United States in building a prosperous, productive society. Individuals, organizations, and nations seek to touch the hem of immortality and hope that their works will endure and breathe and ensure the life and success of their descendants.

Vanderbilt, Rockefeller, Gates, Walton, and others, such as the duke of Wellington, Julius Caesar, Hannibal, William the Conqueror, and Alexander the Great, showed that victory—this earthly reach for a form of immortality—may be grasped rapidly, and within a single generation. However, it requires the toil of generations to consolidate. The Medicis of Florence knew that, and, by nurturing both family interests and the needs of society through involvement in religion, politics, education and arts, and the military, became perhaps the most profoundly influential family in modern history. Their victory transcended that of the Vanderbilts and Rockefellers in scope, but ultimately their victory, too, came to an end.

By the same token, depending on the complexity and pervasiveness of victory, it is rarely lost with a single setback. However, one setback, or a series of setbacks, can begin the process of removing the platform of victory, one plank at a time, until it becomes unstable, collapsing into the dust.

Opportunities, like inventions or battlefield triumphs, are often not created by those who exploit them; some opportunities and technologies emerge from societal or natural situations. Cornelius Vanderbilt invented no new technologies, or even methodologies. He efficiently exploited a market condition and need for transport in a largely unregulated environment. He boldly used some emerging technologies, such as steam power for his ships and railroads, becoming much wealthier than the great pioneer of steam locomotion, James Watt, of Scotland. Bill Gates, on the other hand, like Watt, helped pioneer both a technological breakthrough and a market condition.

While the "will to victory" exists to a greater or lesser extent in all men and women, it is indeed only the art of victory which ensures success. Victory is achieved and sustained by a marriage of the primal drive with intellect and information, plus emotional balance (wisdom, the product of experience), both within the leadership and within society.

That war between England and Normandy was sealed in a single day's action at the Battle of Hastings in 1066. However, the results of the battle and the war would have been overturned, or remained historically of little significance, had they not been consolidated by the zeal of William the Conqueror and his great battlefield commander, Roger de Montgomery, and by the processes which he began to ensure the construction of victory. Apart from the military consolidation which followed the Conquest, perhaps the Normans' most significant contribution to the enduring wealth and power of Britain was the evolution of a structured approach to royal succession in the form of primogeniture. This allowed the eldest son of the monarch the right to succeed to the throne and all its powers, instead of dividing the power and spoils among the late monarch's sons or inviting a power struggle among them, as had been the case in the past.

This was a key beginning of the modern nation-state, moving from the feudal realms of princes, dukes, and kings to defining a state with a legal, geographical, and historical entity beyond merely the lifetime of the ruler.

It was this simple new step which began the development of a formal structure of government and the transition of power down the generations, gradually minimizing internecine contests over power. This led to the development of constitutional rights and modern democratic structures throughout society. It was the beginning of today's forms of representative government, which ensured that conflict was not the only means of changing governments.

Many African states remained in a state of poverty in the past half-century not because they lacked able and intelligent leadership, but because the orderly transfer of power from one leader to the next—something which was in place in traditional African societies for millennia—was constantly forestalled by coups d'état. Ironically, most of these coups occurred to *stop* societal collapse. But the very act of stopping the constitutional processes, and, with each coup, returning to the starting point of government, meant that there was never a base on which to build. At the start of the twenty-first century, the African Union (AU) began a new approach: Build on the electoral process of government succession, even when an election is flawed.

Better to build on a base and keep correcting the mistakes while moving forward than to halt the entire process and return to a "clean slate" with every change of government. The same approach applies to corporations. The success of the evolutionary consolidation of victory is now evident in the way mainland China has skillfully transformed its communist revolution into a classical marketplace evolution since the death of Mao Zedong.

China's lack of wealth and power—its lack of victory—during the twentieth century was largely due to the destructiveness of the revolutionary processes. These opened the door for the Japanese invasion in the 1930s and the subsequent chaos of World War II in China. (The chaos of China, which gave Japan the opportunity to invade, could well be said to have led directly to the Japanese attacks on Pearl Harbor, the Philippines, and Singapore, bringing the United States into World War II, and the British Commonwealth into war with Japan.) Great revolutionary catalysts in societies or organizations are sometimes inevitable, as organizational maturity deteriorates into brittle sclerosis, but those societies which prosper and consolidate their victory do so because they avoid frequent catastrophic firestorms of total collapse and self-destruction.

Britain's loss of dominant status, brought about by World War I and World War II, did not erase entirely the fruits of the long British victory: The United States and the English-speaking British dominions had by then become the broad, enduring flesh of that victory. French setbacks caused by the world wars, however, meant that by the twenty-first century, French no longer rivaled English as the language of world commerce. Thus, despite its successes, the relative victory of France had diminished compared with that of Britain. Similarly, the earlier Spanish victory began its final diminution with the Spanish-American War of 1898. But throughout this, we see in the

Latin and Greek aspects of the English, French, and Spanish languages the continuation of the victory and values of the Roman Empire and earlier Hellenistic civilization.

Victory, in the complex modern world, is no longer possible merely as a result of visceral capability and intuition. It must be conceived, planned, and—as the British and U.S. processes show—pursued over time. And if the initial steps of victory do not commence through the emergence of opportunity, like the eruption of a forest fire, then circumstances can be created to instigate it. Victory is an art which draws upon many sciences.

The victory of a society—even a commercial society, such as that composed of Microsoft the legal entity, Microsoft's employees, and the company's clients and users—is possible only when there is a sense of it as a force within each individual, either to lead to victory or to actively follow. Individuals, communities, and societies which lack the desire for victory will, in all species, risk obliteration. Anything less than victory, then, is unacceptable to nature; anything less than victory risks the future of the line. The impulse toward victory is most strongly manifested when competition exists. This brings out the best in a society so that it can triumph over adversity and adversaries, and also so that it can hone ingenuity to the point that its logic structures and those of its members are refined and adapted to ensure survival.

This logic differs from society to society, and also *within* societies, along the lines of gender, age, culture, and ability. "Culture" itself is merely an outgrowth of logic, as logic is a perceptional evolution of the survival instinct. A culture is that aspect of a group or society which has developed modalities to survive and prosper. So culture is logic writ large.

Those individuals with the greatest natural awareness or perception attuned to the dominance of their interests are most likely to achieve victory. As Goethe said: "Everyone listens only to what he understands." The greater the understanding, the greater the awareness and chances of survival and success.

Victories, then, often begin out of opportunities arising from chaos, decline, or collapse in societies or markets.

What great maelstroms do we see in the early twenty-first century which spell the transition from one dying epoch and the powers which dominated it to the new age, and the new powers which will rise?

THE CHANGING GLOBAL CONTEXT: RELATIVE POWER POSITIONS ARE CHANGING

The unipolar world after the Cold War could never have lasted. Nonetheless, the United States remains the preeminent economic engine of the world, even though it could be argued that fewer Americans than ever are actively engaged in creating new wealth, and a higher percentage than ever are engaged in consuming wealth. Underdeveloped countries are marked by the fact that a very small percentage of the population creates wealth, and the vast majority of the population is either merely a noncontributory sector, subsisting on its own food production, or actively subtracts from the societal wealth. The United States is moving gradually in this direction as a society, whereas once it was almost universally productive and active in building the national strength.

The United States, like Western Europe (only to a lesser degree), is living off the fruits of an economic momentum created by earlier generations who were motivated by a desire to build the long-term victory of their societies. The reality is that to retain global leadership and a victory which cannot be broken by, say, a major war—which would disrupt the flow into the country of foreign-produced energy or essential goods—the United States must continue to be or return to being a producing nation, and not merely a financial services nation.

That is not to deny that the essential platforms of modern victory (including the basic military, industrial, and consumer platforms) can today be produced more efficiently, and with fewer workers, than in the past. The U.S. agricultural industry has proven to be a marvel of technological and scientific efficiency, generating vast surpluses with little manpower. But, arguably, the Australian agricultural sector does the same thing, without the same subsidies which are being paid to U.S. farmers.

The ability to buy whatever a society needs from abroad lies in the value of its currency, and loss of prestige through conflict or relative decline in power erodes the prestige which underpins currency value. Thus, societies which place their emphasis on abstract financial services—as Britain has done—are thinking short-term. Long-term strategic strength (victory) requires that the abstract aspects of wealth creation (capital formation, financial gambling on stock speculation, and the like) be built *on top of* an indisputable foundation of tangible productive output, creating the foods, energy, and manufactures required of a sophisticated society. Only then is a society in charge of its own destiny.

CAN "THE WEST" REINVIGORATE ITS VICTORY?

The great strategic victory of the West is, as we have discussed, already mature. In Western Europe, decline has begun. In North America and Japan, it is wavering on the edge of rebirth or decline. Overall, the West (the current modern industrial powers, including Japan, South Korea, and the like) will, inevitably, become less efficient and less focused, unless it takes some course of action to reinvigorate itself. As Cornelius Vanderbilt said: "Any fool can make a fortune. It takes a man of brains to hold on to it after it is made." His words apply equally to nation-states. We will explore, in later chapters, the factors which can inhibit or help the reinvigoration of the West's grasp on victory.

The West, however, cannot regain its victory momentum without will, and this will can come only from clearly recognizing that decline must lead, within generations, to relative impoverishment and circumscribed strategic options. And yet Western society—fiddling while Rome burns—does not even see the threat to its way of doing business in the thousands of riots which struck France, Germany, and Belgium in October and November 2005. There are many other warning signs, yet the West fails to heed them.

What is the catalyst by which Western societies will awaken and galvanize into action? Will it be a nuclear attack by Iran, for example, against Israel? In all likelihood, Western Europe would rationalize this as having nothing to do with the lives of Parisians or Londoners or Berliners. The United States itself would be relatively powerless to respond. Will it be a nuclear attack by North Korea on Japan, or on a U.S. city? That, perhaps, would provoke a determined response by the United States. But would that also lead to a U.S.-China confrontation? And would Western Europe, again, scurry to avoid involvement, while expressing its regrets?

Clearly, a few terrorist attacks have proven insufficient to awaken the West.

But there are signs that some segments of Western society are growing concerned and are coalescing in their debates about the need for a reawakening of society to face the growing challenges to the great victory which the West has built over the past thousand years. Their first challenge, however, is not to deal with those external threats, but to deal with "the other half" of their own societies, who insist on appeasement, and the consumption of the wealth built over many generations, as though that wealth were inexhaustible and not in need of replenishment.

MILITANT ISLAM: CAN IT CONQUER? AND WHAT OF IRAN?

Militant Islam cannot conquer. That is not to say that Muslim societies cannot succeed. Malaysia, for example, has achieved considerable economic and strategic success, and Indonesia—for all its fragility and problems—holds the potential for success. But militant Islam, which is the transnational Islamist movement based solely on the philosophy of the destruction of the West and of moderate Muslim states, cannot endure, because it is a movement which has no strength except willpower. It does not build on a durable base even of agricultural production. Its tools for success are the technologies and structures of its enemies. It cannot even produce its own weapons.

Can militant Islamists damage the West? They have already done so. But their total success can lie only in the capitulation by Western societies to their demands; in other words, in Western strategic suicide. And even if Western societies do continue their process of strategic suicide, and the Islamist jihadists claim this as their "victory," they will not last because they lack the means to sustain themselves even in food production. They are, in historical terms, a plague of locusts upon the West and upon the core Muslim *ummah* (world), and they will pass like the hordes of

Tamerlane, leaving scars of their passing, but no monuments.

The jihadists, however, are sponsored by the Iranian clerics. It is this, coupled with the monies of Saudi private donors and other Islamist "charities," which gives militant Islam its current traction. Significantly, despite claims that the Iranian clerical leaders are truly committed to "global revolution," the mullahs of Iran engage in this war against the West in large part to project to their own people a sense of authority and purpose, and to engender a sense of siege and threat to the Iranian people, so that they can continue in their suppression of the country.

Can Iran become a major middle power over the next generation? Most certainly. It is a nation with an historic sense of unity and purpose. But the mullahs, rather than maximizing this will toward a revived Persian victory, in fact keep Iran from meaningful success. This, at present, suits many who are concerned at the prospect of a truly powerful and economically productive Iran, independent of the sway of Russia, China, or the United States. The late shah of Iran had envisaged just such an Iran, but one implicitly tied to the West. But that was in the time of the Cold War, when the ideology of the USSR was very different to that of today's Russia.

The overthrow of the clerics in Iran—which can, because of the size and complexity of Iranian society, be achieved only by the Iranian people themselves, with external encouragement—could unleash a major productive power within a decade, truly transforming the Middle East and ending many of the petty squabbles there (including the Arab-Israeli dispute, now, particularly since the end of the Saddam and Arafat eras, funded largely by Iran).

CAN CHINA SURVIVE AS A SINGLE ENTITY?
CAN INDIA ACHIEVE "TAKEOFF"?

China is the most dramatic example of a society in an upwardly spiraling turbulence following the chaos and disaster there of the nineteenth and twentieth centuries. As with all thrusts toward victory, China's path is by no means certain. We have already discussed this, and I will allude to it in later chapters. Similarly, India's quest for true strategic "takeoff" is mired in difficulties. It has, thus far, still rejected some of the key modalities which could create a cohesive power from its disparate parts, but has many strategic attributes which China lacks, with fewer inherent problems.

The potential for rivalry between India and China remains high, and both states are at pains to minimize a return to military confrontation.

THE RISE OF THE AFRICAN
"LION ECONOMIES"

Africa, too, is in transition. By the start of the twenty-first century, much of sub-Saharan Africa had finally begun to throw off the mentalities of both its colonial and its backward-looking postcolonial eras. The inherent wealth of Africa's energy and mineral resources has long been known. Now, as African governments begin mastering the art of the transfer of power without coups and violence, they are beginning to build a pattern of stability and wealth which will become evident over the coming decade.

Africa could well vie with India (which will itself compete with China) by 2015 as a great area for the manufacture of low-cost consumer goods, as well as for the supply of energy and minerals to the world's markets. What is possible (indeed probable) is a new set of African "lion economies" which will do for the world economy what the Asian "tiger economies" did in the 1980s and 1990s. Africa is one of the few areas in the world yet to experience a major modern boom, and all of the underpinnings for security and stability were beginning to come together there by 2006. Africa had been neglected and abused by the world's powers, even as it became evident that, for example, Nigeria provided almost as much energy to the United States as did Saudi Arabia, and that by 2015 it would provide 25 percent of the imported energy needs of the United States.

Parts of sub-Saharan Africa are at their starting point for victory. This will be the venue for many of the new fortunes to be made in the world.

OTHER NEW MIDDLE POWERS: AUSTRALIA, RUSSIA, BRAZIL

Russia embarked after the end of the Cold War on the path to strategic recovery on a more sound economic and structural footing than that of the Soviet period. Post-Soviet Russia could have proven a viable component of the West, but for the fact that the West could not shake off Cold War anti-Russian prejudice. By discarding communism and the oppression of the Russian peoples, Russia had been ready to embrace Westernism, as Peter the Great had attempted to do. Today, the United States and Western Europe essentially work against Russia, although depending on it in many respects. Russia is a key to the stability of today's flow of oil to the industrialized world.

Russia will resume an independent path toward reconstructing itself, over the next two or three decades, as a major power, albeit one which will be unlikely to compete for some time in overall economic terms with China or the United States. Despite structural and social problems, Russia retains at its core a sense of unfulfilled destiny in its quest for victory.

Brazil, with all of the underlying attributes of a potentially great power, continues to lack the will to achieve its strategic potential. Its inherent wealth, however, will continue to impel it toward greater global significance, despite mismanagement and corruption and despite its essentially introspective nature. But because of its strength, China will continue to woo it, and work with it in an economic and geopolitical sense, just as it is working with much of Latin America to counterbalance the United States. In this respect, China understands classical geopolitics, which the United States has neglected at its peril.

But within the framework of rising middle powers perhaps the most interesting is Australia, the smallest in population of the aspirants, with only some 20 million people. What is interesting is that Australia has, after a century of independence and contented basking in the shadows of Britain and the United States, begun to sense an independent identity, purpose, and self-confidence which are combining to take advantage of the country's natural wealth and geographic clarity.

Australian leaders are beginning to understand that modern realities must, of necessity, thrust the society rudely out of the shadows and into a period of self-reliance, given the fact that it will, in the coming decades, be unable to reasonably expect the United States to provide it with comprehensive strategic protection. Japan—the second-greatest economic power in the world today—has also begun to reach the same conclusions about its own future.

Australia has the resources, the productive workforce, and the geography to succeed. Now it is acquiring the sense of identity and will it needs to transform that into a long-term vision of victory. Its principal task in the coming two and three decades will be to skillfully balance relations with the United States, Japan, China, the ASEAN states (the member nations of the Association of South-East Asian Nations), India, and Iran, so that Australian security and economic interests are protected.

Within all of these major trends—and there are many more factors and trends, including the impact of new energy possibilities—we see societies embarking or re-embarking on the quest for victory. We are present at the creation of a new galaxy of states, perhaps emerging in forms we have yet to imagine, deriving their power from different tools—from nanotechnologies to biomass energy production—but all deriving their impetus from a will and sense of right to achieve victory.

Our feet are on the path to victory, but we need to define what victory means to us, in specific terms; we must consider our grand strategy.

DEFINING A GRAND STRATEGY FOR VICTORY

THREE

Victory can be sustained and built only by the conscious articulation of grand strategy objectives, which must be compatible with, and become part of, the society's psyche.

Hurricane Katrina's devastation of New Orleans and much of the U.S. Gulf Coast in September 2005 highlighted the importance of planning for eventualities. Despite ample warning, and considerable funding for emergency preparedness, the people and institutions of the city of New Orleans and the state of Louisiana—quite apart from federal authorities—were ill-prepared for the fate which overtook them. And when Hurricane Rita struck the region later the same month, the effects of the original hurricane were compounded. The actual victims of the disasters had done little or nothing to prepare for the future, and expected "someone else"—the federal government—to shoulder all responsibility for their lives.

Understanding how history—both man-made and natural—shapes societies enables governments, organizations, and individuals to plan for the future, and to master their destinies instead of being victims of circumstance.

The U.S. Gulf Coast will recover, and be the center of a great American economic renaissance thanks to the strength of the U.S. economy, and the commitment of the

U.S. government to spend some $250 billion on reconstruction. But adequate planning and a commitment to strategies and disciplines of disaster prevention and management could have minimized the human cost to the region and those "opportunity costs" caused by the forced diversion of resources away from other priorities. A series of disasters such as Katrina and Rita could, for many countries, spell the start of the unraveling or transforming of a nation's victory.

And despite the scope of the Katrina/Rita disaster and the need for coping strategies to be in place and well thought out, that disaster fell short of the true challenge which faces each society: the creation of a totally embracing national strategy to achieve its long-term goals, as well as strategies to cope with adversity. This is grand strategy: the articulation of the terms and conditions which a nation (or other entity) demands of and for itself into the indefinite future.

Former U.S. secretary of state Henry Kissinger changed an old homily by noting: "If you don't know where you're going, any road will take you nowhere." To grasp victory—the goal to which we aim and travel—it is necessary to understand strategic factors and to be able to develop strategies which define the roadmap, the way stations, the dangers, and the opportunities. Even Kissinger's homily falls short. It should read: "If you don't know where you *wish* to go, and plan and act accordingly, every road will lead ultimately to disaster and defeat." To strive with conscious vision for what is desired automatically strengthens the "auto-immune" systems to spontaneously cope with adversity. This overarching, conscious vision of defining long-term goals, the intermediate steps in achieving them, and the subordinate objectives is called a "grand strategy."

Just as victory can be initiated with the recognition and exploitation of an opportunity, it can only endure through conscious planning and strict adherence to plans, objectives, and time frames. Significantly, the personality types which recognize and exploit opportunities are rarely the same as those that plan the consolidation and follow-up of that initial exploitation.

The current U.S. business maxim, "failure to plan means planning to fail," is understood by all. A grand strategy—to use the statecraft term—is more than just a plan; it is a living process entailing comprehension of the interlocking weave of the broad context which shapes long-term success. It also embodies the selection of short-, medium-, and long-term goals, and the development of strategies and tactics to achieve these goals, all within a multidimensional and constantly changing environment.

A true grand strategy—for a state, a corporation, a family, or an individual—has strong historical as well as social and spatial context. We do not live in a vacuum. Neither do we live in a society unbuffeted by the winds of global economic, social, or political trends. Therefore we cannot successfully plan our futures solely on the basis of linear trends within narrow and localized frames of reference.

The best-laid business and pension fund plans can be turned to ash, for example, by geographically remote wars, famines, natural calamities, or simply by the illness of a key individual. The fortunes of a state—and its inhabitants and the world communities it touches—can wax or wane depending on the health or mental vagaries of a single leader. The unforeseen stroke, and departure from the political scene, of Israeli prime minister Ariel Sharon on January 6, 2006, for example, set in train a strategically significant chain of events in the Middle East. Or consider the long-term impact on East-West relations caused by the ill health of U.S. president Franklin D. Roosevelt at the Yalta conference with Stalin and Churchill in February 1945.

It is the grand strategic ambitions of a society which

define how it sees its own victory. This vision defines how the society comports itself, sees itself, sets its laws and ethical base, and how it organizes itself to achieve its goals. How the society then projects itself defines, too, how it is seen by others. And thus the path toward victory is begun. The overarching nature of the grand strategy is defined by longer-term goals and broader parameters than a single leader, or even a single generation, so that the death or actions of a single individual—in one's own or another society—can be accommodated.

To succeed, the grand strategy must embrace the realistic and the mystical, the measurable and the intangible. Its underpinnings must consist of immutables: goals which will realistically endure even though circumstances change. Its goals must be sufficiently remote to provide a constant star of hope, and its operational strategy must provide recognizable landmarks, links with history, and familiar horizons.

Americans often see themselves as individualists who cannot be constrained by a "five-year plan," or any other kind of plan. The reality is that the great success of the United States lay in the conscious reflection which created the Declaration of Independence, further expanded and elevated by its Constitution and its Bill of Rights. These documents embody the operating principles for the state and its citizens with such forethought that they have enabled almost a quarter-millennium of economic and strategic growth. These three documents are the closest things the United States has had to an enduring grand strategy. Their influence has been profound because they did not so narrowly define the scope of society that their tenets could be readily overtaken by history. These documents, reflecting the profound intellect of their authors, remain fresh today. The United States has foundered, or lost its way, when it has allowed the principles laid out in these documents to be trammeled by short-term political fashions.

Historically, some individuals have led their societies to the first stages of victory without conscious thought about how they achieved their success, other than to attribute it to their own superiority or to the belief that they acted, or re-acted, to situations with expediency. George Washington re-acted to circumstances, and did so reluctantly, and yet opened the path to the victory of the United States. But without the great intellectual talents of Thomas Jefferson, Benjamin Franklin, John Adams, James Madison, and other framers of the great strategic documents which defined what the victory of the United States meant, Washington as a military leader alone would have been a historical figure of but transitory importance.

The essence of civilizational leadership is the *conscious* awareness of the need for victory, the ability to define it in terms of specific objectives, and the capacity to deliver it in physical terms. Most of the process, therefore, is cerebral, or psychological. Victory, then, is what we tell ourselves it is (our self-defined goals), coupled with the validation of his-tory, which determines the durability of our vision. Victory *is* civilization, in its positive and negative forms. The Roman Empire expunged the enlightened aspects of many cultures (such as pre-rabbinic Judaism and Egypt's Greco-Pharaonic society) to win victory to its side, and the civilization which resulted is the base from which much of mankind went for-ward. It was pivotal, and enduring in its effect, even now providing the basis for future Western global cultural evolu-tion, despite Rome's "darkness" in crushing the enlighten-ment and contributions of other societies.

There is, along the path to ultimate victory or defeat, much winning and losing of battles, even the ephemeral winning and losing of wars.

To be truly victorious, the victor must be perceived as such; must be accorded the authority and power which ac-company success and dominance. In that respect, victory is as much perceptual, or psychopolitical, as it is tangible. French emperor Napoleon Bonaparte (Napoleon I) said that in warfare "the moral is to the physical as two is to one." In other words, psychological factors are twice as important as the physical. So it is at the strategic or civilizational level. Prestige must also be planned for in a grand strategy.

If grand strategy is the defining of overarching national or transnational goals and milestones (in essence, the defining of victory), then psychological strategy is the key implementing tool in the achievement of such victory. We will discuss this in detail later.

At a grand strategy level, psychological strategy must embrace an understanding of current and historical factors related to cultures, languages and semantics, religions and belief systems, history, ethnography, geopolitics, conflict, and the relationship of societal survival to climate, technology and sciences, military strategy, and much more.

The world, meanwhile, has just emerged from a half-century of global structural rigidity, which in turn emerged from a century of the construction of that rigidity. But the underpinning of the twentieth century was its constant technological evolution, which gave twenty-first century society a degree of flexibility and opportunity—responsibility for one's own survival and freedom from constraint—reminiscent of tribal societies long since eclipsed. Science and technology have, in a sense, restored the capacity of *maneuver* as a psychological and political stratagem, with human ingenuity in command of such tools providing the elements of surprise.

As victory is a life force, it is, at the conscious level, also a *belief system*. It has throughout history been interwoven with religions and ideologies to give it definition, potency, legitimacy, and authority. Deeply felt and positively motivating belief systems are the result of consciously articulated goals and strategies which consider all the historical, current, and future factors shaping a society. And the more that the operating grand strategy is reviewed and updated to take account of emerging realities, the greater the chance that success will endure. Just as a company cannot expect to operate successfully on an unrevised, five-year-old business plan, neither can the United States expect to be successful into the indefinite future without consciously understanding and "recontextualizing" its Constitution—not changing it, but seeing it in the light of current realities—to ensure that the fundamental document of U.S. self-definition is viable within the changing world.

Almost always, the conscious understanding of what we conceive to be victory implies its possible achievement. Few victories are achieved by accident. The greater and more broadly based the conscious defining of victory as it applies to our individual or collective circumstance, the more likely that such a victory will be broadly and historically enduring.

As with all great human impulses, the compulsion toward victory in those who would naturally lead is absent in others who wish the benefits of victory but feel unable to compete for it. Those who allow others to define the goals of victory, and the methods of attaining it, must live with the consequences of their inaction. However, there are many who are not well-placed to lead but who support the leadership of those who seek victory.

Some elements of society have as their basis for life a fear of change and of strangers, or a sense of self-satisfaction or security which does not wish to entertain the reality that society cannot perpetuate itself without continual striving and risk. In many instances, they exhibit a "fear of victory." These are often the armchair radicals, who indulge in pious criticism to hide their failure to accept responsibility for their own fate. Victory equates to responsibility, in the same way that democracy equates to responsibility.

And if victory is responsibility, it is possible to find the seeds of victory in defeat. Egypt's seeds of military victory in 1973 were in its military defeat in 1967; President Anwar as-Sadat used the six short years between the two wars to totally rethink and replan Egypt's military and strategic capabilities, leading to a rebirth of the country's strategic viability. The results of the October 1973 War were such that both Egypt and Israel could claim victory. For Israel, it was the "victory" of not being defeated; of regaining the temporarily lost momentum on the battlefield, sufficient for the retention of the national sense of self. For Egypt, it was a true victory in that it enabled Egyptians to regain their sense of identity as victors, as masters of their own destiny, not beholden to another for their peace.

It was the mutuality of victory which made it possible for a peace to be codified under the initiative of Sadat. But it was only possible because of a conscious, and rigorously honest, analysis by Sadat of Egypt's position.

Sadat's vision did not survive his assassination in 1981. His risk-oriented, mold-breaking comprehension of realities, and the execution of the necessary steps to achieve success, were not continued with the same verve by President Hosni Mubarak. Mubarak emerged as a risk-averse leader, spending the fruits of Sadat's achievements, to the point where Egypt by 2006 had lost much of its primacy in the Middle East. Egypt had moved rapidly through its period of active pursuit of victory to becoming a reactive power, gradually frittering away its strength. Sadat's actions, however, show how possible it is for Egypt to regain its momentum. It is all a matter of will.

Victory eventually transcends its originating framework, but it rarely destroys that framework; rather, it adds to it, sometimes destroying opposing frameworks. The concepts of "nations" and "nation-states" and "sovereignty" are often frameworks which inhibit the scope of victory (while at the same time providing the vehicles for it). This is why the current trend toward porosity of sovereignty—the reality that the state is no longer in control of the flow of peoples, money, ideas, and forces in and out of territories—and the weakening, through the emergence of globalization, of the traditionally rigid nation-state is part of a dynamic momentum which enables the emergence of new types of leaders and the creation of new wealth. This frightens some, who feel that victory (in this case the status quo) is being taken from them, or who feel that they cannot compete. In fact, *their* "victory" *will* be overturned unless they grasp and employ the realities of the new globalization.

Globalism, changing concepts of sovereignty, and stark threats to the status quo at the opening of the twenty-first century necessitated an end to some fifty years of management-style leadership. The fluidity of the global situation put the necessity for the elemental type of leader—those leaders who reflect the "life force" drive toward victory—back into the consciousness of the world.

The confusion of the early twenty-first century reflected the fact that the established orders of the world—essentially the West—had *not* created new grand strategies based on clean-sheet analysis of their positions and the new realities. The essential basis for operations among Western governments and companies today is a continuation of the status quo ante. But the status quo of the twentieth-century primacy of the West is now gone; victory must be reacquired, and to achieve it new grand strategies must be written.

Recognizing the core, enduring motivations of mankind—and then articulating them into grand strategies—is the first brushstroke on the canvas which is the Art of Victory.

Who would have thought that in this post–Dark Age the West would still be living out the revived victory of the

Romans and the Hellenes? But who would have thought that the West has, essentially, stopped the process of updating its grand strategies?

WHO HAS A GRAND STRATEGY?

The People's Republic of China is constantly writing and updating its grand strategy. So, too, are the leaders of the Islamist caliphate movement, such as Osama bin Laden. Their strategies may succeed or fail, but they are thinking of the future, planning for it, and articulating their overarching grand strategies to achieve it. The West cannot do less.

And in this jostling for victory, we can expect war to play a role. We need, then, to understand where war can help, or hinder, victory.

THE ROLE OF WAR
IN VICTORY

FOUR

War is the most common and successful
catalyst through which victory is commenced,
but once victory is secured, warfare should be
the preferred option only when considered
against lesser forces.

M obs rage through the streets of U.S. and European
cities—burning cars and houses in Seattle, Genoa,
Paris—confronting security forces in melees
which, through the narrow focus of the television screen,
seem like wars within society. The forces of "antiglobalism"
may as well rail against the weather, or bay at the moon,
given that globalism is a natural surge of society in this
time of technology. Not surprising, then, that the antiglob-
alists *do* rail against the weather, blaming its wrath on
human-induced global warming, just as Islamist-jihadists
attributed 2005's Hurricane Katrina to Allah as retribution
for American failings.

All of this is indeed war, and all is an attempt to gain
ascendancy for a way of life. The risk-taking price wars
conducted between Ford and General Motors—cutting
margins to the minimum in order to sustain market dominance or to improve market share—are also war. Indeed,
war is more than just a continuation of diplomacy by other
means (as von Clausewitz said); it is a seamless aspect of

the competitiveness of life. And as with all aspects of life, success lies in understanding and controlling it.

Success in war is often confused with victory. But although warfare has historically played a great and dynamic role in victory, its place within the overall framework of strategic victory is infinitely complex.

The great victory of the West, which has gradually and erratically accumulated since pre-Roman times, but particularly since the Gutenberg revolution in printing around 1450, is directly attributable to the *process* of warfare (as opposed to the results of that warfare). The wars which led to the victory of the West were largely *within* the West; they were in most cases internecine—that is to say, among the Western states themselves—and only secondarily took the form of wars of external conquest. Clearly, this means that the West's strategic victory of today includes and embraces those states which were defeated in the internecine wars. This indicates that their vanquishing—even under terms of "unconditional surrender," as we saw at the end of World War II—did not necessarily exclude those states from the larger victory, but may have even been essential to their ultimate participation in it.

Fundamental to all of this is the fact that extreme competition between societies (and war is the most notable form) is critical to victory.

What warfare provides is the focus of national efforts on creating the tools of survival. It provides ingrained lessons, mostly for those who lose. Few, if any, societies have prospered in a sustained victory at any time in history *without* the regular threat or experience of war. Few, if any, great corporations have survived and grown without competition.

Warfare varies in its practicality or utility depending on whether it is the victorious who are preserving victory, or whether it is used by a state, society, or movement seeking to achieve it. Those states seeking to preserve victory will favor conflicts which minimize casualties. Those seeking to break the status quo will embrace wars which emphasize risk. The innovation and asymmetric warfare techniques favored by the zealous and ambitious may appear to have the virtue of valor, but in reality are short-term gambles. The state which can weigh the threat and hold its fire is more likely to prevail, but it must always find ways—through intelligence and sound intuition—to deny the mobile, intemperate aggressor the option of determining the time, place, and nature of decisive strategic engagements.

How we perceive war and peace changed substantially in the last years of the twentieth century and the first years of the twenty-first century. The end of the Cold War provided a clear break-point to concepts of war and peace which had evolved in many ways over some two thousand years. While clearly delineated rules, laws, and concepts of war—and therefore peace—had been violated or vitiated at various times and places throughout history, it was only with the advent of modern technologies that the standard definitions of "war" and "peace" became obsolescent.

We did not reach this point overnight. Dr. Stefan T. Possony, the great Viennese-born strategic philosopher, was the first to crystallize the new era when, in his 1938 book, *Tomorrow's War*, he looked at the interrelated areas of science, the economy, and conflict doctrine, and how civil society had become integral to all war.

Possony, by understanding the interrelationship between warfighting and strategic depth—including social and economic depth—paved the way for the realization that *all* war is now "total war." All war draws on the comprehensive strengths, and highlights the intrinsic weaknesses, of the total society: The greater the war, the more important these strengths and weaknesses become, quite

apart from the combat strength and military capabilities of
the combatants. (In earlier history, as we saw with the Battle of Hastings in 1066, wars were related more to the outcome of battles, and the results of battles were determined
by the forces which could be fielded on the day.)

Societies demand clarity from their leaders. They demand that wars be seen as such; that enemies be identified;
that forces be arrayed; and that uncertainties be mini-
mized. We need to know our enemies so that, in a sense,
we can know ourselves and how we should respond. The
result is that all societies oversimplify threats and enemies,
and their own strengths and goals, in order to avoid the
anxiety of uncertainty.

Modern technology has ensured that societies now in-
termingle inextricably, both physically and conceptually.
Transnational, or globalist, thinking and lifestyles of large
portions of the world's wealthier and better-educated population—dependent on trade patterns, including food supply, of a totally global nature—combine, perversely, with
transnational movements which play on illiteracy and ignorance. Wealthier, educated societies see barriers breaking
down; ignorant, poor, and emotionalized societies see, because of images relayed through modern communications,
only new barriers arising. The ignorant see clear threats;
the wealthier and supposedly better informed see only confusion and imprecise threats.

The post–Cold War thinking among intelligence services and defense planners has recognized that the formal,
highly structured, mass-oriented military doctrine and systems which had been developed over the preceding century
were no longer universally applicable. Planners have moved
toward recognizing the need for lighter, more precisely
lethal, and more flexible forces to deal with less formal
threats.

Despite this positive move toward recognizing new realities, defense and policy planners still see threats in terms of identifiable, quantifiable forces and opposing methodologies. New forms of warfare between structured, larger forces and smaller, often irregular forces were styled "asymmetric," in order to force the concept of such conflict into some recognizable or codifiable structure. Similarly, the Western focus—both in the media and in defense and intelligence structures—on identifying and labeling terrorist or insurgent enemies as "members" of this or that organization is merely an attempt to quell doubts. The thinking is: If we can label the enemy, we can formulate a coherent response; we can sleep at night.

The emerging strategic framework is, however, far too variable and complex to be merely rationalized into the concept of "asymmetric warfare." Fundamental concepts of "war" and "peace" are no longer even applicable. What is required to ensure the dominance and survival of a society is, more than ever, a total societal commitment to its goals.

All, in other words, is now "total war." And there is nothing resembling "total peace."

The world has become a global battlefield with no "thin red lines" of formal force structures. Conventional force structures have become besieged castles. Psychological factors are paramount.

So what of the role of war in victory? Have the changes put greater, or less, stress on the importance of war in victory? The answer is hedged by ambiguities. The first response is: What is now meant by war? Or, perhaps: What is now meant by peace? These are questions which first began to be answered in the 1930s by the Soviet doctrine of "peaceful coexistence," which allowed for "normalization" of state-to-state relations while conflict was sustained at an informal, often disguised level. When the Soviet leadership spoke of "peaceful coexistence," Western societies assumed that this meant "peace," that is, mutual respect and tolerance of each other's sovereignty. But within Soviet society and the web of Soviet allies, "peaceful coexistence" was seen specifically as a form of warfare. It was, indeed, a form of "asymmetric warfare" to be waged when the time was not ripe for conventional warfare with a technologically and economically superior adversary.

Warfare, however dangerous in a world in which danger is ever-present in so many forms, will continue to provide a pivotal junction in the achievement or retention of victory as it did in the past. There will be other October 14, 1066s; other battles as decisive as the Battle of Hastings.

Literature abounds with studies of war; the path to triumph in battle is exhaustively analyzed, and its rules and lessons are legion. And yet it is clear that victory is neither achieved nor guaranteed through warfare alone, although warfare may be essential to begin the path to victory, to defend it periodically, and to consolidate it. Perhaps, more important, war and the threat of war challenge the victorious to recognize that they must evolve and progress to defend their gains and maintain supremacy over adversaries. It forges the nation-state; it forces technological and scientific innovation. But when war dominates societies for protracted periods, victory may be threatened, put in abeyance, or become absent from all involved societies. Thus, to be most effective in helping to achieve victory, war must be used judiciously, swiftly, and with decisive strength of mind and resources.

To paraphrase the Chinese military-strategic philosopher Sun-tzu: The threat of war through the demonstration of military prowess is the best way to assist in the achievement of victory. To deter conflict through clearly demonstrated strength and willpower—and willpower must itself from time to time be shown—is the path to consolidating victory once its achievement has begun. In this regard, victory achieved without conflict is the acme of excellence. But where the path of victory has not yet begun, warfare or the threat of warfare may be the essential great risk a society must contemplate.

There is no reason to believe that society has outgrown the need for conflict, even if the "territorial imperative" motive, which dominated much of history until well into the twentieth century, no longer has the same appeal it once had. Technology has vitiated some of the purely physical aspects of territorial identification. Nonetheless, since we live in a spatial world, conflict takes place within the context of geopolitics and therefore geography.

While most observers have traditionally associated "victory" with the winning of wars, the real impact of war on victory is how it transforms society as a whole, focusing national identity, innovation, unity, productivity, and other factors. Victory depends not necessarily on winning battles, or even entire wars, but on whether war achieves certain positive objectives before it costs more than it gains. Inevitably, any war can "take time" out of a nation's historical progress, although it can also speed up the process of economic, scientific/technological/industrial, and social development. Wars are crucibles of nations.

Alan S. Milward, in his great study, *War, Economy and Society, 1939–1945*, noted how scientific and industrial productivity compounded dramatically for all of the combatants in World War II, achieving levels of progress which were, in essence, the foundations of unprecedented human development in the years which followed. Even Germany and Japan, which surrendered (nominally) unconditionally to the Allies, forfeiting all their assets and rights, were to emerge from the process with startling strengths, which were to exceed their ambitions in starting the war, in virtually all respects except geographic gain and international domination.

Only Britain, which also gained in many respects, and was the great covictor of World War II, suffered—in some senses terminally—from the war. As a society, Britain had moved beyond its "tipping point," the point at which the gains were outweighed by the negatives. At that point, the victory of Britain finally transferred to the United States, even though the victory of the West expanded to embrace large segments of the old British Empire, as well as the defeated nation-states of Germany and Japan. At the same time, the triumph of the Soviet Union in World War II did not translate into victory.

Georges Clemenceau noted: "The moment of military victory is a moment we must know how to seize if we are to establish and continue it in time of peace."

War is but one handmaiden of victory. And yet war remains a significant undertaking in the achievement of victory. Often it remains the only path to the commencement or defense of victory.

If henceforth all war will be total, in the sense that it rests on the shoulders of all members of the participating societies, there is also another way in which war is total war: It is, in its essence, the manifestation of a society's view of itself, which contributes to the vision of historic victory as a motivational icon. All successful societies have at their core the emblematic image of national heroism, and national heroes.

ANOTHER CENTURY OF WAR

The good news is that apocalyptic, global nuclear wars are now less likely than at any time in the past sixty years. The bad news is that smaller, fierce, almost traditional wars will arise in the twenty-first century with a frequency not seen even in the twentieth century. These, largely, will be wars of national creation—independence, or the foundation of states based on totally new criteria—and they will be fought largely in irregular skirmishes, with political maneuver and psychological operations (including terrorism). Those which make an impact will all be fought with the covert sponsorship of other states and powers.

That is not to deny the need for conventional armed forces and the main platforms of war—ships, aircraft, fighting vehicles—to meet irregular and formal threats. It is just that new rules of engagement will prevail. The Geneva Convention is gone; it remains merely a weapon which the West uses against itself.

But much of the world will remain untouched by these geographically contained, nasty wars, and will go about its business of growth. The United Nations, to an even greater degree than at the beginning of this millennium, will be impotent. The "peacekeeping" approach of the post–Cold War era will not stem the tide. Indeed, it will contribute to the ferocity of the wars, because "peacekeeping" compresses unresolved frustrations of antagonists, which finally give way to an orgy of "resolution."

We are unlikely to see any end to the immediate wave of wars before 2025, and possibly as late as 2050.

WHERE WILL WE SEE THE WARS?

From now and into the coming decades, we will see wars erupt in the Balkans, where low-level conflict has been suppressed and kept at the boiling point because of external interference since 1991. It will also emerge in the former Soviet Central Asian states, possibly Indonesia (an empire of formerly independent societies, chafing under Javanese control), parts of Africa (internally in Somalia, between Eritrea and Ethiopia, internally in Côte d'Ivoire, for example), and South-East Asia (the Philippines). There are many other areas with long-term structural instability: Colombia, Venezuela, and Bolivia; the western Sahara; and so on. South Africa may well, at some stage, move to swallow Swaziland, for example; South Africa itself may also face unrest, possibly triggered from across its borders as Zimbabwe collapses.

Major wars are also feasible, but more likely to be the subject of greater care, on the Korean Peninsula, between China and Taiwan, and perhaps between China and Mongolia; later between China and the United States. Given the tectonic shifts in Eastern Europe, and with regard to the European Union, it is highly probable that a major war between Turkey and Greece could occur within a decade, and that Cyprus—already one-third occupied by Turkish troops—could be completely overrun by Turkish troops, and occupied, spelling the first major formal military assault on a European Union state since the EU was created. Given the complex mosaic of competition between India and China, and China's relationship with Pakistan, the possibilities for renewed war exist between India and Pakistan, and even between Pakistan and Iran.

It is clear, too, that a new and major conflagration—perhaps several—has a high probability of occurrence in the Middle East. An "Arab-Israeli" war may prove to be the tool which the non-Arab Iranian clerical leadership seeks—just as Iraqi president Saddam Hussein contemplated in 2003 and attempted to initiate in 1991—to galvanize the chances for leadership survival in Iran. This would suit Syrian president Bashar al-Assad, and perhaps, if conditions were right, it might also suit a post–Hosni Mubarak Egypt. In the meantime, expect skirmishes between the Iranian clerical leaders and some of the Persian Gulf states, nominally over contested offshore resources, but really to challenge U.S. freedom of movement in the Gulf. It is possible, however, that the Iranian public will react sooner, rather than later, to overthrow the clerics, substantially changing the pattern of Middle Eastern conflict.

We will also see "antinationalist" wars: wars merely aimed at the destruction of sovereign authority, sometimes for religious reasons, such as the creation of a new Islamist caliphate. In this context, and coupled with the mass of underemployed in Saudi Arabia, and its declining per capita income, it is possible that an implosion could occur there within a decade, perhaps upon the passing of the aging King 'Abdallah bin 'Abd al-'Aziz al Sa'ud.

All of these scenarios are short-term and predictable. But what they demonstrate is that the *pattern* of conflict continues, and at an accelerated pace. And many of the conflicts will threaten major U.S. and Western interests. What will the United States, and its Western allies, do?

The nature of war is changing, and not just because of technologies. It is changing because primal human urges for survival and supremacy have been allowed to resurface. The gates of their confinement have been thrown open, and immediate gratification is all that clouds the minds of the great outflow of inmates. In it all, there will be little clarity. We will ask what war is, and what is peace? Even among noncombatants, peace will be accompanied by higher levels of anxiety. Nonetheless, overall human numbers will remain essentially unaffected by war.

All of these scenarios could be changed; the outcomes are not set in stone. Not yet. But we know that there will be more wars, and they can only be prevented or dampened by an understanding of underlying complexities and context. We have, particularly in the modern world, many experts who are specialists with intimate knowledge of different countries, or technologies. They do not always help us, because they often lack contextual understanding and depth of perception within a multidisciplinary framework. They are, as Oscar Wilde once said, people who "know the price of everything and the value of nothing."

We have not seen the end of war, only its transformation.

The successful prosecution of war, or its avoidance, however, requires great mastery over self, and it is this that we will now consider.

MASTERING SELF,
MASTERING FATE

In the commercial world, we can translate "language, belief structures, and lifestyle" into industry standards,
branding, and market domination. All of these are
honed, and made possible, by the challenge of competition
and the openness to adapt to market demands. What holds
true for the victory of societies in the form of states also
holds true for the victory of corporations. In today's society, with greater focus on the entrepreneur within the
economy, functioning in a high-tech environment, the
concept of "personal branding" applies the lessons of society and corporations directly to the individual.

Japan's Sony Corporation was the pioneer in video
recording systems with Betamax, but it soon saw Betamax
outstripped by the VHS system, developed by another
Japanese firm, Victor Company of Japan (JVC). VHS
leaped to market domination through the development of
a two-hour tape, which could record an entire movie unattended.

However, JVC's success with its VHS product was

transitory. By late 2004, VHS players accounted for only 2.5 percent of the market for video players in the United Kingdom, for example, and 80 percent of store video rentals were using DVD (digital video disk) technology. By 2006, it was difficult to find a videotape in the major U.S. video rental chains. This was of little concern to Sony, which dominated the total field of video production software and systems approaches, as well as video content and distribution of television production and viewing systems. By 2004, Sony had sales of $72 billion, while JVC had sales of only $8.7 billion.

Sony's success was that it did not just move to dominate the industry standard for a single aspect of technology, but that it saw its mission in the broader domination of an integrated network of enabling technologies or systems. In other words, it defined the "language"—the industry standards—on a more enduring scale than simply with regard to a single product line.

JVC discovered the reality that winning a war is not the same as achieving victory.

France's acute intellectual observer, Marc Fumaroli, in his important book *Quand l'Europe Parlait Français*, reminds us that, between the mid-seventeenth century and World War I, French was the universal language of diplomacy, culture, and fashion, and that an ability to read and speak it was essential to anyone claiming to be educated. But today, all that has gone with the wind. The government's attempts to protect the French language have failed miserably. Indeed, its efforts have made things worse. By sternly guarding against adoption of foreign words, the French elite ensured that French would lose out to English as the world language of business and communications. By contrast, the ancient Romans embraced the gods of conquered states as Roman gods; the English language absorbed all of the color of Britain's conquered subjects, the refugees it welcomed, and the peoples who mingled with its roving troops over the centuries. English continues to absorb new influences now that the United States has become the dominant power.

Each day we see around us the evidence of victory and defeat. We live the legacy of both, although the survival of our own genetic lines is itself a victory. But victory is relative, only rarely seen in absolute terms. Even vanquishment, when not accompanied by annihilation, attempts to rebuild to victory as remnants of the vanquished society regroup around the victor. Even so, their defeat is in some ways made permanent by the disappearance of language, customs, separate influence, lands, and privilege. The genetic line becomes subsumed, if it survives at all, in that of the victorious society.

In Eastern Australia, transported British convicts in the late eighteenth and early nineteenth centuries were freed at the end of their terms into a society largely made up of former convicts. They married, reproduced, and rebuilt. In Western Australia, transported British convicts were introduced as labor only twenty-one years after a free colony had been formed. The colony was so well established that as the convicts were released into society, they were shunned by it, and virtually all died without issue. In microcosm, the end of their genetic lines made their defeats final.

Victory is the result of the comprehensive strengths of a society, a corporation, or an individual. In geopolitical terms, for a society, this takes into account its strategic industrial depth, its access to resources, the ability to mobilize the national (and transnational) will of its members and allies, its economic and political complexities, and so on. All victory today is the result of total war in that all aspects of society contribute to success or failure. In corporate life, or the challenge to achieve dominance for one's family and heirs, the lessons are the same: The battle for victory is end-less and requires constant attention to the comprehensive nature of the context and individual strengths. In all areas—societies, corporations, and individuals—arrogance begets complacency and diminished sensitivity to change, chal-lenge, or opportunities. Arrogance is the dark side of pride, the sentiment which should be a motivating and assuring factor.

Victories, like all other aspects of civilization, are the re-sult of patterns of thought and behavior which evolve over time. Perhaps more important, victory is brought about by a profound disturbance to those patterns. Complete victory requires a symbiosis of the pattern's evolution and its subse-quent disturbance. And yet societies, corporations, and in-dividuals cling to continuity and fear change. Perhaps this is because continuity is the function of a society's members when represented as a mass, and change is the instrument of the individual. In this regard, as Gustave Le Bon noted: "A people is an organism created by the past, and, like every other organism, it can only be modified by slow hereditary accumulations. It is tradition that guides men, and more es-pecially when they are in a crowd."

He went on to say: "Civilization is impossible without traditions, and progress impossible without the destruction of those traditions."

Victory, then, is in many respects the harmonious compo-sition and destruction of traditions. Success lies in achieving and maintaining that harmonious balance, on an ongoing—even intergenerational—basis. All things must be considered in balance in building victory, and the will to exercise control over one's own sovereignty is part of the equation. Subject na-tions—like dependent corporations, or dependent people—are not only those that must beg for food and existence; subject nations are also those that must beg for protection.

The hallmark of the rising world power, the rising corporation, and the rising individual is an energy and zeal which thrive on competition, dreams, and an acute awareness of others. In many respects, the energy is possible only because of the awareness of other powers, other corporations, other individuals, and the desire to emulate or exceed them. Arrogance arises when other powers, corporations, or individuals no longer seem worthy of respect or competition. When challenged, the response of the arrogant will be either to awaken and revive the concept of victory as a yet-unfinished thing, or to turn over in its self-absorbed slumber and drift away.

The global empire of the Netherlands is no more; Britain's once vast multinational corporation, the East India Company, has vanished; neither do the Medicis dominate as a family, nor do the Vanderbilts.

Will Microsoft prevail two generations after the passing of its founding leader, Bill Gates? Any corporation, even Microsoft, which does devote enormous resources to divine future trends, must ponder deeply the underlying goals which will still translate into action and motivation generations hence. We know that Microsoft has attempted to plan even beyond the present generation, even given that markets and economic cycles have narrowed into periods measured three months at a time. Few individuals, corporations, or states can clear away sufficient time to gather together the knowledge of historic trends and context, and to then learn to understand them so that they can think about and plan for the future. We're too busy fighting the immediate fires which threaten to engulf us to plan for the future.

As we have noted, victory requires tradition and history, building belief and goals. But it also requires "the destruction of those traditions." This present Age of Global Transformation is part of the breaking of all of our traditions.

Osama bin Laden and his coterie strive for the opportunity to create a new caliphate which would be a major geopolitical power, but which can only come into being if the West colludes by committing political suicide. The West's suicide would occur if the component Western states continue to refrain from cooperation, and do not show zeal in their own defense. Even so, the radical Islamists are dependent not only on the West providing the rope for its own hanging, but also on Western technologies for their own movement, communications, and weaponry. It *is* possible that the Islamists can achieve a strong measure of success in securing territory—a state of sorts—and in creating chaos in the West, but the Islamists have none of the fundamentals to achieve victory.

They lack the tools to create the food and other mechanisms for long-term survival of large population bases. They could, ultimately, only prevail over a period of declining productivity, increasing poverty, and ultimately famine and declining population. They would, given present approaches, fail within a generation or two. On the other hand, the Iranian Islamists recognize the failings of their temporary allies and surrogates—the bin Ladenists—and have attempted to build a balanced empire, legitimized by religion but in fact committed to developing the tools of language domination, technological competence, and productivity which would enable them to overwhelm all of the Islamic *ummah* (world). Ultimately, then, the vapid zeal of the bin Ladenists serves only Iran's clerics.

The West, failing to comprehend the delicate choreography between the historical and intelligent organism which is Iran and the simplistic and unproductive force which is the fundamentalist caliphate movement, has been surrendering its options and credibility. The probable result—absent an uprising of Iranians to remove the clerics from power—is that Iran will be a major power later in the twenty-first century. An overthrow of the clerics could see a moderate, free-market, secular Iran as one of the emerging great powers even sooner, given its geopolitical position, its resources, its historical identity and sense of self, and— most important—the fact that it has participated in the destruction of traditions. Iran is ready to break the mold, and is preparing to recast it, in the words of Persian poet Omar Khayyám, "nearer the heart's desire."

Europe has also "broken the mold," but has failed to create a new grand strategy for the future. Unlike even clerical Iran, it has avoided defining what it wishes to be. Despite the efforts of Napoleon and Hitler, there has never before been a "European." And no attempt has been made, even now by the European Union (EU), to create a European culture, language, or overriding identity and set of principles. The attempt in 2005 to create an EU constitution was merely an attempt to impose and legitimate a set of laws which confirmed the separate cultural identities of the member societies.

The Chinese example, however, is more like the Persian or Iranian: It presents a conscious vision of victory in the longer term, embracing a unifying language and culture, built from the broken—and then reconstructed—mold.

The Chinese and Persians are consciously attempting to master themselves and their fate. The Europeans and West in general are attempting only to legitimize a status quo which, in fact, has already been eclipsed. The Western tradition has been broken. It could again form the basis of a revitalized and continuing victory, but not in the absence of a vision which embraces the opportunity of the present chaos.

HAS THE WEST LOST MASTERY OVER ITSELF?

It is not a question of whether the West has lost its cohesiveness and momentum toward a consolidation of its longstanding victory since the end of the Cold War. The question is whether the West can *regain* its advantage—its victory orientation—over the coming years before the crystallization of a clear and unambiguous threat.

The West has been in "strategic decline" since the end of the Cold War, largely because the galvanizing external nuclear threat from the USSR disappeared. The only new "threat" to emerge in a way which galvanizes society since that time has been terrorism, but that challenge is so amorphous—and to most people so nonthreatening to victory—that it has been the cause of fracturing, rather than uniting. Great opportunities have been lost by the West, perhaps the greatest being the failure to comprehensively embrace Russia as an integral partner. To many, however, the lingering comfort of the Cold War and its clear delineations have encouraged the continued perception of Russia as a more toothless "enemy."

That is not to say, for example, that the West should be forced to think in terms of characterizing China as the "enemy" of the West. China will rival the West in many ways soon enough. Indeed, the principal threat to the West remains a clerically controlled Iran; it is, through sponsorship of terrorism and political action, the true, unrecognized focus of anti-Western activities. But this is solely because of the nature of the Iranian leadership, which had been put in place by the actions of then-U.S. president Jimmy Carter in 1979, when he destroyed the Government of the Shah of Iran. If Iran can be restored to moderate, nationalist government—sending the clerics of Iran back to the mosques—then it will transform from implacable adversary to an integral part of "the West."

Ending the rule of the clerics in Iran would help both the West and the Iranian people. But that does not solve the problem of how the West can reignite its passion for victory. Indeed, it is possible only that an unambiguous military attack by Iran, or North Korea, on U.S. or European targets would be sufficient to shock the West from its slumber. Even the firestorm of deliberately engineered riots and terrorist acts across Europe—from the bombing attacks on Madrid and London in 2004 and 2005, to the riots through France, Belgium, and Germany in October-November 2005—failed to awaken Western societies. In France, the government specifically chose not even to identify its assailants in the great weeks of rioting and destruction.

The biggest threat to Western revival, then, is not a strong military power, such as China promises to be. Rather, it is the creeping cancer of the division of society into pockets by apathy, anomie, and angst. The "salami strategy," it used to be called: cutting the opponent down, slice by slice. We have responded with a "war on terror." It might as well have been a "war against unhappiness." Threats need to be identified with specific people, nations, and governments. Osama bin Laden and his terrorist colleagues have ensured that this clarity has been denied to the West. But Iran, and its clerics (but not the Iranian population, which remains intrinsically pro-Western), have yet to be understood clearly as the source of the threat they represent to the West.

This does not mean that the West should galvanize behind the concept of a war with Iran. That would merely punish the Iranian people, who are themselves victims of their leaders. But absent some galvanizing force and action, the West will likely resist revitalization until China itself emerges in a "checkmate" position, having developed its economic, political, military, and social power to the point where the West awakens to find the giant already supping from its table.

The West could have mobilized in the 1930s and helped ensure that Hitler, for example, did not develop Germany into a threat to global stability. But then, too, the West chose to sleep, forcing it into a great military conflict which could have been averted. Must we again await the full swing of the pendulum, sleeping all the while until it reaches its apogee?

Achieving decisiveness and self-control, and seizing fate, are critical elements in securing victory, but the triumph requires a strong self-belief system to achieve and sustain. We must now consider where God—or a belief system—and victory coincide.

GOD AND VICTORY

SIX

No victory was ever begun, or sustained, without a belief system that was greater than the individual. However, reliance on belief alone, without the balance of other strengths, is the path to defeat.

Philosopher Gustave LeBon in the late nineteenth century touched on the potency of the relationship of God to all societies, and he understood that the more mystical and unassailable the inspiration of the divine to society, the more potent its force. He said: "The most redoubtable idols do not dwell in temples, nor the most despotic tyrants in palaces; both the one and the other can be broken in an instant. But the invisible masters that reign in our innermost selves are safe from every effort at revolt, and only yield to the slow wearing away of centuries."

Iranian President Mahmud Ahmadi-Nejad said on October 25, 2005, that Israel should be wiped from the map, a taunt he kept repeating in the coming months. Whether or not this was cynical politicking to galvanize domestic Iranian support, this was conscious religious warfare in a pure form, ostensibly pitting Muslims against Jews and Christians. As Ahmadi-Nejad intended—because he repeated the sentiment a day later—the Western media and political leadership responded with horror and disgust, attacking the newly elected Iranian President. Ahmadi-Nejad intended that this should force Iranians—who are overwhelmingly disenchanted with the clerics who hold power—to rally together, around the government, in the face of Western hostility, giving him a unified state and the ability to eliminate dissidents.

Ayatollah Ruhollah Khomeini, facing similar domestic unrest and dissatisfaction in 1982, took Iran to war with Iraq as a means of galvanizing national support. Ahmadi-Nejad was playing on religious fears to forcibly create a new climate of threat and trigger war.

We believe in the West that we live in an age of rational enlightenment, and yet religion plays as vital a role in war, peace, and development as ever it has throughout history. The wars of the 1990s and today are inspired by religion, not economics or territory, and this trend will continue into the indefinite future. It is part of us. Moreover, the subtle schisms in Christianity caused the inflammation of the wars of the former Yugoslavia in the 1990s, with Western Christianity supporting Muslim extremists against Eastern Christianity. Many in today's culture of materialism remain unaware of the extent to which religious foundations affect their ethical positions and decisionmaking.

In Iraq, Iranian Shi'a leaders support Sunni Muslims against the Iraqi Shi'a leadership. And the corrupt election process in Ukraine at the end of 2004 was about liberal Western media and political forces manipulating the system in support of Western Christians (Ukraine's Uniate Catholics) against the majority Ukrainian Orthodox Christians.

These were not portrayed as religious conflicts, but that is exactly what they were. We have learned in the West to cloak our religiously based prejudices in more abstract cultural arguments, because we believe that we are today more pragmatically and scientifically grounded in our beliefs and reasoning.

Our belief in ourselves as a species has never been

higher. All things are possible for us, given our scientific and technological prowess. If there is something we cannot have now, then in time it will be ours, given the inexorable march of human endeavor.

And yet.

And yet there is a growing sense of isolation, of being removed by our "technological independence" from our neighbors. We often work during the day in relative isolation from others; we return home at night to our own world of artificial companionship with the television or the internet, our views shaped by remote voices, and our ability to debate and reason through argument and social intercourse withering from the lack of a stimulating variety of companionship.

Human survival is dependent upon the cooperation of individuals within a society and our ability to mate and reproduce from a pool of potential partners; we know this emotionally and intellectually. It is therefore a physical and psychological need. But we are replacing this process of normal human interaction—which satisfies our physical and emotional hungers—through our ability to work, often, from home, connecting remotely to our employers' databases. We select mates through "internet dating," our language skills reduced to iconic grunts and groans, often electronic, our mating rituals reduced to shorthand symbols transmitted through text messaging or email.

Oratory is removed from society; televised presidential debates are determined not by great intellectual argument, but by sound bites, phrases too brief to provide a basis of reason; by images of expression flashed across a candidate's face.

And yet it seems to work. But at the same time, societies—particularly in advanced technological countries—begin to lose their cohesive nature. Society narrows into zones—pools of light—consisting of the immediate home and family, the immediate needs of survival.

There is, as a result, a large part of Western society which begins to doubt itself, and views this progress as fragile; perhaps, in its isolation, beyond nature's intent; beyond God's intent. Who are we? Are we different from our neighbors? Are they our enemy or competitor for survival? Or our essential companion in achieving it? There is now, as there has been throughout civilization's development, an awe of those who appear to know exactly who they are, and what they are intended to do, people who are motivated solely by belief, rather than knowledge, the holy man who is a tool of the divine.

Our very isolation and lack of cohesion as a society make us vulnerable in the face of the "true believers," who appear filled with a certainty of mission and a divine inspiration.

Modern Western society is today assailed by small bands of people—the jihadists, primarily—ostensibly motivated *solely* by beliefs, rather than what we could call rational thought, or empirically based knowledge. Modern society, isolated and divided, and despite its aggregate wealth and power, is easy for a cohesive belief-based opponent to weaken or destroy. Remember Napoleon I's maxim: The moral is to the physical as two is to one (psychological, or belief, factors are twice as important as physical factors). It applies not just to the battlefield, but to all of society.

The sense of isolation within society is not new. Remote villagers and herders felt it in ancient times, and even in living memory, before electronic communication. What is different is that the sense of isolation is today felt in the midst of the urban roar. Within the deafening ocean crowd there is silence. Yet we know there is a life force within us.

And the concept of a life force beyond oneself is expressed in a belief in God or in gods. This belief, and the worship of the greater power, the deity, has in all cultures led to expressions in art and architecture, and in written language, intended to glorify God. It is a thing beyond human individuality, and given that society is a gathering of individuals, it is also something beyond society. Thus the belief in God leads mankind to art, architecture, intellectual expression, and unified activity in the creation of orderly society and moral or ethical standards.

The path, then, from religion to art and architecture, intellectual rationale, and civilization leads on to the gathering of power by a society: to victory. It is no wonder that societies have always believed that God, or the gods, was the key to their survival, strength, and power. The instinct to organize, in the name of the moral or ethical structure which grows out of religion, is indeed part of what gives victory to societies.

In essence, then, belief in God represents an inherent "natural order," which is at the core of victory, but there is always the element of human will, skill, and wisdom, which either moves along this path or slips from it.

Rome, Jerusalem, Angkor Wat, the ruins of Persepolis, the Acropolis of Athens, or of Alexander's birthplace at Pella, the pyramids of Giza: These are direct examples of enduring edifices built on faith. When greatness of civilization is built, and victory created and sustained, it is achieved out of the belief in the society's implicit justice and rightness. When victory is lost, and only the shells, the physical temples, are left, these serve as reminders that victory was once won and can be regained.

The right to survival and perpetuation is therefore intellectualized and emotionalized as justice. Each person has innate knowledge of the external aspects of survival (and therefore justice), but the concept of justice, being outside the control of any single individual, becomes mystical and abstract because the source and grantor of justice always lies beyond each individual. It becomes the eternal un-known; the subject of conjecture and wonder. Mankind's need to understand his environment leads to the conceptu-alization of this abstract and implacable justice as God, or the gods, codified as religion. This explains why so many religions, evolving in different regions, have so many as-pects in common. Religion is innate to mankind, and is di-rectly linked to the will to victory.

Those who stray from the religion (or even the pseudoreligion of ideology) of their community, or from the mainstream functions of the day, frighten the society by challenging its belief in the justice of its victory; they are therefore vilified as apostates and heretics, threatening unity and survival.

Where societies are organized along very direct hierar-chical lines, there is a greater reliance on religion or social conformity. This implies a relatively simple structure, which also often implies an economically poor and less-developed society. In complex, highly urbanized, and wealthy societies—where there is a greater tendency to a laissez faire attitude toward divergent lifestyles and the del-egation of the functions of societal administration to elected or appointed officials—there is less demand for reli-gious conformity. At the same time, in all societies, when threats to unity or welfare (or survival) arise, the group ten-dency toward religious conformity strengthens.

As philosopher Eric Hoffer (1902–83) pointed out in his brilliant 1951 thesis, *The True Believer,* "The discontent generated in backward communities by their contact with Western civilization is not primarily resentment against ex-ploitation by domineering foreigners. It is rather the result of a crumbling or weakening of tribal solidarity and com-munal life."

The frustration felt by some in the Muslim *ummah* in the late twentieth and early twenty-first centuries directly parallels the frustration of the societies of European Christendom in the late Middle Ages. The introduction of new ideas and debate brought about by the innovations of movable type and the printing press in the mid-fifteenth century compounded the schisms which already existed in Christianity, polarizing society and effectively creating a revolution in which the forces of modernization eventually triumphed.

Little wonder, then, that the victorious society is one in which the zeal of the galvanizing and unthinking passions is ultimately tempered by individual thought and action. This is the balancing of the mystical with the temporal: the harmonizing of God, government, and the individual.

But what if "God" takes another form? Utopianism—the belief in collective perfection, often expressed in Fabianism or socialism—is clearly derived from the same genetic impulse as belief in God or the supernatural forces of destiny. It is the belief in the power and righteousness of a force beyond the individual. Modern utopianists and socialists believe their interpretation of the collective spirit to be infinitely superior to, and more explicable than, religion. Traditional religions often see heresy in socialism. But they derive from the same source—the innate belief in the salvation which is delivered by a collective spirit, greater than the individual—and compete for man's passion for a stern, guiding presence to take ultimate responsibility for the meaning of life.

So delicately balanced is this belief—because nothing tangible unquestionably validates it—that those zealously committed to their religion or dogma brook no opposition to it; neither do they tolerate any variation in its application.

But the essential difference between those who shape their God as "utopia"—whether socialist or democratic—and those who see God as the mystical king of all creation is a difference not between "science" and "mysticism" but between short-term and long-term desire. "Scientific socialism" promised heaven on earth (but not quite yet); traditional religion promises heaven in a more remote and less tangible place.

Gustave LeBon noted: "Were it possible to induce the masses to adopt atheism, this belief would exhibit all the intolerant ardor of a religious sentiment, and in its exterior form would soon become a cult." The collapse of communism, which became starkly apparent around 1990, ended the dogma of communism's "inevitability," leaving "post-communism communists" to rely on arguments about security and social justice to defend their beliefs. This demystification of communism meant that it held no competitive allure against, for example, mystical Islamism, that amalgam of politics and revisionist (and frequently heretical) versions of Islam.

Imbuing leadership with legitimacy and the moral authority of God—or the pseudogod of the collective—has had profound effects on victory throughout history.

In simple societies, however, the already close bond between the belief system and power is hammered by crisis into a more brittle and rigid fusion. Either the society wins at a great, single toss of the dice, or it fails and victory is lost. The enormous absorptive powers of complexity are unavailable to such societies to cushion or suffuse the pressures applied either by the society itself or by a foe.

What is widely seen, but seldom mentioned, is the reality that societies of direct structure and religious orthodoxy or zealousness are also often poor, in both economic and infrastructural terms. The question arises, then, whether complexity causes wealth and victory, or the other way around.

Societies which blossom into victory are increasingly—as technology develops—those which have achieved a viable balance between "discipline from God" and "discipline from society": the inspirational and the immediate; the emotional and the physical. Hence the compunction to follow fashion: fashionable ethics, fashionable ideology, fashionable manners, fashionable dress, food, and habits.

That belief systems and the natural urge to victory are linked should be obvious: They are merely different expressions of the same impulse. There is a balance in, and natural order to, how societies strive competitively for victory. Failure to strive for victory invites the excessive demands and depredations of others.

Victory and God are inextricable, because both represent the societal struggle to survive and prosper through history.

THE COMING AGE OF RELIGIOUS WARS

The West will call the wars which are now developing attacks by extremist fanatics against the reason of an enlightened age. But that is just semantics. In reality, the "fanatics" merely wear their beliefs on their sleeves; in the West, beliefs are submerged beneath a complex web of societal behavior, wealth, and established success. It is as important to understand Western underlying beliefs as it is to understand the beliefs of the West's opponents.

Can Western society remain cohesive and successful without God? That is the center of the great debate between "urban intellectualism" or "modern materialism" and the more religiously oriented parts of society. Between the "red states" and the "blue states" in the U.S. voting pattern, if you will. History shows that societies do, in fact, lose their ability to defend themselves if they are preoccupied solely with individual greed or excessive internal competition. Equally, however, the abandonment of great scientific inquiry, and reversion to religious absolutism—as we saw in, say, fourteenth-century Christianity, prohibiting, as far as possible, all dissent and inquiry—also ultimately leads to the collapse of societies.

Religion and religiously oriented conflict will not disappear as long as human society exists. It will constantly change in form, and religious conformity will attempt to suppress any dissent to its orthodoxy. But all victory derives from the balance between the inspiration of religion—expressed often as ethics and societal values—and the self-discipline of the individual. Significantly, Western society has today drifted substantially from its traditional ethical values, and this is demonstrated by short-term thinking and greed—the opposite of the long-term requirement of victory. On the other hand, the West is being assailed by an extremist Islamist-jihadist force bound solely by belief, and not by the balancing power of individual responsibility and human inquiry.

The world is thus in a race between a force which is, without any external pressure, allowing itself to abandon its historical victory and to disintegrate in many respects, and a force which has no inherent strength other than its belief and its willingness to destroy all in its path. The jihadists may well expend all of their power before the West surrenders its wealth. But we in the West would do well to remember that the "dark ages" were caused by the gradual collapse of the great Roman civilization, falling under the weight of its own self-consumption, to be overrun by barbarian hordes.

The world is essentially on a knife-edge. The "modern world" (the West, including most Muslim states) could see its unity, wealth, and security wither away in the face of extremists who claim nothing but God as their strength. Or the "modern world," by skill, resolution, and cooperation, could create a climate of education and prosperity which could, within a decade, end the basis of support for the jihadists' momentum toward a victory which could—like that of the hordes who overran Rome—never be sustained.

Depending, then, on the steps we take now, the West could retain its momentum and victory, or it could abdicate victory and begin its slow decline. But even if the West refuses to save itself, the jihadists will not attain their own victory unless they transform into a society which has the responsibility to create the tools needed to feed, sustain, and protect its members. In terms that matter, neither do they reap, nor do they sow. That is not the same for Muslim societies in general; for them, they will succeed as all powers have succeeded, by balancing God and Caesar.

In the West, there is a growing debate over the role of God in society. In China, as the great internal migration leads to yet bigger urban societies, there will be an increasing demand for religious expression, and this will threaten the rule of the Communist Party of China. Denial of a place for religion in Western society will weaken national harmony and productivity. In the United States this factor already contributes to the schism which has seen the creation, essentially, of two American societies, inhabiting the same nation. Denial of a place for religion in Chinese society could be the tinder for a new revolution, fueled by massive unemployment and unmet economic expectations.

Looking into the twenty-first century, Western societies have victory which is theirs to lose; China has victory to grasp; jihadist Islamism may flower briefly in the sun, but, as with all power based solely on belief without responsibility to build, it will never attain victory.

But forget the jihadists for a moment; the West itself is engaged in religious conflict. The majority Catholic and Protestant Christian community has been drawn into confrontation with Eastern Orthodoxy. The religious, cultural, and geopolitical aspects of this schism cannot be separated. But when the European Union itself increasingly absorbs Orthodox Christians by expanding eastward, and when, as is now the case, more than 30 million Americans are Orthodox Christians, perhaps it is time to see whether Christianity is subtly at war with itself, and whether this matter, after almost two millennia of religious schism, can be addressed before it is exploited by militant Islam, as is now the case in the Balkans.

But Islam itself—within both the main Sunni and Shi'a branches as blocs—tends to look within itself and to artificially created Western "enemies" to exert pressures which enforce solidarity within its own ranks. Osama bin Laden, the Iranian Shi'a clerics, and Sudan's Hasan al-Turabi, all try to force the West, en masse, to oppose Islam en masse, so as to cause Muslims to rally under the jihadists' own banners. Thus far, the West has resisted characterizing all Muslims as "enemies," but the October 25, 2005, outburst by the new Iranian president, Mahmud Ahmadi-Nejad, stating that Israel should be wiped from the map and that the United States was a defeatable enemy, was all about consolidating an increasingly restive Iranian population around the clerical leadership.

God, then, is not dead in the struggle for victory. He is used to create a siege mentality, or to engender pride, identity, sacrifice. Moreover, the need for a god figure is innate within us, and those societies which deny this potent and unifying force—in favor of short-term consumerism—are, in essence, denying the need to act collectively and in the longer term.

How societies react in the face of the growing mobilization of Islam—largely financed into effective jihadist action now by Iran's clerics—will determine whether the West falls into disunity and declining productivity over the next decade. It is as serious as that. But for Iran's clerical leaders, the coming few years represent a life-or-death struggle. If they fail to galvanize Iranians by creating a siege mentality, then they will be gone from the political scene.

And right now, God is their *only* tool for survival.

The place of societal belief systems in victory is clear, but there are other strengths we must now explore on the path to victory.

THE PREREQUISITES OF VICTORY

SEVEN

Belief in a greater power than one's self is essential to victory, but self-belief is of equal importance in obtaining and sustaining victory.

J. Paul Getty, the late oil tycoon, once said, when asked how to make a fortune, that it was necessary to work eighteen hours a day, seven days a week, for ten years. And then to strike oil. Success, in other words, was a matter of luck, or opportunity, but with the understanding that opportunity—"luck"—comes only with preparation and positioning.

All victory is the result of a combination of preparation, skill, fortitude, and opportunity. Of these, preparation, fortitude, and opportunity are by far the most important. Preparation can, in many respects, compensate for lack of skills, but skills alone cannot always compensate for lack of preparation. The greatest preparation lies in the acquisition of understanding on many levels.

There will always be a temptation, particularly by those who have achieved early success, to forgo the demanding processes of preparation. Thus, early failure is the best base for preparation: It cautions the true leader of the need for vigilance, but early failures will deter the faint-hearted and shallow, who at best should be followers and in some cases should be avoided altogether within the cam-

paign for victory. It is debatable whether, in fact, meaningful victory can be achieved under the leadership of someone who has not experienced failure or challenge; who has
not had the opportunity to acquire wisdom. The path to
leadership, and therefore victory, is incremental. It is true
that some acquire wisdom, and attract good fortune, faster
and more easily than others. This is true for institutions as
it is for individuals.

FAITH IN SELF: The confidence with which victory is
sought is the result of an inner knowledge. Only through
such perception can a self-*belief* be stimulated to pervade
and motivate the individual and society. The bulk of society moves according to a sense of collective self-belief, a
faith. However, those who need to master their society in
order to achieve victory need first to understand the underpinning realities which have contributed to that faith, so
that the faith may itself be better understood, nurtured,
and led.

An understanding of self requires ruthlessly honest introspection, which is possibly the thing resisted most
fiercely by all, for fear of questioning—and thus losing—
one's sense of identity. The irony is that such a process inevitably leads to a stronger sense of identity, and therefore
to a stronger sense of confidence and destiny. Faith in self,
and in one's own society, does not preclude a sensitivity to
the needs of others, but it enables the strength to place the
victory of one's own society above the needs of others.

Fear and frustration, self-doubt and insecurity are more
often what govern those individuals who sublimate themselves in group identity.

UNDERSTANDING HISTORY: Individuals resist a true, deep
understanding of history because this often raises questions
of one's own relationship to it, which again touches on the

question of personal identity. As a result, the study of history has, in virtually all societies, been reduced to iconographic symbols, to motivate members and to help reinforce the sense of context—comfort, really—of their citizens.

During World War II, for example, an understanding by the Allied leadership of the ways in which the closed crowds around both Adolf Hitler and Hideki Tojo separated them from their respective societies would have made it possible for the Allies to split the German and Japanese leaders from their support bases. Stripped of faith in their own leaders and relieved of the belief that they would suffer true "unconditional surrender," as promised by the United States (the loss of all rights, including the right to life), the German and Japanese people would have been more amenable to the sanity of a negotiated surrender.

UNDERSTANDING THE SCOPE OF OPPORTUNITY AND POSSIBILITIES: We are prepared for confrontation, but the greatest scope for victory comes from opportunity. Victory does not derive from conquest alone; conquest must be the final resort when opportunities for seizing the initiative peacefully—through superior vision and sensitivity to surroundings—have been lost. Sun-tzu said: "If the enemy leaves a door open, you must rush in."

Napoleon, too, did not look for generals merely anxious for the fray. "Give me lucky generals," he said, in the knowledge that "luck" comes to those who recognize opportunity, and seize it, as the path to victory. "Opportunism" has become a pejorative term precisely because it implies a tendency to rely solely on the emergence of good fortune instead of undertaking the hard work necessary to fully exploit opportunity.

Failure to understand one's own goals, and failure to understand one's own values, means that opportunities may lead to the wilderness, and the transitory success of opportunism—which we may interpret as the *abuse* of opportunity—will not lead on to victory.

That many opportunities fail to yield their anticipated potential should in no way diminish the delight in finding each new possibility.

IDENTIFYING GOALS AS THE BASIS OF A GRAND STRATEGY: As we discussed in Chapter Three, articulation of goals—personal or societal—is one of the most difficult human tasks. On a personal level, the revelation of true and overarching goals, even to oneself, entails risks. Failure to achieve articulated goals means, on a personal level, the prospect of the collapse of self-image, and the risk of ridicule or ostracism by peers and competitors. There is the risk of ridicule even due to the unique (or alternatively the uninspiring) nature of the goals. The identification of goals—representing a person's innermost desires, beliefs, and rational thoughts—lays bare that person's soul, exposing it to vulnerability.

Two things are fundamental:

- Without definitive goals, definitive victories cannot be achieved. The more vague the goals, the more vague and unsatisfactory the victory.
- The articulation of goals invites challenges, because even the goal of a victory—whatever its specific subsidiary goals—implies a threat to another society. Therefore, it will always be the case that some goals within an overall grand strategy for victory must remain either secret or disguised by a cloak of mystifying nuance.

Failure to define goals renders the architecture of victory incomplete. No victory exists without goals. Some goals may be articulated openly; some may be kept secret, or semisecret; but all should derive first from the *needs* of the society, and secondarily from the *wishes* of the society. Where a need is clear but wishes have not yet been formulated, it is the function of a leader to lead.

IDENTIFYING THREATS AND OBSTACLES: History is replete with nations capable of survival but which have refrained from their own salvation.

It is usually easiest to identify—although not necessarily to understand—the threats, or potential threats, from outside one's own society. Equally, it is more difficult to identify the obstacles to victory *within* one's own society. Damage to the foundations of victory lies most often in the unwittingly corrosive behavior of individuals who, following a natural impulse, place their own security ahead of that of the society. And there are those whose innate timidity or desire to sustain the status quo blinds their judgment to what is required to defend victory in changing circumstances.

UNDERSTANDING DESIRES AND BELIEF SYSTEMS: When most people talk of desires, they mean solely emotional desires; when they talk of goals they mean rational or intellectual objectives. Leadership and the will to victory usually fuse emotional and objective functions, because the real security of victory requires both tangible and perceptual recognition. It is important, therefore, to ensure that *desire*, which dominates and sways the immediate consciousness, does not detract from the process of achieving strategic objectives.

It is the function of psychological strategy to help structure perceptions so that the emotional and objective goals are harmonized within one's own society and confused in the mind of the adversary.

IDENTIFYING ALLIES AND TEAMING PARTNERS: There are two main times when it is important to identify allies and partners in the quest for victory: when the need for victory becomes apparent and the battle for it is commencing; and after victory has been secured and it is necessary to embrace others in its warmth in order that they be restrained from becoming adversaries. When the initial victory has been achieved and is being consolidated, it can thrive only by expanding. This expansion need not be territorial, but it must represent an expansion of the ability of the victorious society to protect itself in an evolving world, and to enhance its leadership by constantly improving its welfare and knowledge.

Enduring victory, then, is an expanding universe which must be ready to embrace new, and sometimes formerly hostile, societies. However, new alliances and partnerships cannot endure if the other countries are held at arm's length, or treated paternalistically. It quickly becomes apparent to an ally or partner whether the relationship is one of mutuality, or merely one of convenience.

Understanding allies, and potential allies, is as vital as understanding adversaries. To be failed or abandoned by an ally at a critical juncture sets back the cause of victory. Therefore the understanding of, and respect for, an ally must be equal to the understanding and respect held for one's own society and for an adversary. Any diminution of understanding or respect for any of the three sides of the triangle is a weakness which will damage the cause of victory.

Even the denigration of an enemy must be conducted with great caution for fear that it will breed arrogance within one's own society or among the allies, opening the door to complacency and vulnerability. Similarly, praise and respect for allies must be based on genuine understanding and the sentiment this engenders, or it will ring false and the ally will not remain firmly on the flank toward victory.

WHERE SELF-BELIEF IS DETERMINING HISTORICAL OUTCOMES

Who today sees opportunity in the confusion of the Age of Global Transformation? Who is laying the foundations for a future twenty, thirty, fifty, or a hundred years hence? Only China is thinking deeply and comprehensively in this context. Despite the reality that the future belongs to he who will seize it, and that, for example, India and China are more or less equally placed for future leadership, it is only China which has an almost wartime belief in the inevitability and justice of its victory. Indian leaders, however, are gradually awakening to the necessity for comprehensive long-range planning.

Because of China's sense of destiny it will not act precipitously to grasp at victory, but will await and pursue appropriate opportunities. U.S.-based Russian philosopher Lev Navrozov believes that China will pursue an ancient Chinese strategy called *shashou jiang* ("assassin's mace") entailing surprise and fatally decisive ruthlessness, maneuvering outside the historical rules of international society. He is certainly correct in this. China is indeed thinking in terms of *shashou jiang*.

Let us examine some of Beijing's options. China is now, for example, with Iran and certain members of the European Union, negotiating oil contracts in euros, rather than in dollars. Iran in 2006 created an "oil bourse," denominated in euros. Iraqi president Saddam Hussein had also toyed with this idea. Such a bourse could help break the market for oil in U.S. dollar terms, and weaken the U.S. currency, perhaps saving the euro from the weakening

EU political momentum. Would it help China at this time? It is to its benefit to see Europe strengthen as a counterweight to the United States. But the West could unite again in the future, this time against China. Moreover, the markets and resources of the West as a whole, including those of the United States, are vital elements of China's prosperity.

So an attempt to undermine the U.S. dollar is unlikely to be China's *shashou jiang*. A premature move by Beijing could reinforce a rift between China and the United States, regalvanizing the United States into strategic resurgence and destroying China's own economic base.

China, more likely, will use science, technology, and space to achieve its *shashou jiang*. China is investing heavily in space capabilities—including permanent moon basing within a decade or so—which would enable it to use space-based weapons to neutralize strategic ballistic missiles. Chinese leaders have taken seriously Ronald Reagan's and Stefan Possony's Strategic Defense Initiative (SDI), and have begun to implement it in a new sense. By neutralizing the U.S., Russian, Indian, Iranian, and all other ballistic missiles and the potential nuclear threat they carry, it would render the global playing field more equal. China is not attempting to go to the moon merely for "national prestige"; that would be wasteful.

At that point, China's nanotechnology lead would ensure its ability to fight an essentially robotic war against the United States and all others.

The potential timeframe for a Chinese checkmate capability could be less than twenty years, if China does not first implode—or stall—politically and socially. The West does not have to stand idly by and allow China to achieve a strategic checkmate. But first the West must awaken and, like China, "break the mold" and see opportunities from new perspectives. Moreover, a rise in China's strategic and economic capabilities does not in itself portend disaster for the West. Given the global transition, over the coming half-century, to new energy forms which could dampen the competition for available fossil fuel resources, it is more than possible that China's rise as a victorious power could complement and enhance the victory of the West. Indeed, in the future the West—which already includes Japan, South Korea, and India (to a large extent)—could be seamlessly partnered with China and Russia.

The marriage of Russia and China into "the West" was a major possibility as the post–Cold War period came to an end with the September 11, 2001, attacks on the United States. It was thwarted then by bureaucrats in the East and West who did not trust such an outcome. It could be derailed again. But the possibility exists for a "super West" involving virtually all of the modern economies of the world.

Perhaps it's time to stop referring to "the West" as such. We are already in a new geopolitical and market construct, the "modern world."

We have been looking at the historical and, in many ways, obvious factors which go into the history matrix. We must also examine the vital role of abstract factors and the pursuit of "organic complexity" in cementing the achievement of victory.

ABSTRACTION, COMPLEXITY, AND VICTORY

EIGHT

Organically evolved complexity defines and sustains victory.

Singapore is an island chain of some 699 square kilometers, 84 percent of it covered in urban development. It produces little in the way of agricultural or manufactured goods. It has no natural resources, save its position astride major sea routes, and was, only two centuries ago, a festering mangrove swamp of malarial mosquitoes and the ills of other tropical vapors. By 2005, it had a gross domestic produce of $107 billion—$25,236 for each of the approximately 4.24 million Singaporeans—and, in the final quarter of 2005, an annualized 9.7 percent average annual growth rate.

Singapore achieved its success and stability by embracing complex abstraction in almost all aspects of its social, political, and economic structure. Most sub-Saharan African states, by comparison, still labor along with cash economies, unable to extract and exploit the value of their asset bases through various forms of credit. By "abstract" I mean separated from direct action. For example, barter is a direct form of payment. The creation of coinage began to make the trading process less direct (more abstract) and required mutual acceptance by traders of an entirely artificial value for coins, though the coins originally reflected the desirability of the metals with which they were made. Paper currencies required more rationalizing, and faith. Credit, then, is even more theoretical, or abstract in some respects, although like barter it usually gets back to agreed values in tangible objects, such as land, buildings, or "things."

Credit, this abstract phenomenon, then, is the leveraging of assets (whether tangible or intangible), just as, for example, a spear leveraged human strength, allowing early hunters to strike a target at a greater distance. The thrown rock or spear, or the conversion of a stick into a hammer, may have been the first human movement toward acquiring abstract strengths, strengths enhanced by the use of value-added leverage.

Mankind's pursuit of victory may be punctuated by sharp watersheds of military success, or the granting of national independence, but true victory is achieved only in subsequent years through a society's successful embrace of what I term "abstraction." The longer a society delays its movement from that initial, direct physical success on the battlefield or in the attainment of sovereignty—the grasp of power over its own destiny—to the consolidation of victory through abstract means (that is, the development of a jigsaw of elements which bear indirectly on the shape and direction of society), the less likely it is to compete successfully with other societies.

This is the real distinction between successful and unsuccessful societies and states: Those which historically succeed embrace abstraction; those which labor to eke out their existence are those that cling to direct approaches to their economies, military doctrines, and social structures and interactions. The failure of struggling states reflects this. And yet some societies poor in resources, remotely located, and historically without great records of achievement, such as Singapore, have suddenly prospered.

All societal evolution is marked by the progress of technology, tools, or systems which are, by definition, abstractions. These technologies, tools, or systems make direct wealth, and direct strength, more effective and useful. The military term for something which adds power or effectiveness to a system is "force multiplier." Adding a guidance system to an aircraft's bomb, for example, makes it better able to hit a specific target, which means that it is possible to achieve more success with fewer bombs. The added guidance system, then, is a force multiplier.

Credit takes the value inherent in a piece of property and turns it into cash, which can be used for, say, education, or to buy additional property. So, by embracing abstract concepts of value, one can turn a piece of property into an engine of wealth creation. By creating many social structures within a society—one to collect garbage, another to fight wars, another to build roads—we also create a capability greater than the direct action of an individual. We have created a society based on abstract principles. And more successful societies usually have more complex and layered sets of interlocking authorities and technologically enhanced tools than unsuccessful societies.

Victory is conceived in the absolute simplicity of its immediate objectives and driven by the simple necessity of a society to achieve dominion over its own destiny. But victory is sustained and defended against collapse by the construction of increasingly complex and interlocking modalities which buffer a society against weaknesses in individual areas. Watersheds create or destroy victory, but, as the maxim says, it is the *organically evolved complexity* of a society which defines and sustains its victory.

Watersheds in history are often most visible because of destruction by direct and brute applications of force. While direct action initiates a catharsis—it is necessary to break the egg before an omelet can be made—only the appropriate use of abstraction can transform and cushion that brutal, primal action into long-term success, or victory.

From the military standpoint, the initial success is caused by the primal leadership qualities of the commander. It is this "commander at the watershed" who takes the pivotal risk, without a great supporting structure or history to guide the action. George Washington, Mustafa Kemal Atatürk, Tamerlane, and Alexander the Great were examples of this initial form of leadership. The first use of force—direct action—must be decided by primal leadership instincts, requiring courage, intuition, and wisdom.

But the defense, consolidation, and expansion of that initial success must—as history demonstrates—be achieved by reduced risk-taking; the fate of the society cannot, once it has something to lose, be gambled at each threat or opportunity. The great risk for any leader, any society, lies in that initial gamble; the life-or-death decision to end subservience and seize self-dominion. Thereafter, at all possible times, success is best not so daringly gambled, but rather defended and built by a web of abstract and mutually supporting complexities.

The initial use of a force multiplier occurred when man, having learned to walk upright, picked up a rock or stick to kill an opponent or prey at a distance, or to defend with more than bare hands. The use of fire to preserve meat, to provide food beyond the immediate killing zone, was equally critical to the mobility of mankind, and therefore to human expansion and the construction of societies larger than a band of hunters.

Today, more than ever, *the victory of a society is measured more in terms of its abstractions than of its tools of direct force, or even direct productivity.* Societies which depend solely on their standing military capability, or their food or energy reserves, or even their industrial capability will be outpaced, outlasted, outmaneuvered by societies whose strengths are complex, abstract, and flexible.

The evolution of strategic power, then, should be seen not only in direct, physical terms—the strength of an armed force, the strength of food production or weapons manufacture, and the overall strength of the economy—but also in terms of the complexity and abstractions which become rooted in a society and grow with it. Abstraction and complexity are not measurable in finite terms, which is why they have been so often overlooked as strategic factors, and yet this feature of society was fundamental to the West's success over the Soviet Union in the Cold War, and even of Ethiopia's success over Eritrea in the war of 1998–2000.

Complexity and abstraction embrace all aspects of society, not only its military might.

Complex and abstract societies have depth; they reach down beneath the surface. They have reserves of strength which can be drawn up to meet needs and challenges. The USSR had enormous military strength and natural mineral wealth, but it could not sustain the multigenerational challenge of societies with more complex, interactive strengths, such as the West had developed.

Perhaps the most significant, identifiable aspect of this complexity as it contributes to the strength of a society—and therefore to its survival and ultimate victory—is the degree to which the society is *quantified*. Ideally, all the values in a society can be identified, quantified, and therefore made available to the greater good.

The first great task of King William I, after he consolidated the Conquest of England, was to take a census of all his new realm. The result was the *Domesday Book*, commissioned in December 1085 and completed in its first draft in August 1086. The collection of the wealth of data found in this book laid the foundation stones for Britain's, and the

West's, subsequent thousand years of victory, more surely than the chance military triumph William secured in 1066.

At first, the quantification of a society merely enabled the most efficient use of that which was obviously available. Today, quantification and abstraction—the addition of psychological aspects, such as "trust" and "value"—go hand in hand to create strategic strength.

This is most dramatically exemplified today in the real difference between rich, powerful societies, and poor, weak societies. One principal "abstraction" of the successful societies lies in moving from cash-based to credit-based economies. The development of more and more abstruse forms of credit—implying greater and greater leverage and flexibility of economic resources—is the hallmark of inherent strategic strength in a society. This gets back to the question of not merely what assets we have, but how creatively we can use them.

Complexity is the enemy of the achievement of victory, and the greatest tool in its sustenance. Complexity of decisionmaking processes and of etiquettes within society ensures that, in times of peace, the path to leadership is slow, and negotiable only by patience and compromise. More store is set in the legalities, modalities, and prerogatives of tenure than in making the best decisions for society. Security is perceived to be preserved by minimizing change and thwarting radicalism, even forms of radicalism which would serve society better than stagnation.

Complexity of social and bureaucratic structures makes *the process* more important than *the ends*. As a result, complex institutions, governmental or otherwise, become blind to the fact that they are embarked upon a path, a timeline, in which change will occur, regardless of (or perhaps because of) their blind inertia. Large and complex institutions, and the people who thrive in them, are *process-driven*. They are not *victory-driven*.

So successful complex societies recognize that, in times of crisis, complexity must give way to direct, victory-oriented decisionmaking. During a crucial period of the Cold War, the United States was able to design, build, and deploy the Pershing battlefield missile within about nine months. Later, as the Cold War became more like grinding political trench warfare, with both main power blocs locked into the process, the United States took ten years to design, build, and deploy an upgraded version of the great Pershing system. And the cost of the Pershing II was commensurate with the decade of labors of the bureaucratic managers who inched it into existence.

The British armed forces had been languishing through neglect by the time the Falkland Islands were invaded by Argentina in 1982. The procurement of major defense systems was excessively process-driven, expensive, and unending. But when Prime Minister Margaret Thatcher committed the United Kingdom to repelling the Argentine invasion, all bureaucracy fell away. Weapons systems procurement occurred with the stroke of a pen; new systems were devised almost overnight. When one deploying British regiment did not have the equipment it needed for the Falklands conditions, it purloined it—unauthorized—from another regiment the night before embarkation. Ferries which had been plying the North Sea instantly became troop transport ships. The will to victory displaced the tired bureaucracy. And, as with the powers given to Prime Minister Churchill in World War II, some of the debates and checks and balances of democracy fell away to allow decisions to be made appropriate to the situation.

The move from complexity to simplicity—as required by a situation—can occur overnight. This was evidenced to a startling degree twenty-one years after the Falklands War by the U.S.-led coalition war against Iraq. More than a decade of indecision had attended military thinking in the wake of the Cold War, as bureaucracies, particularly in the United States, eased themselves into modest debates about the "Revolution in Military Affairs" (RMA) and force restructuring. But two weeks of actual conflict in March and April 2003 saw old doctrine swept aside and new thinking emerge as a result of the exigencies of the drive toward military triumph.

There were those who said on many occasions following the end of the Cold War that the institutions and people of the United States were too seduced by the ease of their victorious lives to be able to respond to threats to their interests. Those who held that view were surprised, then, when the United States became galvanized by the attacks against symbolic targets on September 11, 2001. It responded rapidly, sharply, and in relative unison. Much of the United States' indecision and process orientation dropped away, allowing a victory-oriented leadership to do its duty.

The attacks on the U.S. victory would, almost certainly, have been rationalized away with apologetic gestures and inaction had a management-oriented, process-driven leadership remained in place.

Those embarked upon seizing victory need quick decisions, short lines of communication, and the ability to distill counsel so that it does not destroy clarity. Equally, this applies to those engaged in defending against serious threats to their victory.

But once victory is attained, its consolidation and security depend upon weaving the complex web which ensures that victory does not become hostage to the fragility of unsupported leadership. The argument against dictatorship is not that there cannot be a wise, benevolent, and visionary autocrat. But what will happen when this leader dies or is displaced? Hellenism's march toward global domination halted with Alexander the Great's premature death, for example. Complexity of sociopolitical customs and structures may, in times of unchallenged victory, produce mediocre leaders, but it also ensures that there is always the platform of strength and productivity needed to allow a victory-oriented leader to rise when the challenge emerges.

The task of the victory-oriented leader in times of strength and power, when threats are minimal, is merely to prick at the self-satisfied managers of society to ensure that they do not allow the fruits of victory to be squandered beyond reconstruction. There will always be, in halcyon times of long victory, leaders who remain uncalled to the challenge, like de Gaulle before World War II, when he was unable to arouse the French General Staff, the National Assembly, or French society to the impending disaster. But society hopes that when the crisis does arise, a victory-oriented leader will emerge with the times. And it is the task of each individual to nurture a belief in victory—not just a desire for it—so that when the need comes for victory to be won or defended, the spirit rises naturally and quickly.

BRITTLE VERSUS SUPPLE?
COMPLEXITY LEADS TO FLEXIBILITY,
UNTIL IT LEADS TO ATROPHY

China and India are potentially the rising great powers of the coming decades; Iran, Australia and Brazil the rising middle powers. India is mired in complexities and bureaucracies more suited to a society long into a victory cycle, less able to respond to the challenge and opportunity than China. India proved, though, with the Kargil conflict with Pakistan in Kashmir in 1999, that it *could*—like Britain with the Falklands War of 1982—break through the red tape and respond quickly and effectively with its military.

But then it returned, in some respects, to torpor. China, on the other hand, has been on a "wartime footing" at all times in the past decade or so. It moves in a fashion designed to seize victory. India, as yet, does not. But it is stirring.

China's governing structure, however, is still—despite recent evolutions—brittle and unsupported. One giant human tsunami of political unrest could snap the structure. Beijing's leadership is aware of this, and is moving, as best it can, to adopt a Singaporean approach to democracy: strong and stern in its leadership, but with flexible institutions to withstand the public pressures that arise during times of crisis.

China is now in a race with itself, then, even more than with the outside world. It is in the position of the company director flipping a coin and saying, "Heads we go global; tails we liquidate." The destruction of arable lands in China's pursuit of the raw materials of growth, and the loss of inland water, coupled with the rise of economic opportunity in cities, has driven Chinese internal migration. The massive rush to the cities will create seething, difficult urban clusters, political and criminal upheaval, and national collapse before the economic powerhouse can deliver solutions. This is the other side of the coin to the innovative thrust toward global leadership we discussed in Chapter Seven. Cracks may begin to appear in China's structure in less than twenty years. And if an implosion occurs, India could emerge as the more stable Asian giant.

By 2006, India had begun to make its run to compete with China, and the battle for global energy resources had begun. Even by mid-2005, India had quietly begun acquiring 17 million barrels of oil a month from Nigeria, and by the end of 2005 it was competing to acquire large offshore oil blocs in Nigeria, ultimately teaming with Chinese partners to develop the resources. But more significantly,

India's naval chief had begun openly talking about India's mission to dominate the entire Indian Ocean—which contains sea routes and resources critical to the West and to China and Japan—as India's right. The changing dynamic served notice to Australia, for example, that its geostrategic position had changed forever, and that it had to negotiate a path into the twenty-first century which was not dependent on U.S. military power.

But the current shakeout period of global change and upheaval, and the uncertain direction (and results) of the Chinese and Indian searches for victory, will all begin to affect the global financial markets. Already we can hear the tinkling of chandeliers in our salons in response to the distant rumble of the artillery of change. The battle is drawing close. We must ask, then, how financial markets and economic values will be sustained during chaos.

We have only to look at the collapse of the USSR and its control over Eastern Europe, which occurred in 1990 without a shot being fired. Currencies, hierarchies, lifestyles, asset values—everything—changed overnight. Little wonder that nuclear scientists, unable to buy food in Russia, could be persuaded to move for a pittance to Libya, Iraq, and other countries. And right now, in the decades after the collapse of the USSR, we see the West fracturing and preoccupied with its petty squabbles, facing the threat of paralyzing and highly organized chaos in the streets (as we witnessed in France, Belgium, and Germany in November 2005).

The complexity of the West saves it, at present, from imminent disaster. The growth of complexity in credit and money supply even since 1973—the year of the economically depressing OPEC oil embargo—has helped insure it against sudden and total economic collapse. Certainly, Western stability rests on a more complex basis than did the stability of the Soviet bloc in 1990, when the single thin and brittle basis for power—military strength—was marginalized as funding ran out and exposure to external psychological factors sapped the energy from the Soviet system.

Even in a Western society so totally dominated by underpinning asset values—which provide the basis for credit and therefore capital formation—there comes a point at which the collapse of societal cohesion could begin to affect the overall economic position. We have already seen that a string of hurricanes devastating much of the United States had virtually no impact on the economic viability of the United States or the West. The terrorist assault on the physical assets of the pivotal New York financial hub in 2001 did not even halt the U.S. recovery from the Clinton-era economic recession (although it did affect the U.S.'s and West's collective psyche).

Significantly, in the global rivalry for victory, China is dependent on integration with the classical, existing Western framework, but the leaders of Iran and North Korea are not. China, while successfully seeking (along with others) to break the U.S. domination of conventional energy markets and resources, does not wish to see its growth cause a collapse of the U.S. dollar, nor even the value of the euro. Neither does the bulk of the Iranian population wish this, but the Iranian people by late 2005 were increasingly in the grip of a leadership which cared little for the views of their population. Both Iranian president Mahmud Ahmadi-Nejad and North Korean leader Kim Jong-Il were indifferent to the stability of the global economic structure. Both leaders, along with the advocates of a new caliphate—such as Osama bin Laden and his followers—welcome the prospect of the collapse of the Western system.

Both Iran's and North Korea's limited supplies of nuclear weapons—which face increasingly capable antiballistic missile (ABM) defense systems—could do enormous damage to Israel, Europe, North America, and the Middle East. Even if such a watershed encouraged, say, an Indo-Pakistani nuclear exchange (which could destroy the cohesive Pakistani state and set back India's quest for strategic parity with China), it is probable that the modern system of economic progress could survive. It would, of course, change the balance of power. In the short term (next half-century), it would give greater importance to West Africa's energy resources, which would supplant in significance the unstable resources of the Middle East.

Perhaps the United States could fare better than much of the rest of the world given such developments. There is no likelihood that, even if the Iranian leadership survived a nuclear exchange with Israel and the West, Iran itself would emerge significantly enhanced from such a conflict. Victory requires the complex development of economic and societal structuring—the very thing the Iranian leadership has avoided building, just as the Soviet leadership, obsessively grasping for power since 1917, failed to focus on fundamentals, which saw to its ultimate collapse.

This returns us to the thesis that only the West can throw away the vast margin of victory it built up over the past thousand years. And it *could* throw it away by the abandonment of unity and purpose. This process is, in fact, well advanced in parts of Western Europe, whereas the former Eastern bloc states in Europe are, by and large, anxious to assert their chance for victory and do not take their growing wealth for granted. But in the United States and Canada, the abandonment of unity and purpose is also on the march, perhaps stopped only by the catalyst of the September 11, 2001, terrorist attacks and the subsequent assertion of national will.

It is possible that the slide of Western Europe could continue to worsen, particularly with the thrust of radicalism and terrorism from the jihadist base in Bosnia and

Kosovo, and even exacerbated by a war promoted by the Iranian clerical leadership. But as the world reshapes, the "new West"—which already includes Japan, South Korea, and the ASEAN states—could (as we discussed in the previous chapter) fully begin to embrace China and Russia.

But if *anything* saves the West, it will be the cushioning effects of its complexity, which reflects the accretion of history.

What has occurred, however, is that, once again, something has come along to demolish the traditional hierarchical structures. This time, wealth, computers, communications, and transportation technologies have leveled the playing field, giving new elements of societies the chance to rise to the surface. In many respects, there has been a great leveling of opportunity. The advantage will accrue to the societies which can galvanize this new situation with the will to achieve cohesion.

Those societies which have will, assets, and secure geography will have the edge. And they will create new hierarchies. The "leveling of society"—of which we will talk more later—is a feature of eras of transformation.

These complex, abstract institutions and practices with which we have grown ensure that we have sophisticated, multifaceted societies. How we reach out and shape opinions and motivate action, then, is one of the great challenges.

POSITIONING PERCEPTIONS FOR VICTORY

NINE

Only the mind can conceive victory, comprehend threats and possibilities, and accept defeat. All victory is more easily achieved and maintained by placing twice the emphasis on psychological strategy as on physical force.

Raymond, the savant figure played by actor Dustin Hoffman in the 1988 film *Rain Man*, said that Australia's national airline, Qantas, was the safest in the world because it had never experienced a major crash. In fact, until that time, it had suffered eight accidents. This remark in a fictional movie had the significant consequence of catapulting Qantas's prestige and passenger appeal, but it was, nonetheless, misinformation, inserted into a film for artistic purposes.

In 1999, the Clinton administration caused NATO to attack Serbia on the basis of something far more sinister: disinformation. Time has since revealed that the Clinton White House and State Department used carefully timed, deliberate distortions of reality as well as outright lies by key officials to create a national security emergency to distract from domestic U.S. political pressures. In essence, the disinformation and the war which followed relied on what propagandists call "the big lie technique," with the knowledge that—by the use of shocking and overwhelming state-

ments, repeated with the force of a supportive media—
some of the mud would stick.

Misinformation is often accidental. Disinformation is
deliberate. But both have an effect on the political and economic environment. Disinformation and propaganda are
essentially tactical devices, or stratagems: They fall far short
of psychological strategy. And while psychological warfare
is often discussed, psychological strategy is virtually never
discussed or considered, despite the fact that psychological
strategy is the core of the Art of Victory. It gets to the motivations which bring victory, as well as the ability to control
the perceptions and therefore the actions of one's allies and
adversaries.

Psychological strategy is employed in *defining and
achieving* grand strategic goals, which reflect the desires—
which are psychological/emotional—of a society. How
goals are identified determines their appeal and motivational value. How perceptions are shaped in target audiences will determine success or failure in achieving goals.
The art of psychological strategy will either motivate or
paralyze or confuse, divide or unite, thus determining victor and vanquished.

As we have noted in the maxim, only the mind can
conjure and achieve victory or defeat, and the mind is the
master of the physical action. To parallel Sun-tzu's maxims
on the art of war, the acme of victory is its achievement
and sustenance without physical war. Next is the achievement of victory through disruption of an enemy's plans,
which means disruption of his collective mind, will, image,
and ability to influence and communicate. Third is the
achievement of victory by the efficient use of force under
the guidance of a comprehensive psychological strategy.
But all victory is more easily achieved and maintained by
placing twice the emphasis on psychological strategy as on
direct physical force.

Psychological strategy is the functioning mechanism of a national (or corporate) grand strategy and includes those measures required to achieve the grand strategy which are dependent upon human motivation, including:

- The creation and empowerment of the leadership of one's own, or one's allies', political, military, and economic structures, including the shaping and motivation of the necessary social and structural bases;
- The destruction, diversion, subversion, paralysis, demotivation, or surprise of opposition leadership and opposing political and social structures;
- The motivation in a chosen direction, or the paralysis, of societies or target groups, including military forces, on a broad strategic scale.

All of these missions include the use of many specializations, including political and psychological warfare, information warfare, and public relations. It is often necessary to undertake some action in the physical world in order to achieve the appropriate intellectual-emotional motivation in a target audience. This could include anything from the control of an architectural environment to the staging of a rally or a terrorist incident. Different symbols can be used together, as in the case of Hitler's Nuremberg rally and the Olympics in 1936, a combination of architectural, human, and audiovisual stimuli.

We live in societies which already have shape, beliefs, motivations, customs, leaders, and capabilities. Individuals and groups routinely undertake activities which affect other individuals and groups, often with unintended or unexpected consequences. Most often, we undertake actions based on our own motivation and what we wish to achieve. But in psychological strategy, the goal is not to allow the "normal" course of social events to govern the success or failure of our plans. Rather, the goal is that, *by planning, understanding, and acting within a conscious framework, we control the outcome of events.*

That is the essence of psychological strategy: to shape events so that our national grand strategies can be achieved—can bring victory—at the minimum human or financial cost, and within the time frame we have set.

America's first department store magnate, John Wannamaker, once said that half of his advertising budget was wasted, but he didn't know which half. That's because he, like most corporate leaders, did not consider professional psychological strategies before embarking on advertising campaigns, which are only the "propaganda" element of what should be a larger framework of grand strategy.

Psychological strategy is national mobilization. It transcends the components of military strategy, political strategy, and economic strategy. Psychological strategy should help create the appropriate climate so that all of the economic, military, and political strategies work. Conversely, the political, economic, and military strategies should fall into an overall unity of purpose determined by a psychological strategy, so that the national grand strategy can be achieved. Grand strategy and psychological strategy are therefore "bigger than war," in the sense that war is merely a tool for achieving a national destiny, a national grand strategy.

In all human achievement, the thought precedes the deed: Substance is built around dreams, illusions, and perceptions. So psychological strategy is the tool with which to achieve national goals, regardless of the context.

And the global context has been transformed substantially by technology, particularly communications technology, which includes information-processing technologies as well as the physical movement of people and goods. What this has led to has been an increasing focus by strategists and planners on the actual technologies and capabilities themselves, on what is technologically feasible. This has had the effect of substantially moving attention away from the national goals and national grand strategy. It focuses on what is, rather than on what we want or determine our world to be.

Marshall McLuhan, the Canadian media expert, was correct when he said that the medium had become the message. It has been our unfortunate obsession with the *media* of communication which has taken our focus away from the creation and achievement of national goals. Of course this is not to deny that modern information-handling technologies do in large measure shape perceptions in target audiences, often to a far greater degree than the intended message.

Only an understanding of individual and group psychological factors can permit us to ascertain relative strategic values. In other words, as threat analysts are fond of saying: we can never completely ascertain the *intentions* of a potential adversary, but we can quantify *capabilities*.

Whereas classical intelligence is merely the collection and assessment of information on a target, reported to a policy apparatus, psychological strategy is a process of complete interaction among collection, assessment, and, often, policy implementation, not only on target countries, forces, or populations, but also in our own policy apparatus and societal structures. And in every government and organization there needs to be this process, providing the leadership with an overview to ensure that all the functions of administration interrelate in an optimal fashion to achieve overall grand strategy goals.

Unless that function is in place, any government or organization, no matter how professional in other respects, will run into problems. One department or service may move off in one direction, and a different department in another. Or one part of government may be more zealous in pursuit of a goal than another, creating a disjointed result.

In today's conditions, *belief* becomes accepted as *reality*, and *truth*—that is, indisputably fact-based truth—is a totally inadequate strategic defense.

This is not a recommendation that truth or honesty should be abandoned as an underpinning of government or of strategic planning. Rather, it is an assertion that *truth and honesty are not weapons* which will defend a nation or further its strategic objectives: They are merely principles which need to form the *basis* of policy. On the other hand, *belief, or structured belief systems, can be both weapon and defense.*

What is critical, then, in today's psychological strategy environment, is to understand *beliefs*, and that beliefs are the result more often of *perceptions* than of knowledge. It is also important to understand what types of conscious or unconscious image stimuli are involved in creating and controlling beliefs, or what sorts of processes can alter embedded existing beliefs. These must come in forms which address individual as well as collective sensibilities.

Having achieved this understanding, it is necessary then to understand what constitutes the appropriate action or nonaction needed to affect the target audience in the desired way.

The conscious actions of the psychological strategist occur in an environment already rich with naturally occurring sensory phenomena. Things happen through normal societal interaction, creating a dense forest of psychological clutter around which the strategist must maneuver. It is the strategist, however, who controls events and destiny, rather than letting the natural sequence of events control the fate of the nation.

Again, we need to stress the difference between psychological strategy and operational functions.

Psychological strategy is involved in the planning and conduct of policies which involve *belief systems,* while information warfare is concerned with offensive and defensive operations related to *knowledge systems.* Psychological strategy, psychological operations, perception management, and psychological warfare aim directly at the human brain. Information warfare aims at the systems and architecture carrying, storing, and presenting information and beliefs. Psychological *warfare* is the offensive and defensive operational aspect of military-political psychological strategy.

To give one last anecdotal example: During World War II, Allied intelligence discovered that the Japanese government was conducting the war against the Allies in isolation from the emperor of Japan, although the war was being fought in the emperor's name. To give himself some measure of control, or at least understanding, the emperor had his own small private intelligence collection operation within the Imperial Army, with messages radioed in from the field to his office, and then presented to His Imperial Majesty for consideration. Once this was discovered by the Allies, and it became apparent that the emperor was struggling to be able to make and impose decisions of his own on the conduct of the war, a small group in the United States, including Dr. Stefan Possony, went about formulating a way to get an appropriate message to the emperor. They knew, from monitoring operations, the radio frequencies which were being used by the emperor's field collectors. But they also knew that a message inserted into that wavelength would be subject to translation and interpretation before it was shown to the emperor. Receipt of such a message might confuse the intelligence staff, and the message could be discarded or be passed on in an edited or distorted form.

Possony and his colleagues knew that it was imperative

to get the message totally intact to the emperor, and that meant not only getting the message taken seriously by the receiving staff, but also ensuring that the staff did not modify or hedge the content in presenting it to the emperor. That message, in 1945, was this: "Unconditional surrender does not mean unconditional surrender." Both President Franklin Roosevelt and his successor, Harry Truman, had told the U.S. public that only "unconditional surrender" would be acceptable from the Germans and Japanese. To the Japanese, this meant that there was no motivation for surrender; they would lose everything in any event, so they might as well fight to the last. The message that "unconditional surrender does not mean unconditional surrender" was to advise the emperor that, while the U.S. public wanted to hear the jingoistic cry, it was not to be taken literally. Surrender, although nominally unconditional, would not mean the end of Japan, would not even mean the end of the imperial structure, and Japan would be helped to rebuild.

To get this delicate message across in such a way that it would not be disturbed required someone special: someone who understood the particular form of the Japanese language used by a commoner speaking to an emperor. Such a person was found in the Japanese-American community, and the message was phrased and sent—repeatedly, over a period of time—until it was accepted and conveyed to the emperor. Japan then agreed to "unconditional surrender" under those terms, and at the emperor's insistence. Everyone, the emperor included, had agreed that with "unconditional surrender" in its original context, they would fight to the last Japanese. But once the message was rephrased, a totally different outcome to the war was possible.

In this context, then, the two atomic weapons used on Nagasaki and Hiroshima became the symbolic icons—

elements of psychological strategy—of a very different purpose: to halt the Soviet advances in the East, and to establish
U.S. dominance in the post–World War II era. They made
it clear to the USSR that, in the postwar period, the United
States would not tolerate Soviet expansion.

Within the context of psychological strategy, information warfare and information policy, on the other hand, are
very much the operational component or operational tools
in certain situations. If we look at the Japanese example just
mentioned, information warfare would have been the actual
implementation of the transmissions; the intelligence-
gathering needed in the first place to understand the wire-
less transmissions from the field, and the breaking of the
Japanese codes.

A WORLD YEARNING FOR CLARITY

The irony of our age of mass communications is that,
while more voices can be heard, it is fewer voices which
people crave to hear. The more complex an issue, the more
deaf an audience is to complex debate, and the more it
craves simplicity. We see this increasingly, with the almost
childish simplicity of political debate in the modern world,
where intelligent, well-educated people repeat sloganized,
iconized propaganda and see no inconsistency in their approach.

Lenin perceived this reality early in the twentieth century and worked to reduce the complexity of the arguments
he made to the public. That is what led to the communist
approach of sloganizing all aspects of crowd control and
communication. Visitors to the Soviet Union right up
through the seventies and eighties were struck by the red
cloth banners hung from buildings in every city and town,

with statements such as, "Communism is Soviet power plus the electrification of the whole country."

Soviet sloganizing under Lenin, and later under Karl Radek and Radek's successor as chief propagandist, Boris Nikolayevich Ponomarev, also included the reduction of entire concepts and attitudes to single words. So effective, for example, was the Soviet use of the words "capitalist" and "capitalism" that they became negatively loaded words: pejoratives for the entire basis of Western strength, and words which were embraced in their Soviet negative connotation even by most Western audiences. *Forbes* magazine in New York, however, struck back. It seized the phrase "capitalist tool"—one of the Soviet insults to those states and leaders allied with the United States or United Kingdom—and transformed it into a message of pride in the free-market system.

And now, moving into a time of even greater sensory bombardment, the path to uniting societies and influencing them toward positive and cooperative development will become increasingly difficult. Computerization and globalization have leavened Western society, flattening traditional hierarchical structures, which means that the authority of information delivered by leaders no longer has the impact it once had. Information, then, now travels more effectively laterally through peer networks, rather than vertically, and now lacks the reassurance of authority. This means that fear and paralysis are far easier conditions to convey, and such emotions travel more rapidly and effectively through society.

More than ever, then, good news travels slowly, if at all; bad news, and more particularly, bad beliefs, unqualified by any unimpeachable authority, travel quickly. This means that angst in modern industrial societies will grow at a greater rate than it did in more primitive societies. These less sophisticated and often poorer societies are less wired in to the modern systems and are still structured into a vertical hierarchy.

At the heart of all individuals—the core of their motivation—is their identity, set within a social framework. So the impact of "identity security" is what we must consider.

IDENTITY AS THE
CORE OF VICTORY

TEN

Victory is achieved and sustained in direct
proportion to the level of "identity security"
of a society and its leaders.

Why, in 2005 alone, did some hundred people commit suicide as terrorist "martyr bombers" in gestures of political defiance? Why did nonviolent Buddhist monks pour gasoline on themselves in Saigon, during the Vietnam War, and set themselves alight in suicidal acts of theater? Why did successive generations of Indian widows for centuries perform suttee, ritual suicide, by throwing themselves onto their husbands' funeral pyres, until this practice was banned by the government? The answers get to the root of why societies survive or why they ignite in rebellion, or why they disappear altogether. It is a phenomenon—with very real, physical symptoms—which, in studies for UNESCO and other audiences, I labeled "identity security."

In the next chapter, we will examine how terrorism works as a weapon, and how it must be dealt with at the symptomatic level. But before suicide terrorism can be conquered in the long term, and while immediate steps are taken to deal with an urgent threat, it also must be understood as a phenomenon of societal development. In the late nineteenth century, and then again in the second half of the

twentieth century, terrorism was clad in the colors of bol-
shevism, and we thought that by reading Marx and Engels
we would comprehend it. In the transition from the twentieth to the twenty-first centuries, terrorism was mostly clad
in the colors of Islamism—not Islam, but Islamism—and so
we read the Koran to better understand it. But the terrorism
we face today is more complex than that, and deeply rooted
in the human soul. Thus, while we deal with the symptoms,
and with the people who are prepared to perform the seemingly irrational acts of suicide terrorism, we need also to understand what is at terrorism's heart, and to start to address
that reality.

And the reality is that the entire global dynamic has
changed. Tools of communication, travel, and wealth creation have developed to the point where the most fundamental bearings of human societies—geographical, cultural,
historical, religious, and linguistic points of reference—have
become clouded, and often lost. Great segments of the dramatically increasing human population are on the move.

If, within this global, moving crowd, peoples lose their
sense of identity and historic points of reference, they lose
much of their ability to act collectively for their own survival. Disorientation leads to panic and chaos. That is what
began to occur following the end of the Cold War: Horizons and historical reference points were being swept away.

This led to a critical dichotomy between the growing
global reality of seamless human interaction on the one
hand, and the eternal, visceral human necessity for a sense
of societal identity on the other. This will lead to further
global strategic unrest, because an *aspect* of all humanity is
at war with *another aspect* of all humanity.

The success of human society has been in its ability to
perpetuate itself and to grow, all the while sustaining its expanding numbers through organizational structures of increasing complexity, and through evolving adaptability and

productivity in the supply of food, water, and shelter. Of critical importance in this organizational process throughout history has been the cohesion of the family, clan or tribe, nation, and, ultimately, the nation-state or supersociety. This structured approach—essentially dictated by a natural evolutionary process—provided protection, cooperative achievement, and a continuity of experience and learning which built upon itself, generation on generation.

Now, the technologies of communication and computerization, transportation, life sciences, and wealth creation, coupled with population growth, have challenged or displaced what had become the clearly defined structure of societies and geographical states.

The collapse of the bipolar global power structure by 1991 freed the technologies which had been developed for national competitive purposes and defense. These technologies are now used in *counternationalist* communications—that is, communications which link nations rather than separate them—bringing societies for the first time into an integrated and often commingled status. Technologies of computerization, telecommunications, and transportation, which had been developed in the forge of the Cold War to reinforce *separation* between strategic blocs, had overnight *reversed their roles* to become the tools for global social *integration*.

The wave of global integration created a reaction based on the resultant threat to identity: an urge to return to some aspects of the ancient "natural" nationalism which defines who we are, and where we belong. It was this urge to find something familiar, something comfortable, something identifiable, which struck all societies, while the waves of globalism seemed to be surging over them, sweeping away the familiar landmarks, obliterating history, overturning long-held beliefs.

For some societies, everything they believed, everything

on which their lives and confidence had been based, was washed away, the few mementos of their past now worthless in the new world.

The concept of society, which had evolved fairly constantly over some ten millennia, is now challenged by a tantalizing and radical revolution embodied in the possibilities offered by technologies, which had been created originally to protect and preserve *individual* societies. Turning these tools of human communication to the service of *global* interaction at the end of the Cold War seemed to be a logical sharing of human wealth; it was inevitable. Perhaps the last parallel we saw to our current situation was in the rapid conquest of most of Asia and much of Europe and the Middle East by the Mongols in the twelfth century.

In part, the global interaction which began with the end of the Cold War reflected a newfound sense of safety, as societies intermingled at an unprecedented rate and scale. Yet basic human needs remained essentially unchanged. After food, water, shelter, and a pool of reproductive partners, the next most basic need is for identity. Identity and context give us purpose. These human needs—identity, purpose, and context—are now being swamped by globalism.

History has demonstrated that instability and conflict follow when belief foundations are challenged, when societal and contextual affiliations are removed, when identity is erased or forgotten. This applies equally to individuals and to societies. The expanding surge of technology outpaces our understanding of how underlying human needs for identity and context can be satisfied within the new global environment. And the crossroad is as threatening to U.S. society as to the smallest tribal groups in Africa. Loss of a knowledge and sense of history, and of identification with the continuity of history, disorients us all.

This globally pervasive, although far from uniform, transformation of realities—in which change is apparent to all, and disquiets more people than it can immediately sat-isfy—generates reactionary movements. These reactionary movements are visceral in their appeal, and either attempt to return a society to a utopian view of the status quo ante, taking us back to something we can recognize and which comforts us, or attempt to sweep aside the past altogether, denying the validity of historical identity issues in order to take us in another, equally utopian direction, toward a fu-ture its proponents believe is unrelated to the past. That was the supposed appeal of communism in the late nine-teenth and early twentieth centuries: Its legitimacy was rooted in a vision of the future. It could afford to be utopian, because it could not be disproven, except by time. But it compared itself with the ills and injustices of the world, which at that time was in the process of massive so-cial change.

We are at that point again, only on a more global scale.

The early twenty-first century is the "eye of the hurri-cane": a brief period between historical eras during which the role of past human societal development can be evalu-ated in the light of opportunities available as a result of new and potential technologies.

The challenge, then, is not how human society should halt or reverse the progress and abandon the tools of ad-vancement we have created, but, rather, how these tools can be made to fit with the human requirement for group identity, and how societies can strengthen their underlying sense of identity and purpose so that they do not feel the need to lash out in order to protect their survival.

The end of the Cold War was, of course, the collapse of the global bipolar strategic framework: East versus West. We then relearned what history had proven: that a "unipolar" world—one governed by a sole superpower or single gov-ernment—cannot last for long before it automatically splits into factions, reaffirming the competitive nature of life. But this process of change, beginning with the end of the Cold War, created or resurrected a sense of uncertainty and fear in many societies. This has been coupled with a compounded sense of frustration in some societies as modern transnational media portray the apparent stability, wealth, and seemingly unattainable benefits of other societies.

The frustration is *not* caused, or even seriously compounded, by *differences* in cultures, identities, or civilizations. Rather, it is caused by differences in the levels of *perceived* societal security and identity confidence; by one society looking at another and feeling threatened, lost, or inadequate. It is the *sense* of the inability of a society to progress (the sense that it is trapped and faced with extinction), when seen in comparison to other societies, which provides the high- and low-pressure zones of global life. And, as with the weather, such barometric differences generate turbulence.

History shows how frustration, and the fear caused by loss of stable societal parameters, can generate reactionary responses from individuals and groups threatened with being bypassed by history and trammeled by victorious societies. Responses to this frustration include communal anger, anarchic behavior, terrorism, and insurrection, and those responses are designed to reaffirm or create the sense of identity and purpose necessary for the survival of the challenged society.

The late nineteenth century in Europe saw an almost direct though small-scale parallel to today's terrorism response, when industrialization and urbanization swept societies, transforming entire patterns of life and introducing anxieties and uncertainties. From this emerged the bolshevik and anarchist attempts to force new definitions of society. They were movements which generated support because they offered a new sense of identity in a transforming world. Then, as today, the loss of traditional structures led to terrorism. Significantly, the tenor of the language of the late-nineteenth-century bolshevik terrorists mirrored almost directly the language of the twenty-first-century Islamist terrorists.

Today, because the technologies of communications and wealth creation have become global, so, too, has the response.

Inevitably, this frustration is primarily manifested as anger, and has as its goal the destruction of the unattainable—and seemingly unjust—symbols of the alien threat. Far from achieving "justice" or improving the survivability and welfare of the frustrated societies, such anger and destruction tend to further polarize communities, reducing still further the opportunity for mutually achieved benefits.

Such schisms have been characterized, with dramatic and misleading oversimplification, as "clashes of civilizations," which has led many to accept such confrontations at face value rather than searching for options to address underlying causes. At present, the options available to most societies are seen as either embracing "globalism"—in a way which denies many of the essential historical cultural/identity building blocks—or opposing "globalism" in the sense of seeking a utopian fundamentalist society, usually based on one which existed only in myth.

Utopian, fundamentalist societies cannot endure; ultimately, they cannot even feed themselves. Modern technologies and methodologies are available to aid societies which reject utopian fundamentalism. But aiding those societies through the introduction of prosperity is not enough; they need to reorient themselves to their sense of identity.

And societies which reject the modern world cannot stave off the siege of the global mainstream. The rise of frustration in such societies is inevitable and galvanizing, their fear, anger, and frustration focused toward external targets. Their rejection of education, inquiry, and dialogue only serves to compound their disadvantage.

Instability and frustration are not cured by prosperity alone: It is the balancing of wealth with identity confidence which is the challenge of the twenty-first century. The Kyrgyz Republic was, for example, a poor but relatively confident society from 1990 (when it was founded as a modern state) until 2005, when an externally supported coup changed the government. Another example: Swaziland, despite substantial external interference, is a state of relatively modest economics, but with a strong sense of identity confidence. Today, as prosperity levels continue to rise globally—albeit unevenly—the concern is the loss of confidence and identity in some societies.

But no state or society can give identity to another society. No state can give another society a guarantee of survival, prosperity, and cultural and linguistic dominance or independence. Each society must *achieve* its own identity. Palestinian leader Yasir Arafat struck a chord when he said that any state given to the Palestinians by their enemies was not worth having. There is an innate recognition of the fact that people have to feel, viscerally, who they are, and to what they belong.

Dealing with the symptoms of terrorism, or attempting to address the heart-wrenching issue of poverty, is important but totally inadequate. In the absence of historical context, and an understanding and reaffirmation of cultural and societal identities, the results of our "wars on terror" and our "wars on poverty" are only tactical and transitory. They are Band-Aids. The more difficult and more complex and time-consuming answers to the anxieties and insecurities which create terrorism and poverty lie in helping to ensure that national and cultural identities are valued, and are worthy of nurturing.

The real war in which we are now engaged is one within ourselves; within mankind as a complex whole. Our right hand holds high the tools man has developed for his security and survival. Our left hand clasps to our heart our most valuable, innate tool: the sense of identity and the contextual logic of our survival.

It is important, then, to understand how terrorism—an extreme reflection of identity insecurity—works in the overall quest for, or defense of, victory.

THE FAILURE—AND
PROMISE—OF TERRORISM

ELEVEN

Terrorism is a tool for an imperiled society
to use in order to avoid vanquishment and
disintegration. It is not a war-winning weapon,
nor is it a tool to gain or sustain victory.

errorism cannot by itself achieve victory, but it can
sometimes stave off defeat. Terrorism, in its natural
form, captures the angst, despair, and loss of identity
security of a society. Left alone, it is the death throes of a
people. But, as a collective energy force captured by leadership, and fed and directed by sponsors, it is a weapon.
Rarely, however, is terrorism actually a weapon of the despairing society which supplies the combatants; it is usually
the weapon of the sponsoring state, not the despairing state.
In other words, it is invariably the remote tool of indirect
warfare of a covert sponsor. The leaders of the despairing
themselves—even if they use the blood of their society to
wage terrorist war—rarely survive long or victoriously.

When conducted by a third-party covert sponsor, as
part of an overarching and well-conceived psychological
strategy, terrorism can, however, be used as a national-level
weapon. It can be used as a decisive political trigger, and can
be employed either in the context of a comprehensive conventional conflict or by itself as a weapon of psychopolitical
warfare. But terrorism is a war-winning weapon or strata-

gem *only* when the principal and declared enemy target voluntarily surrenders or when terrorism-induced political paralysis allows other military-political strategies to succeed where they otherwise might fail. In the case of Jewish terrorism against the British occupation of Palestine, for example, the British—almost exclusively because of domestic considerations following World War II—did, in fact, surrender Palestine, not because of the terrorism, but, because of budget constraints and a war-weary population at home.

Terrorism, however, is often a tool through which the user society, or sponsoring elite, survives politically, by creating a sense of purpose and positive momentum in the society from which the terrorists or their sponsors come. It is a weapon employed to sustain a group or society which might otherwise lose all cohesiveness and identity in the face of a more unified and capable adversary. The Palestinians facing the Israelis in the late twentieth century and early twenty-first century in some respects provide a case in point, although here, too, the Palestinians have been used as ruthlessly by foreign sponsors as by some of their own leaders.

Terrorism is a natural tool of groups—both the society which fights and the state which sponsors it—which lack the ability to achieve military parity on other terms. It can induce confusion, paralysis, despondency, and division within the societies of superior forces. To this end, for example, the use of narcotics and media manipulation (what we might today call "perception management") by the People's Republic of China (PRC) and North Vietnam during the 1960s and 1970s was a classic form of indirect terrorism.

The previous chapter described some of the deep, underlying social causes of terrorism. But putting aside the historical motivations, once the conditions exist for terrorism and both the cause and combatants are ready, and sponsoring or manipulating powers emerge to enable it, terrorism becomes a system of warfare. In this context, terrorism is defined only by its actions, not by its motivations: It is an action designed to create terror, a psychological condition, usually by the selective application of violence or the threat of violence in a manner which relies on unpredictability to achieve maximum impact.

The war on terrorism which the West is fighting today has been to a great extent ill-planned, largely because the phenomenon of terrorism is itself not understood or adequately defined. Even the concept of a "war on terrorism" addresses only the phenomenon, the symptoms, rather than its combatant society and its sponsors and manipulators. It is axiomatic that it is difficult to fight an enemy who cannot be identified or understood.

Conventional warfare has the maxim: If you can see it, you can hit it; if you can hit it, you can kill it. The parallel in psychological strategy is: If you can understand the threat or opportunity, you can address it; if you can address it, you can triumph. The difference between direct warfare and psychological strategy—and its subordinate, psychological operations—is that conventional warfare is based substantially on finite objects and objectives; psychological strategy and psyops (including terrorism) are all about context, history, and abstracts.

Terrorism has taken many forms over the centuries. It usually comes in two basic streams: the response of a weak force against a superior force (asymmetrical warfare), or the attempt by a great force to suppress all opposition. In both instances, terrorism is a psychological tool. When the sponsor is a weak power, that state attempts to obfuscate its sponsorship, in order to avoid being the target of the overwhelming capability of the greater power to respond. When terror is used as an overt, or thinly disguised, tool of state, it is usually—but not always—used by autocratic rulers against their own people to create conditions which discourage dissent.

What is new is that terrorism has, in the past decades, become a national-level, offensive strategic weapon of greater utility and viability than nuclear weapons. Terrorist leaders have begun to employ national-level technologies and concepts. Terrorism can now inflict national levels of damage (but rarely war-winning levels) to major economies by causing physical damage to infrastructure—which is the sabotage aspect of the phenomenon—while at the same time ensuring psychological paralysis and depression in the human component of the economic infrastructure. The possibilities for such action should have been apparent more than two decades ago, when very low-cost, low-risk terrorism by al-Gama'a al-Islamiyya caused great hardship to Egypt by stopping inbound tourism almost overnight, robbing the country of half of its foreign exchange earnings for a considerable period.

Like air power, terrorism is a superb strategic weapon which is incomplete by itself. Just as the overwhelming and successful use of air power as a strategic weapon still requires the insertion of ground forces to occupy territory and complete the process of victory, so too strategic-level terrorism still requires the essential complementary action or reaction of the victim to complete the process.

Terrorism is a psychological weapon and can only be defeated by psychology, even though terrorism and counterterrorism use physical imagery—like "performance art"—to achieve their goals of psychological domination. We cannot properly counter terrorism if we fail to understand what it is. Just as rape is a crime of violence, not just of sex, so terrorism is a weapon of emotional manipulation, not just of violence. It requires, and often needs to create, a receptive psychological climate to be successful. Therefore, counterterrorism implies the necessity for defensive conditioning as well as offensive operations.

But the phenomenon of "terrorism" is interpreted differently and selectively by almost all who use the term.

"Terrorism" and "terrorist" have become loaded words: They have an iconographic meaning which calls up images, almost always of acts or individuals hostile to one's own interests. But the terms "terrorism" and "terrorist" are often used and misused indiscriminately, making clear policy responses to the phenomenon difficult.

TERRORISM IS A STRATAGEM, employed to create a certain effect, and a tool which reflects the resources and disposition of the group or nation-state which employs it. It does not represent a holistic approach to conflict, nor is it an entity in itself.

TERRORISM IS AN ASPECT OF PSYCHOLOGICAL WARFARE, falling under the overarching umbrella of grand strategy. Where it is coordinated into a grand strategy of the sponsoring state, and implemented under a defined psychological strategy, it can be an effective force multiplier in the conduct of an overall war. It may even be a decisive psychological tool, but it requires a comprehensive political strategy on the part of its sponsors to be anything other than an antagonism, unless the target group or state willingly surrenders.

"TERRORISM" IS NOT A DIRTY WORD. The word "terrorist" is often used as a pejorative, a loaded term. However, a "terrorist" is merely an individual who uses actions to create the psychological condition of "terror" in a target audience in order to achieve a desired social or political effect. That effect could be paralysis, retaliation, or polarization of communities brought about by engendered bigotry or pseudospeciation (the transformation of an opponent, in one's mind, into a lesser species, unworthy of equality with ourselves). This in turn could push decisionmaking in a particular direction.

A humorist uses humor to create a desired effect in his target audience; a terrorist instills terror in order to achieve a social or political result.

Within the normal framework of conventional warfare, civilians are a key component of national capability and decisionmaking, and are therefore the primary targets of terrorism. On the other hand, terror can infuse military as well as civilian targets; terror can paralyze or distort the minds of professional leaders as well as the minds of "innocent bystanders." From time immemorial, but certainly with the great example of Attila in the fifth century C.E., we see that all war is "total war," and that the psychological component—including terror, but also including hope, optimism, and charisma—is its critical element.

The Cold War itself was *entirely* about the use of terror against civilian targets. The "balance of terror" was the essence of the mutually assured destruction (MAD) strategy adopted by the Soviet bloc and the West, specifically implying that civilian targets—cities—would be held hostage to possible nuclear attack, thereby forcing a decisionmaking mode in the opponent's body politic which would respond to that threat.

WHY DO WE FEAR TERRORISM? Quite apart from the fact that terrorism does, in fact, create terror in the target community (and in other communities who fear that the same thing could happen to them), terrorism often creates almost irrational responses among professionals in the policy, defense, and intelligence arenas. People who talk rationally about nuclear threats often talk irrationally about more localized forms of terrorism.

This is because terrorism is, by definition, a stratagem of surprise, deception, informality, and manipulation of perception. It is employed specifically as a tool of asymmetrical warfare, usually (but not always) by a weaker or smaller force against a stronger and more fixed target. Military and intelligence officers within the major powers have been predominantly trained and disciplined in conventional, structured warfare; normal defense depends upon cohesive unit action against a similarly trained adversary. But it is laughable to suggest that a less-advantaged adversary should feel compelled to fight on terms defined by the more powerful foe.

Major powers throughout history have felt it their unique right to act and force others to react. But this is a luxury. Similarly, major powers, with everything to protect, cannot afford to disband their conventional capabilities in order to fight an unconventional foe. Unconventional response capabilities must be added to their force mix, and, of necessity, unconventional capabilities require unconventional thinking and structures. It is not unreasonable to suggest that the formal, conventional structures of policy thinking, defense forces, intelligence, and law enforcement are inadequate to the task; even that those individuals who have grown up in such structures may be unable to adequately respond to psychological threats.

The fear of losing control is the most significant aspect of the impact of terrorism on the national security professional. This is closely related to the fear of the unknown. Professionals who can with valor engage in mortal conflict with an enemy state peer find it difficult to know what to do in the face of an unseen, unknown adversary who fights by different rules.

"TERRORISM" IS AN ASPECT OF "UNCONVENTIONAL WARFARE." Terrorism is one of several forms of unconventional warfare, along with guerilla warfare, sabotage, and insurgent warfare, but they are not interchangeable terms. Some acts of "terror" are not themselves actually acts of violence or destruction, but most need at least the threat of violence or the removal of a sense of safety. Because terrorism entails, by definition, acts which are not covered by a declaration of war by a nation-state, or are not permitted under international law governing the conduct of war, they are usually criminal acts, beyond normal state protection.

Terrorism can also be employed by military units on a battlefield, exempting it from the legal ramifications which apply to terrorism performed in a nonwar civilian environment. Battlefield terrorism—such as the kamikaze attacks during World War II—is designed not only to inflict operational damage on an enemy, but also to confuse, distract, and paralyze.

CAN TERRORISM BE DEFEATED? Sun-tzu said in *The Art of War* that the highest form of generalship is to balk the enemy's plans; the next best is to prevent the junction of the enemy's forces; the next is to attack the enemy's army in the field; and the worst is to besiege a walled city.

If we are to balk the enemy's plans, those plans must be understood. In the case of the current broad war, the West in many instances has attempted to divine its enemy's plans either by believing what sympathizers of its enemy are saying are its plans and causes for war, or by using Western logic (mirror-imaging) to deduce the enemy's intent or goals. This is a reactive process, relying on intelligence structures which are not equipped to handle the task.

According to Sun-tzu, "All warfare is based on deception." And terrorism is, by definition, entirely about deception. It intends to deceive a populace into believing that it is constantly at risk; it deceives as to the perpetrators of the attacks; it deceives as to the real purpose and cause of the hostility; and it deceives by creating the belief that it cannot be stopped because of its "irrational" and "unpredictable" nature.

Sun-tzu also said, "Indirect tactics, efficiently applied,

are inexhaustible as Heaven and Earth, unending as the flow of rivers and streams." At present, only the terrorists are employing indirect tactics with any consistency. The West has not yet grasped that the response must also be indirect.

The response to terrorism must be to strategically outflank it. This does not mean abandoning physical protection against it, but such protection and direct responses should not become the strategy. The answer to terrorism in its present form is to change the shape of the world.

The essence of this, in the counterterrorism sense, is to reshape global alliances to reduce the pool of states or communities which see the need to employ terrorism. The USSR throughout the Cold War employed and supported terrorism against the West; the PRC once used narcotics trafficking and narcoterrorism against the West. These were asymmetrical forms of warfare to be employed when direct confrontation was impracticable. Now other powers—particularly Iran, Syria, and Libya—sponsor terrorism by proxies because they cannot afford direct confrontation with the West.

Within this framework comes the need to address the broader human issues of education, opportunity, communication, and—as a direct result—a particular psychological condition: identification *with* a civilization rather than against it. Inclusion rather than exclusion.

As long as groups feel frustrated and unable to break the cycle of suppression or containment by which they subconsciously believe their society is doomed (usually by their own leaders, but blamed on outsiders), they will resort to terrorism. In a sense, terrorism is the only form of nobility still available to those who perceive that they have no other options.

This sense of doom or extreme frustration in those sections of the societies from which terrorists come contributes to a feeling that the people's lives and the

present—in which they live—have been irretrievably ruined. The glorious past and the glorious future are all that
are worthy, and individuals achieve glory in sacrificing
their bodies and lives to the future.

Eric Hoffer, in 1951—long before the Islamist "martyr
terrorism" of the late twentieth and early twenty-first centuries (and even before the protesting self-immolation of
Buddhist monks in Vietnam in the 1960s and 1970s)—
identified the causes and processes of self-sacrifice for mass
movements. These were causes and motivations which de-
fied the logic of victorious societies, which are rooted in
their satisfying circumstances.

Coupled with the frustration over the "irretrievably ruined life" in the societies from which terrorists and suicide
bombers are recruited is the sense of satisfaction derived
from serving as a conduit to a glorious future, a future
which, to outsiders satisfied with their lives, seems fantastic
and implausible. As Hoffer notes: "Glory is largely a the-
atrical concept. There is no striving for glory without a
vivid awareness of an audience—the knowledge that our
mighty deeds will come to the ears of our contemporaries
or 'of those who might be.' "

To the victorious, relatively contented society, this frustration and the luminous appeal of a glorious "transition" appear irrational, largely because, as Hoffer notes: "A pleasant
existence blinds us to the possibilities of drastic change. . . .
The tangibility of a pleasant and secure existence is such that
it makes other realities, however imminent, seem vague and
visionary."

Thus, not only does the victorious society not understand the logic behind the threat, it is seduced into not
comprehending that a threat is real and urgent. This accounts not merely for the failure to recognize imminent
terrorist threats, but for the failure to recognize almost all
forms of external (or internal) threat.

The key, then, to eliminating terrorism and terrorist threats lies to a large extent in ensuring that the societies from which terrorists emerge have avenues by which they can avoid the frustration and disorientation which the combination of poverty, ignorance, the breakup of family and tribal units, and a loss of personal identity bring. And often, to achieve this, it is necessary first to reduce or eliminate the influence of those demagogues who attempt to ensure that these frustrated societies remain frustrated, ignorant, and disoriented.

Most societies which successfully resist the mindlessness of mass movements do so because they feel that they have a national—rather than antinational—culture of worthwhile ethics, rooted in historical examples. This does not deny the appeal of religion, but subordinates it to national identity, which has a greater, although by no means total, appeal to individualism. Hitler demonstrated that nationalist mass movements could also be mindless and xenophobic, but President Askar Akaev in the Kyrgyz Republic between 1991 and 2005 showed that pride in national identity, coupled with a sense of purpose in building a newly sovereign state, could be an effective antidote to a form of radicalism which would induce a sea of despair and create a breeding ground for terrorism.

The development of antidotes to terrorism requires a depth of understanding of historical, cultural, and sociological context which is too often bypassed by those who claim to be practitioners of counterterrorism. Terrorism clearly must be confronted at the practical level when it occurs, but it is most effectively deterred by addressing the roots of despair and offering alternatives.

And, as President Akaev demonstrated, poor economic conditions do not automatically engender despair. Pride, ethical values, and self-confidence can also be engendered in circumstances of poverty. These, in turn, are the tools which can be used to build the economic and social well-being of the society. Therein lies the defeat of terrorism. The demagogues who remove hope from society must be removed before such seeds of thought can be planted in the breeding grounds of terror.

Terrorism, however, is not our only enemy. It may well, in fact, distract us from the consideration of more substantial and enduring threats.

THE CARE AND FEEDING OF ENEMIES

TWELVE

Victory can never be given, it can only be achieved, yet enemies are vital to victory as the stimulus for its defense. Therefore embrace, nurture, understand, and respect enemies.

C ould the West have united after World War II into such a vibrant, cohesive, and intellectually productive society in the absence of a common enemy, the USSR? Indeed, could the USSR—the leadership of which ignored economic wealth in the pursuit of military strength—have lasted as long as it did in the absence of an overwhelming rival, the West?

Victory is essential on a societal level if mankind is to find new ways to feed the growing multitudes, to meet the increasing demands on viable water supplies and other resources, and to cope with epidemic or pandemic illnesses which threaten the health of the entire human population. But challenges such as water shortages, starvation, and pandemics often rally us to our own defense, only because we had not earlier aroused ourselves to face a clear threat from a human adversary. History has shown that human competition, including war, helps stimulate the disciplines and science which also help address challenges from nature.

Competition in any event is fundamental to nature, because all peoples wish for their own victory. They wish to live neither as a subject people, nor as a people given their peace, wealth, and freedom as a dispensation. This is as fundamental for the individual as it is for a society. Gifts can be exchanged between equals; that connotes respect. There is no victory in the acceptance of "freedom" or "independence" as a gift from a stronger power, despite the desire for such a wondrous prize. Victors dispense largesse; subject peoples—vassals—accept it.

Victory must be won if it is to satisfy the visceral need which drives the competition for the survival and progress of the species. Anwar as-Sadat's relative military triumph of 1973 gave Egypt the sense of completion—at least for a period—to enable the country to move forward, in command of its own destiny and able to treat with others as equals.

One of the difficulties of great and protracted victory is that it becomes the habit of the victor to reward the "loyalty" of its vassal states. It offers these vassals the fruits of its own victory, particularly "peace" and prosperity. There is almost always surprise among the victorious people when this "peace"—whether it is the *Pax Romana*, the *Pax Britannica*, or the *Pax Americana*—is rejected by the ungrateful subject state and its people who at the same time tread underfoot the trappings of prosperity.

They do not want the peace given to them as largesse by the great power; they want their own victory, their own peace.

However, they recognize the asymmetry between their position and that of the great and victorious power. They couch their rejection—their hidden rebellion—in subtle terms, often turning the words and arguments of the great power against it. The intellectuals of the great powers call for the perpetuation and expansion of "peace" because that is the great prize for which their societies had fought. From the smaller, subject peoples comes the echo of the cry "peace," but it has a different connotation: It is, in large part, a call for their own victory.

Those in the peaceful, victorious societies of the great powers who have not understood that victory, and its byproduct of peace, is something which must be won and protected, tend to try to bargain with those who threaten the peace. Their first reaction, when the calm is disturbed, is to appease the noisemakers.

Those in the victorious society calling loudest for peace are usually calling not for peace but for appeasement. They are, in fact, calling for "peace at any price"; calling for someone to remove the fear so that they do not have to understand what brings peace.

Peace—which implies a condition of prosperity, freedom, and the ability of society to cope with challenges—is the product of victory. There are those who believe that victory is the destruction of an adversary. This is not so. The destruction of an adversary may be a transitory triumph on the road to victory. But victory itself is the construction of a positive and evolutionary civilization, based on the triumphs of politics, sociological evolution, and military conflict.

The Western world, so accustomed by the early twenty-first century to the fruits of victory, had come to believe that peace was something which could exist in the absence of victory. When the West talked of "peace," it meant its ability to impose that "peace"—in this instance meaning the values and modalities of the West—upon the world. When adversaries of the West talk about "peace," they, too, are talking about victory, but one which would enable them to impose their own language, beliefs, and modalities, at least upon their own world.

As we discussed earlier, Palestinian leader Yasir Arafat, in the 1990s, stumbled upon this great truth when he told colleagues that any state given to the Palestinians by the Israelis and the West was one they did not want. The only state they wanted, and of which they could be sure, was one they seized for themselves. They did not want to receive a gift from the victor to the vanquished; they wanted their own victory.

This is a fundamental driving force in mankind.

Only by recognizing this underlying aspect of human nature can the West actually start to understand what needs to be done. The West needs to identify what it considers to be its necessary victory, and act to achieve or perpetuate it.

One goal for the West may be to find a way to embrace all of the Middle Eastern peoples firmly into Western civilization itself. If that attempt does not succeed there are many in the Middle East who will seek their own separate victory, which demands the dominance of their values over their own, and other, spheres. Such victories can neither be achieved nor sustained without struggle.

Thus, for the victorious power or society, the road to the perpetuation of victory is not to attempt to grant largesse to lesser peoples, but to treat with the potentially rebellious societies in such a way as to make them integral with the victorious society. Do not dispense peace and justice; share the victory and make it also the victory of the societies which would otherwise rebel. Britain dispensed "peace and justice" in much of the twentieth century to subject dominions such as India and Kenya, but many there resented this "kindness" and rebelled, demanding the victory of self-determination. Other subject dominions were, in essence, invited to share the victory—Australia, Canada, New Zealand—and remained part of the victory of the West. Even so, Britons in time forgot even to share with these loyal subjects, and while they remained part of the West's victory, they walked away from the paternalism of the United Kingdom, and thus allowed the United Kingdom's separate and historic victory to diminish.

President Askar Akaev of Kyrgyzstan noted: "The well-known Russian historian, Prince N. Trubetskoy, who passed away abroad after the [Russian] revolution, states in one of his works that people integrated into a state cannot voluntarily allow the destruction of their ethnic identity in the name of assimilation, even to create a more perfect nation." This highlights the importance of sharing victory in a way which embraces different origins and different points of pride in origin and achievement (nationalism), and which tolerates imperfections, rather than attempting to create total commonality within an alliance.

The remaking of the global alliance system was feasible when the world finally broke out of the rigidity of the Cold War era on September 11, 2001. At that point it was conceivable to bring together former adversaries under the framework of a common civilization, a common victory. The so-called war on terror declared in response to the attacks of September 11 provided one of the great opportunities for the West to expand and strengthen its victory by reappraising attitudes toward old adversaries and bringing them into the West as true partners. Despite the Middle East conflicts of 2002–06, it is not inconceivable that the West could strategically outflank the potential hostility of some or all of the Muslim world so as to embrace the Muslim *ummah*—along with Israel—into the victory of the West. Then again, the situation may now have progressed beyond that possibility, and once again the West may have to face war to defend its victory.

The end of the Cold War in 1990–91 saw the start of a widespread perception in the West—in Western Europe and North America, and from Australia to Japan—that military power was no longer necessary. But by the late 1990s, it was apparent to many jihadists and others that the West, having abandoned military defenses, had become decadent and weak, ripe for attack.

The attacks were broadly based. They were direct terrorist actions supported by states and ideologies which openly declared their hostility to the West, and which began developing tools of warfare designed specifically to achieve parity with the West in order to challenge it. This amounted to a message the West found unacceptable. It challenged the West to a response, which would have necessitated great effort and change. So it was ignored. The more the challenge was ignored, the more it was escalated, with growing militancy of action and word.

The United States responded to the 2001 attacks with the avowed aim of totally suppressing the opposition. Other Western states had disarmed to the point where they could not lead such a response to the challenges. Thus, from the apparently egalitarian "peace" which followed the Cold War, one power re-emerged with both military capability and political will. The victory of the West then appeared to be transformed into the victory of the United States; the shared victory of the West no longer seemed to guarantee the innate demand of other Western societies that they be in control of their own destinies, languages, and cultures. However, these societies had, by abandoning their defenses, placed themselves in the intolerable position of being dependent upon the United States for their continued survival.

It was a condition which was intuitively unacceptable to the dependent Western states. Those dependent societies therefore rationalized that the fault lay not with themselves, for failing to commit to their own defense—and for allowing the United States to bear the burden of it—but with the United States. Thus the real enemies of their own societies were in turn rationalized, because they were also enemies of the United States, into the status of victims, with which the Western European (and other Western) societies had common cause. In other words, the French government, and many "intellectuals" in the West, in their anger with the United States, chose to align or empathize with people who were, in fact, enemies not just of the United States but also of all the West, people such as Saddam Hussein and the Palestinian and Wahhabist jihadists.

In reality, given the impracticability of Western European (and other Western) societies challenging the United States, and the unwillingness of the United States to view its erstwhile partners as enemies, it was necessary for all of the Western societies and the United States to rethink how best to share the new era of their joint victory.

The Western states must, then, if they are to survive with their victory still dominant, find new ways to work together. Failure to hang together will result in the victory of some or all of the Western states succumbing in the fratricidal rivalry. Thus do dark ages begin.

Rather than face this stark dilemma, the intellectual approach of many outside the United States was to demand that the United States voluntarily subjugate itself to a collective authority of those states which had failed to strive for their own victories. For the United States to agree to such an abdication of its success would be tantamount to suicide; the pursuit of mediocrity over excellence. It would reduce all of modern civilization's defenses against the depredations of anticivilizational forces. The Continental European states, by the early twenty-first century, while protesting the United States's seemingly aggressive defense of modern civilization and attempting to separate themselves from the U.S. position, were not prepared to assume the burden of their own defense. There was some question whether, given a half-century of gradual abstraction by the intellectuals of Western Europe from the hard realities of survival, they even knew the cost of their own defense, quite apart from any willingness or refusal to pay that price.

However, just as victory cannot be given, its voluntary surrender challenges nature.

APPEASEMENT IS NOT THE TOOL OF A VICTOR: A victorious society starts to lose its victory when it begins appeasing smaller powers which are snapping at its heels and demanding spoils. Appeasement flows only in one direction: from the victor to the challenger. The arguments for appeasement are those of the competing power put into the mouths of individuals in the camp of the victor. Appeasement is often mistaken for—or misrepresented as—the trading of land or rights or values for peace. It is never that. It is merely a disguised form of surrender by a society which values the peace of today more than the peace of the future.

Appeasement for "peace in our time" is the act of a society which does not think in terms of perpetuating its values, which does not think of the welfare or even the survival of succeeding generations. Appeasement is the enemy of victory, disguised as "reason." Appeasement is the last stages of the squandering of the victory won earlier, and then gradually spent by successive degradations on the part of "managers." When appeasement begins, either the society comes to the end of its victory or a new victory-oriented leadership emerges to reclaim the victory.

We have seen, in commercial terms, appeasement by corporate managements faced with unrealistic union demands, when long-term pension and health-care benefits have been promised to achieve short-term labor peace. Invariably the price for such appeasement is paid for later by shareholders and future management, either with the loss of corporate viability, or with the need to undertake painful restructuring.

THINKING BEYOND GRATIFICATION: The fruits of victory are narcotic and delusory. Security and wealth are secured; the ego is gratified; a sense of omnipotence pervades the second generation of victors. They are the masters of all they survey. Constant challenges, with frequent small failures—or other instruments to sustain humility—are necessary to ensure that the goal of victory is constantly pursued. Finding realistic challenges to sustain the adrenaline which motivates the will to victory is the most difficult task for the victorious. Constant sensitivity to one's surroundings is necessary to avoid the xenophobia which feeds delusions of omnipotence.

Often that which sustains victory is the constant existence of an enemy.

THE CARE AND FEEDING OF ENEMIES

The hardest thing to achieve is victory in the absence of an enemy. Therefore it is important to recognize who, or what, is the enemy of one's desired victory. This recognition is a key motivating and concentrating factor in the achievement of success.

Despite the need to recognize the enemies of victory, true victory is rarely achieved by those who are lost in the emotion of hatred for enemies. Enemies are tools to be used carefully, reluctantly, and respectfully. Despite this, there is always an eagerness to raise the specter of the enemy in order to motivate the population to support the leadership's will to victory, or to suppress opposition to the leadership.

In almost all instances, even with the best intentions, the nature of the enemy is misrepresented.

To the fearful or complacent, who wish to avoid pursuit of the expansion of victory, the enemy is a threat understated. To the ignorant—steeped in the belief of the universality of their own logic and values, and ignorant of the logic, values, beliefs, and needs of other societies—the enemy is rationalized or explained in one's own terms: This is mirror-imaging, and is the most common failing. To the zealous supporters of victory, the enemy is overstated and often distorted to the point of unrecognizability.

Nowhere is the truth to be found.

It is in this fertile environment that enemies are also created out of thin air by opportunists in their quest for dominance and victory. History almost always shows the folly of the artificial creation of enemies, either because the lie is transparent, or because it causes a distortion of the leader's own strategic priorities. It is therefore a distraction from the path of victory.

Hitler's persecution of the Jews entailed enlisting the support of the Grand Mufti of Jerusalem in an anti-Jewish scheme which, for the most part, was designed to assist Germany in undermining Britain's control of the Middle East's oil and the Suez Canal. While Hitler's effort played on Arab concerns over the post–World War I Balfour Declaration, which promised a Jewish homeland in Palestine, his actions substantially aided in the destruction of the millennium of mutual trust and partnership which had been the hallmark of Jewish-Muslim relations. So, by the early twenty-first century, the legacy of Hitler's messianic anti-Semitism could be seen in the inability to achieve an harmonious relationship between Israel and many Muslim states.

Similarly, the legacy of Clinton's demonization of the Serbs, which was aided by virulent Croatian-led propaganda stemming from the remnants of the defeated World War II Ustaše extremists, was the process of dismemberment of Yugoslavia as a state, a process which continued into 2006 and will cause still more chaos in Europe.

In almost all instances of the artificial creation of an enemy, and in many instances where desperation causes the dramatic overstatement of an enemy, the phenomenon of pseudospeciation—the characterization of enemies or outsiders as another species, less than human—arises. And in almost every instance where this distortion occurs there are long-term and destructive consequences. Two generations after World War II, the pseudospeciative images of "the Huns" and "the Japs" color many people's views of Germans and Japanese, hindering productive relationships.

Pseudospeciation often harms the nation which uses it. The demonization of the Jews by the German nazi leaders was a critical element in the destruction of Germany. It is, more than sixty years later, a critical element in the lack of stability and progress of many Arab societies. When enemies are reduced unnecessarily to emotional icons, this ultimately reduces, negates, or distorts victory or diverts from the path to its achievement.

Where concern over enemies turns to hatred and a preoccupation with destruction, we stray from the path to victory.

WHEN DESTRUCTION IS THE AIM, VICTORY IS NOT

THIRTEEN

Destruction can never be the quest of victory.
Destruction may merely be a step in the path to
construction, which is the hallmark of victory.

Most structures created by man have a finite life,
whether they are nation-states or corporations.
Whether, in their lifetime, these structures become
the basis for greater things is determined by how well they
are run and whether they have in place a grand strategy
which addresses, among other things, intergenerational
succession. Many states have disappeared throughout history, and many corporations. Trans World Airways (TWA)
was swallowed into American Airlines, for example.

But we have, in the twentieth and twenty-first centuries, seen corporate raiders lay seige to companies, acquire them, and break them up to sell their component
parts. Living things—for societies of people brought together in commercial organizations to provide goods and
services needed by the world are indeed living organisms—
are destroyed for immediate gratification, just as grave rob-
bers took the brilliant artistry of the funereal regalia of the
pharaohs to be melted down, their gems prized off.

The death of a corporation, or the destruction of art,
or societies, or bloodlines, is also the death of someone's
victory.

Pilgrims and travelers have labored up into the Bamiyan Valley of central Afghanistan, 230 kilometers of winding, rock-strewn track north from Kabul, for a millennium and a half, to gaze at the great standing statues of Buddha, carved over decades into the sandstone mountainside some eight thousand feet above sea level. These giant figures marked more than the teachings of the Lord Buddha; they represented the grandeur of a civilization striving for eternity. But they were destroyed by the Taliban in the space of a month in 2001. The act of destruction galvanized the world community in support of U.S. efforts to destroy the Taliban itself within a year or so.

In the moments before his suicide on April 29, 1945, as the Third Reich was collapsing under the hammer blows of Allied military power, Adolf Hitler crafted and issued his last testimony, blaming the destruction of his Reich on "the Jews." Germany came within a hair of success in establishing a strong, undefeated, and enduring nazi state. Hitler might have succeeded had he not diverted so much of the Third Reich's military might, resources, and political capital into the destruction of entire peoples: Jews, Gypsies, and Serbs. And Hitler's obsession with destruction—which was only marginally less obsessive than his desire to build—cast a dark scar upon the German people for a half-century and more beyond his death, skewing the destiny of Europe.

Competition along the path to victory often entails confrontation and the destruction wrought by war. Victory, however, is beyond destruction, and those who seek victory must think and plan beyond the carnage which may occur on the journey to victory. That which was counterproductive and hateful in the society of both the victor and vanquished will, in any event, largely be swept away or rendered meaningless by victory. To minimize threats to the victory, the goal of the victor should also be to minimize the motivation toward destructive and hateful reactions among the defeated.

World War II sprang from the nurtured hatred of the vanquished Germans of World War I. The October 1973 War sprang from the loss of self-esteem visited upon the Egyptians by the Israelis in the war of 1967. And so on.

Planning for victory should entail a conscious orientation toward constructive goals. The victorious society must be open to all stimuli and see the humanity and possibilities even of its enemies.

In the early 1970s, Dr. Stefan Possony forecast the collapse of the Union of Soviet Socialist Republics in the 1990s, based on a variety of factors, such as demographic and economic trends and political stagnation. By 1989, I was lecturing in Europe and elsewhere about the impending withdrawal of the Soviets from Eastern Europe, and the collapse of Soviet ideological motivation.

The most ardent Western Cold Warriors were reluctant to accept the scenario which Possony and I, years apart, had painted. We had predicted the victory of the West, which President Ronald Reagan and Prime Minister Margaret Thatcher ultimately delivered. But because it was the challenge of the Cold War's bipolar rivalry which sustained the motivation of the Cold Warriors, many could not envision peace, or welcome it. Their "rice bowls"—their careers, and to an even greater extent their self-perceptions—depended on continuing competition. As a result, the West had no plans for its victory. Indeed, there were even attempts, perhaps largely unconscious, during the Clinton administration—by individuals who had to a large extent played down the threat to the West from the USSR during the Cold War—to re-establish Russia, as the USSR's successor, as an enemy of the United States once again.

Thus, in the absence of planning and understanding, victory can be thrown away by a leadership which refuses to recognize when it has been achieved and what then must be done with it.

The Cold War is now over, but the deeply ingrained passions of that conflict have not yet completely dissipated, and the decision by the Clinton administration to continue to pursue the war against Russia was sustained by many bureaucrats in Washington after Clinton left office. And that, too, has skewed Western strategic policies, reigniting resentments against the United States in many parts of the former Soviet Union. The refusal by some Western officials to know when the time had come to end the war and to start to bring the Russian Federation—as the remnant heart of the Soviet Union—into the West has reinforced traditional Russian concerns about the intent of the West.

Indeed, much of that continued urge toward the destruction and punishment of Russia emanates from the desire of some in the West to gain dominance over the treasures of the former Russian and Soviet empires in Central Asia and the Caucasus. That treasure is energy and access to the strategic rear of the People's Republic of China. But the methodology adopted by the Clintonites has been short-term and flawed. It was based on the assumption that Russia could not respond; that the Central Asian and Caucasus emerging sovereign states could, and would, abandon all allegiance to, or concern for, Russia; and that China itself would not assert its influence in the region.

As a result, the United States has been frustrated by the fact that, although most of the Central Asian and Caucasus states have expressed a desire for "democracy" and friendship with the United States and the West, they recognize and welcome the fact that their geography determines much of their politics and culture. They cannot ignore Moscow, or forget that—now that they are no longer under the umbrella of the Soviet Union—they are vulnerable to China, with the new ally, the United States, far away.

The lack of subtlety in the United States's attempts to force the Central Asian and Caucasus states away from geopolitical realities has not gone down well, and could end in failure for the United States and the West's instrument in the region, the Organization for Security and Co-operation in Europe (OSCE).

The concept of knowing when to end hostilities—and when to commence them—is not new. The lines from Ecclesiastes 3, written in the pre-Christian era, tell it all:

> *To every thing there is a season, and a time to every purpose under the heaven:*
> *A time to be born, and a time to die; a time to plant, and a time to pluck up that which is planted;*
> *A time to kill, and a time to heal; a time to break down, and a time to build up;*
> *A time to weep, and a time to laugh; a time to mourn, and a time to dance;*
> *A time to cast away stones, and a time to gather stones together; a time to embrace, and a time to refrain from embracing;*
> *A time to get, and a time to lose; a time to keep, and a time to cast away;*
> *A time to rend, and a time to sew; a time to keep silence, and a time to speak;*
> *A time to love, and a time to hate; a time of war, and a time of peace.*

These are words of strategic advice, and yet we persist in continuing old habits and patterns when the time has come to abandon them. If we look at the loss of victory throughout history, it has frequently been caused by not matching the deed to the appropriate hour.

Now, for reasons of immediate energy needs, as well as because of the legacy of obsolete geopolitics, some corporate and diplomatic officials persist in attempting to destroy the indigenously developed democratic structures of Central Asia, Eastern Europe, the Caucasus, and Africa in order to ensure more extensive U.S. control over strategic resources. This carryover from the Clinton policies—with many Clinton officials still in place within the U.S. bureaucracy—will ensure long-term harm to U.S. interests worldwide.

HAS THE UN RUN OUT OF TIME?

The sense of timing governs much of success and failure on the path to victory. The world was fractured, uncertain, and engulfed in the potential for change at the end of World War II. It is possible that humanity could have faced then the uncertainty that we face now. Instead, the uncertainty was quelled by the conferences of great powers at Yalta and in San Francisco, resulting in the arbitrary—and often sweepingly inequitable—division of the world's people into a structure of nations which were immediately given "permanent" legitimacy.

The decision to create the United Nations locked the spoils of war into the responsibility of the conquering parties, and the subsequent decolonization of much of the developing world was automatically swept into this process. Indeed, it was an essential component of the move from colonial state to recognized sovereign entity. And many in the world believed that a permanent and defined structure had come as the salvation for all humanity, the start of a world government capable of ending the rigid state structures which "had caused war," and which would henceforth become structured elements within a global government.

The United Nations was blindingly successful in resolving the immediate threat of postwar chaos and uncertainty. But it was never likely to be anything other than a temporary solution to humanity's perpetual internecine competition. It is difficult to say whether President Franklin D. Roosevelt, who was present at Yalta, or British prime minister Winston Churchill viewed the United Nations as a permanent force; it is probable that they did not. It is clear that Soviet leader Joseph Stalin did not view the UN as a world government, nor as a permanent fixture. It was a temporary solution which enabled all the great powers, but particularly the Soviets, to regroup to later find ways to shape the world "nearer to the heart's desire."

Yet today we view the UN as a permanent edifice, a promise of tomorrow, freezing the comfortable status quo into a definition of the future. History has shown that there can be no such permanence in a world constantly changing. We must recall with humility that the same beliefs shaped the creation of the first "United Nations" at Delphi—the *amphictyony* between the constantly warring Hellenistic city-states—twenty-five hundred years ago, and the formation of the League of Nations after World War I.

The chaos of population growth and population movement, as well as the accompanying new age of the birth and death of nations (which we will discuss in Chapter Twenty-one), spells the end of the artificial rigidity which the UN brought to the world. The antagonisms which many in the United States feel toward the UN will not be the cause for the UN's gradual disappearance into insignificance. Nor will it be saved by the hopes of its supporters, who hope for the UN to be their guardian and substitute for their obligations to strive individually for victory.

The United Nations will soon become largely irrelevant because its principal job, the freezing of the status quo in 1945 terms, is finished. The UN staved off, for as long as possible, the chaos and lawlessness which—because of globalization and the movement of humanity, searching to find its own boundaries—will now define itself in natural terms, not through the artificial construct of the old men of Yalta. That is not to say that some UN-created institutions will not continue to play an effective role in coordinating the societies of the world. But humanity is on the move as never before; the boundary fences have been trampled by people, ideas, electronic signals, and the flood of goods and money.

The UN belongs now to a bygone era, just as Delphi's *amphictyony* and the League of Nations and other confederal structures of multisociety governance come and go.

Victory requires "legitimacy" and prestige to ensure a stable transition to the next era over the coming decade.

MAKING VICTORY ENDURE THROUGH "LEGITIMACY"

FOURTEEN

Victory must be recognized and venerated by the victorious as well as by the outside world if it is to be truly durable.

M ayer Amschel Rothschild (1743–1812) had a vision of victory for his family when he founded his banking dynasty in Frankfurt am Main in the eighteenth century and dispatched his five sons to establish additional branches of the Rothschild banking house in four European cities. Today, globally, the Rothschild name connotes respectability and prestige. Of necessity—being Jewish and therefore unable to take on direct influence in politics and in the establishment religion of the day— Mayer Rothschild was unable, when he began his House, to take the path toward victory which the Medicis took in Florence. But, from a position of great social disadvantage, Mayer Rothschild and his descendants came to dominate society and finance in many areas of the world.

The effects of success must be durable—lasting over generations or centuries—to be considered "victory." A single triumph may constitute the commencement of victory, if it is sufficiently pivotal. However, victory is the *dynamic possession* of an individual, group, or nation, and it is the victory of its possessor which endures to embed into civilization and history the profound new course. The vision of victory must therefore be greater than the attainment of its first success, embodied in a transitory event. While victory may be marked from its point of inception, it is not remembered until it has consolidated its achievement. Victory must be won every day, or it will erode and ultimately die.

It is often said of President James Earl Carter (1977–81) that his only vision was the attainment of the presidency, and that he had no strategy for his country or his office beyond his election. Indeed, it seemed as though his only mission, having attained the presidency, was to continue to run for the next election. Having no comprehensive vision, no articulated posture other than self-righteousness, he squandered the strategic position which his country had already attained, so that a quarter-century later his failings still haunted his successors and the global strategic environment. Carter epitomized the leader who believes that his victory lies in the mere *attainment* of leadership and power, rather than believing that the attainment of leadership is merely a *tool to attain victory* for his people.

Then there are others, who believe that the attainment of power and authority is a tool to ensure control over a population, whose task is then to serve as the tool for the *leader's* own greater victory. German Führer Adolf Hitler, Iranian "Supreme Leader" Ayatollah Ruhollah Khomeini, Iraqi president Saddam Hussein, the USSR's Josef Stalin, and even the United States's president Bill Clinton were modern examples of such leaders, even if the actions of Clinton were nowhere near as barbarous as those of the others. But each saw victory as a solely personal thing, and their population as pawns to their own ambition.

LEGITIMACY: THE FIRST TASK OF VICTORY

Victory becomes durable only when it is widely recognized within the victor's own society and is acknowledged broadly in the outside world. It must pass through the phases, in foreign eyes, of acknowledgment, acceptance, and respect. The process of legitimizing the victory must be consolidated at all stages. Legitimacy acts as a barrier to usurpation of the victory by an opponent. The quest for victory by any individual or society is made easier by the acquisition of legitimacy.

Legitimacy, which is widely perceived as a legal matter, is, in fact, a psychological or perceptional state. History is replete with instances in which legal authority has been overridden by force and by *perceptions* of right or wrong. Appropriate legal structures are, of course, critical to the acceptance of a state's legitimacy. Beyond that which is often arbitrarily given and removed, the durability of legitimacy is the product of *prestige*. And prestige is most definitely a perceptional or psychological condition.

Possony was fond of saying that prestige was the credit rating of nations. It is a great observation and truth, which governments and individuals forget at their peril. The achievement of prestige, and therefore legitimacy and authority, is the direct product of a credible grand strategy pursued with the tools of a broad psychological strategy.

The creation and entrenchment of symbols as guardians of victory is the hallmark of human progress. Symbolism is the most fundamental mark of the evolution of mankind into civilized societies. The earliest representations of Stone Age communities, pictograms on cave walls throughout the inhabited world, were meant to reflect man's comprehension of his place in nature's hierarchy, and his dominance over it. They were essential symbols connoting his own perception of his victory, or drive toward it, and his demand for acknowledgment. The symbols marked man's claim on the specific territory in which he lived by expressing his knowledge of it and its inhabitants, and by illustrating for his contemporaries and his descendants the nobility of his victories over nature.

Pictographic symbols, icons, and statuary have constantly evolved throughout human history, including the development of pictograms into written language, but the evolution of society also included, at its earliest stages, another representation of structure: the tribe or community group. Within this group was an accepted hierarchical pattern, initially based on the strength of natural leaders, and later—in addition to strength—on an appreciation of wisdom, leadership powers, and the rude natural politics of the group. Leadership connoted power, then and now, and leaders coopted the use of symbols which reflected and reinforced a mystical projection of power. And we must acknowledge that leadership, power, and authority *are* mystical: they can only be described in emotive, imprecise terms. Leadership, power, and authority cannot be precisely quantified, and yet they exist. They are the attributes by which things are made to happen. Food is gathered, territories are secured, learning occurs, victory is achieved, and societies prosper, all as a result of these human qualities.

We tend to believe, in this "Information Age," that all matters are quantifiable. We have to a large degree, as a society, made the mistake of believing that "information" is "fact," and even that "belief" equates to "knowledge" and therefore "fact." But this is far from realistic. There is also a tendency to believe that modern society is managed properly through the exchange of information, and that romanticized iconography and symbolism play no role in the way in which society is governed today.

We need only look at the rise in the use of iconography and symbolism in the marketing of goods and services—in the form of trademarks, slogans, and brand identities—to see that we are now more than ever living in a world in which beliefs about almost every aspect of our lives are controlled by symbols, rather than by deep understanding. Lenin, the first man to seize power and implement it under the banner of communism, was far ahead of his contemporaries in the early twentieth century in understanding the power of symbols and slogans to control crowds. He—like the often less doctrinaire communists who went before him in Western European café society—coopted the royal color red as his own, and with magical and majestic effect. Red was traditionally a royal color not because it was innately more regal than any other color: It was used because *it worked*; it stimulated passion, response, positive reaction. It was one of the earliest colors for which a consistent dye could be developed and, as with all new and striking discoveries, this dye was costly, and therefore affordable only to the powerful.

Stefan Possony, discussing "Communist Psychological Warfare," in the *Stanford Research Institute Journal* in 1959, noted that the communists had "learned a great deal about the interrelationships between physiology and psychology," and that "they approach the mind through the body." He went on to say that the Soviet view of conditioning and controlling societies and human masses was that "the propositions of the doctrine [which they wished to impose] must be *attached to the person* by extreme emotion." This, of course, is how society has evolved in its natural state: Events sear themselves into the collective psyche, resulting in a societal or group tendency to act in a certain manner. This natural state creates what we call "logic," and we tend to think of it as merely a normal part of life. Military units, thoroughly conditioned to the need for efficient and unquestioning obedience and response in the chaos of battlefield conditions, induce the desired group and individual responses by artifi-

cially "attaching" doctrine, discipline, and appropriate behavior to the person of the unit leader by the use of "extreme
emotion." The punishment of boot camp and the ferocity of
regimental sergeants-major have always been known to help
create well-trained and efficient soldiers, and this is a part of
the phenomenon Possony describes.

But the conditioning of a target group in a selected,
controlled environment—such as boot camp—is one thing;
the conditioning and shaping of an entire society, even one's
own, is something else again. And the fact is that the emotions by which a society at large is conditioned into a
happy, efficient, productive, and mutually supporting unit
are the product of generations of welding and shaping
events which contrive to build values and ethics, response
patterns, "logic," discipline as a group characteristic, and so
on. What the major communist leaderships attempted to
do—and what they did quite well in the twentieth century—was to isolate the values and response-predictability
factors which they wished to inculcate into the individual
and collective psyches of their target audiences and then to
hammer them home in a short space of time.

What the collapse of Soviet and Eastern European communism in 1990 proved was that the seventy years of communists' conditioning had failed to remove the generations
of conditioning which had preceded the communist efforts.
The reversion by these societies to overwhelming national
characteristics and religious and cultural beliefs showed that
the Soviets had not hammered their doctrine onto empty
slates. Pre-existing tendencies seemed to be perpetuated,
even when the Soviets—and such leaders as Romania's
Nicolae Ceausescu—worked on artificially isolated groups
of children, growing up in controlled environments.

That is not to say the Soviets failed. In many respects,
they achieved in their target audiences the degree of subservience and acquiescence they sought. They retained con-

trol of the societies they governed until other events made their continued rule of their empires no longer tenable. But clearly, where they succeeded in the longer term, they did so by drawing upon conditioning and symbols which had a far deeper hold on their audiences' souls than the modern or new concepts of communism which they attempted to introduce. The use by the Soviets of the color red is a classic case of drawing on an already powerful eidetic image. Eidetic imagery includes the use of some sensory factor to trigger reactions based on the memory of the target. A fairly basic example would be the smell of baking bread arousing in an individual a feeling of well-being based on his or her recollection of the childhood security of a mother's kitchen. The image of a populist politician "wrapping himself in his country's flag" also conveys the point.

The use of eidetic imagery in psychological operations takes a sensory approach to the subject. As Possony noted of the Soviets, the way to the mind is often through the body, although where the body ends and the mind begins—or vice versa—is equally a matter for debate by the psychological strategist. Inherited genetic memory, something only now being explored, is as much physiological as psychological.

Societies which have deeply ingrained hierarchical traditions and structures and clear-cut forms of recognition tend to have higher levels of societal discipline or compliance with the wishes of the state. This seems to be true in both military and civil life. In most places, people seem more ready to abandon financial security than they are to abandon the honors and prestige of rank and recognition. This may be partly a practical matter: If one loses a fortune, but retains a noble or military title of substance, rebuilding one's life is far easier. But the desire to cling to rank, title, and orders seems stronger than that sort of calculation. Often, it seems that the ego is a far greater driving force than is comfort and well-being. Furthermore, the desire to be an accepted, respected, and "safe" part of a larger, inclusive society—as Elias Canetti noted—is perhaps the overriding motivation for many people. This would explain why certain people can excel in a military force and face conflict with an extraordinary degree of calmness, and yet cannot function well in civilian life when confronted, alone, with the demand to perform in what seems a lawless or at least less-structured society.

Those societies which are new and have no visible legitimate traditions often go to great length to create or recreate traditions.

What we have seen in Africa in recent years has been a revitalization of interest in traditional symbols of African societies, gradually being integrated formally into the structures of the present-day states and their armed forces. Where African armed forces have been successful it is because they have finally come to terms with the marriage between traditional local cultural approaches to organization and the military structural legacies and traditions welded onto them by the colonial powers. We have seen structures of orders, decorations, and medals become more potent and more respected when they have been redesigned to reflect local traditions and incorporate local symbols.

Perhaps it is also time in the West that traditional motivating and structurally stabilizing symbols be reviewed from a positive perspective to help reburnish their luster as tools of national and military management.

THE RECREATION OF LEGITIMACY

Legitimacy and prestige are the things which suffer most in revolutions. And our Age of Global Transformation is a revolution which has toppled much of the older, vertical hierarchical structures. Leaders today are pilloried and destroyed in the media, just as the leaders of France were humiliated in their tumbrel ride to the guillotine in the French Revolution of 1789 to 1799.

Today, the destruction of prestige and legitimacy is part of that process of leavening which globalization and computerization, the main components of the current revolution, have wrought on the hierarchical structures of society. As a result, we ascribe social prominence to individuals of fleeting, fashionable significance, rather than to structures and positions within a social or governmental framework. Clearly, this creates an unstable situation.

This "revolutionary situation" in the West today creates—as with the French Revolution—a form of mob rule. At present, the "mob" is, to a large extent, the media: the surging voice baying from the streets; the fickle and self-appointed arbiter of fate. But as with the French Revolution, the situation ultimately comes to an end, and structure is recreated; new hierarchies formed. The French mobs ultimately clamored for the kind of order which Napoleon Bonaparte provided with great strictness. And the laissez-faire swagger of today's Western society will, of its own accord, give way to social militancy and political correctness.

It is up to Western societies whether, through thought and conscious action, they return to some of the legitimating and prestigious icons of the past—which gave credence and continuity to the entire rise of Western civilization—or abandon such things as the U.S. Constitution, the British Crown, and the like, in favor of new structures.

When communism fell in Russia in 1990, the most stabilizing aspect of the revolution to replace the communist structure was the restoration of old imperial Russian symbols—the double-headed eagle, the uniforms of czarist guards at the Kremlin, and the like—which helped legitimize the new leadership. And if the great and patient construction of victory in the West is to be sustained, it will be achieved only by carefully protecting, preserving, and burnishing the prestigious symbols which can help reinforce the legitimacy of the societies.

Prestige and legitimacy are the result of enduring institutions and outstanding leadership.

THE TRUE LEADER

FIFTEEN

The true leader is in harmony with the times, and comprehends the place and role of past leaders while building a foundation for future leaders. Only through leadership can a society be greater than the sum of its parts.

Management is prose; leadership is poetry. . . .
The manager thinks of today and tomorrow.
The leader must think of the day after tomorrow.
—RICHARD M. NIXON, PRESIDENT,
UNITED STATES OF AMERICA, 1969–74

Each of us can name someone we think of as a great leader, and usually it is someone who has been vindicated by history. Only with the hindsight of history can we determine the true worth of a leader, by seeing that his or her leadership qualities translated down the generations to the victory of society. Vice-Admiral Viscount Horatio Nelson, the hero of the battles of the Nile and Trafalgar, counts as a leader whose standards, ability to inspire loyalty and performance, and vision substantially defended and added to the victory of Britain over two centuries.

But someone you may never have heard of, Sir Charles Court, ranks up there with Lord Nelson. A dynamic and decorated army officer in World War II, Court, as premier of Western Australia, was the man who in the 1960s and

1970s put in place the political and trade agreements and policies which ensured that today Australia is one of the wealthiest, most dynamic, and most stable societies. And to do so he had to draw on a wide range of diplomatic and intellectual skills to totally change the course of Australian history.

Each time we think of those people who continue to motivate us, years, decades, even centuries after their death, we recognize the compelling power of leaders who have transcended the generations. Not all leaders are perfect; not all are suited to each occasion.

Today, because of the flattened social hierarchy in which traditional structures are neither trusted nor respected, it is difficult to identify the true leaders among us, and even more difficult for leaders to rise out of the cynicism and self-absorption of society.

To seize or seek the leadership of men or ideas is to grasp for immortality. It is an innate urge, like procreation itself, to play out life on a stage beyond the moment: to be larger than life, and therefore to defy time and to ensure the survival of one's dominance beyond a single life. It is a parallel instinct to that of the suicide terrorist, who also attempts—in that case out of frustration or desperation—to play out a "larger than life" act to affect his society's life beyond the immediate.

That leadership is a quest for immortality is often demonstrated by the fact that positions of leadership—whether of nations, organizations, or ideas—are usually viewed, or prized, as being hereditary in nature. Even in egalitarian societies, such as the United States, leadership, once seized, is often regarded as being an intrinsic "right" or privilege of the family of the leader. Historically, such rights have been enshrined in royal and aristocratic prerogatives. The urge toward nepotism—to hand leadership to one's own kin—exists, however, in all tiers of society, and confirms the tendency to use leadership to ensure the victory of clan, society, or state down the generations. We see this in all walks of life: the Medicis, Vanderbilts, Rockefellers, Murdochs, Rothschilds, and Waltons all seek to perpetuate their "aristocratic rights" in business.

True victory transcends the life of a single generation, so the victorious leader must be at one with—or in harmony with—the continuum, even though it is the function of a leader to change or adapt that continuum to cope with evolving realities. The leader must instill, at the beginning of a new epoch, the belief in the possibility, perpetuity, and safety of the victory.

A victorious leader is one who can absorb all the complexities of his own and other cultures and yet display a distilled image of simple clarity, unambiguous and certain.

The ability of a leader to lead depends on his or her ability to retain intellectual functions separate from those of the crowd, and yet to understand and identify with the crowd. Leadership, however, is compromised, or lost altogether, when the leader becomes part of the crowd. And when leadership is lost, so, too, is victory.

The relative rarity of true leadership is in line with the relative rarity of all other forms of genius. And, as with all other forms of genius, leadership may go unrecognized, unfulfilled, if the appropriate circumstance and context does not occur. Former French president Georges Clemenceau, who demonstrated many of the great qualities of leadership, as well as philosophical introspection, noted in his book, *Demosthenes*: "Now and again in the cities—caldrons, full of the ideal and of the basely turbulent, to which all the sorcerers had brought their spells—a man would rise who showed an energy beyond his times, occasionally beyond himself, and who marked his city with the stamp of his passage."

The containment of military leadership within the

bounds of national, societal—civic or civil—control is admirable as a concept, but the bounds of conflict and physical and structural threat have often, as at the start of the twenty-first century, returned to an almost primeval and amorphous anomie, lawlessness. It is a threat environment which must be faced on many levels, and in some senses neither politicians nor soldiers are ideally equipped for the task, while bureaucrats and economists are unsuited to it almost completely. What, then, must now emerge, or re-emerge, is the "natural" leader, but one now fitted to the task by decisiveness, and by combined skills and vision in statecraft, force, and motivational capabilities. A strategic leadership structure is required, supported by an intelligence, power projection, and force structure matching the greater flexibility and subtlety of stealthy and indirect threats, as well as the "clear and present" conventional dangers.

Where will we find these new leaders? All our systems, in the firm structures of established societies, block their evolution and prohibit their creation. There is no apparent home for them. But they emerge automatically in shapeless, natural crowds. Osama bin Laden took on such a mantle and attempted to sustain a transnational power in the latter years of the twentieth century. In some senses he was a multifaceted leader in embryonic form, but without the necessary comprehension of the need to create an enduring society.

Napoleon attempted to create a comprehensive strategic leadership but was thwarted by an imbalance which allowed his military ambition to move ahead of economic consolidation. It was a function too great for a single lifetime.

But it is clear that a more broadly evolved strategic leadership pattern must be commenced—with the emphasis on natural, multidisciplinary balance—and be gradually incorporated into the evolution of existing systems and structures. And the new support entities, such as professional psychological strategy bureaus, must be there to assist such leaders.

In many respects, Western society—because of the breakup of traditional hierarchical power—is coming to represent a version of the shapeless, natural crowd. But it is not the angry, frustrated crowd which gave rise to such people as Osama bin Laden. The first leaders who arose in the West, as the old systems shattered with the end of the Cold War, were merely those who wanted to spend the fruits of victory; they gave the crowd what it wanted: release. The crowd wanted its "peace dividend," and frittered away that dividend on indulgences. But the release is now spent; and the hollow, morning-after emptiness has settled in.

It seems clear that a new generation of leadership will emerge which will demand the reconstruction of vertical hierarchies in society and will demand a discipline and militancy which has been lacking for several generations. This is the natural pendulum of society.

What Constitutes Strategic Leadership?

Great strategic leadership involves more than the innate talent and vision of the individual who is offered up to shepherd a society to safety or victory. The leader who may serve well in one society, one situation, or one time may fail completely with another people, another situation, another time. Sir Walter Scott, in his novel *The Heart of Midlothian*, noted poignantly: "The hour is come, but not the man." Indeed, such is our love for and dependence on a leader who has saved us by being the "man of the hour" that we tend to devolve all trust on all issues and in all situations upon this person, often with unrealizable expectations.

It is true, however, that the characteristics of great leadership include the ability to match behavior to the society, the situation, and the time. This enables the leader to apply reserves of courage, and the willingness to make difficult decisions, along with knowledge of when to defer a decision, within a receptivity to the climate of the times in the context of historical trends and needs.

The great strategic leader, who is essential for the achievement and sustenance of victory, is the one who can manage the status quo in times of peace and yet move it forward without chaos. In times of danger, this leader can anticipate threats and mobilize resources to pre-emptively deter an enemy's hostility. Such a leader must have an implicit understanding of the historical and social motivations of his society and must also understand when, and how, to employ the simplistic cohesion of "mass motivation." Equally, he must have the ethical constraint to know when to refrain from such motivational behavior, and must recognize the distinction between the long-term good of his society and the short-term appetites of either that society or himself.

Some leaders—motivated by the retention of personal power—rely on the constant *absence of hope* in their society in order to achieve maximum compliance, rather than address the fickle and erratic behavior which hope and rising expectations create. By denying personal freedoms, removing all hope of moving the lives of their subjects out of the ruin which the leadership in fact ensures, such leaders generate an illusory appeal to the populace that their only meaning lies in sacrificing to a "greater cause" and a societal future, beyond their own lives, filled with glory. This creates a tool which cannot build, only destroy. It may be used to destroy an enemy, but it cannot be used within a state to build its own victory. And yet this is what is attempted where the leader capitalizes on the natural tendency of societies to galvanize around a simplistic mass movement, especially at a time when the present life of the people appears to have been ruined and become hopeless, and then relies on perpetual subjugation of the society to sustain his power.

Lenin understood this philosophy; Stalin employed it. So did Khomeini and Arafat. But this is not victorious leadership, which knows when to unite and motivate society and encourage collective sacrifice for survival, and when to harness individual freedom, inquiry, and hope to the unpredictable advancement and consolidation of success.

Significantly, the U.S. media in 2005 and into 2006 played on the fact that President George W. Bush had, in 2002, authorized changes in the U.S. national security structure, allowing the National Security Agency (NSA) to eavesdrop on the electronic communications of people inside the United States. This had hitherto been banned. The change was, of course, intended to address the presence of suspected terrorists and their supporters inside U.S. territory. The fact that the media, "intellectuals," and populist politicians were "outraged" by President Bush's decision contrasted dramatically with the significant support or acquiescence which the action generated in the public at large.

The public view reflected the reality that a yearning was beginning for a return to vertical hierarchical structure in society. It was the same reality which had ensured that President Bush was elected, and re-elected, to the presidency: People sought a leader who would, even imperfectly, but with true passion, be dedicated to their protection and the preservation of what they perceived were their historic values. In that regard, Bush was more attuned to public sentiment than were his political opponents, who sought to continue the "peace dividend" party.

Society demands special qualities from its leaders, the most significant of which may be passion.

THE PASSION OF LEADERSHIP

SIXTEEN

Collective leadership does not exist. Collective
responsibility is the abdication of responsibility.

I f anything emerged from the U.S. presidential elections
of 2004 it was that "primal," visceral factors dominated,
and "intellectual" approaches failed, even though the
United States was, at that time, still very much dominated
by the belief that individual rights predominated over the
security of the collective or nation-state rights. The United
States was still—as much of Europe remains—in the mode
of spending the fruits of the long Western victory.

Despite this, sufficient angst had begun to permeate
the U.S. electorate to the point where many voters felt that
the peace dividend festivities would come to an end unless
the country returned to a sense of national purpose. Most
notably, this was felt outside the major urban areas, because in the cities there was a greater preoccupation with
the newfound powers and gratification which accompanied
the breakdown of the older hierarchical mode.

It was, as a result, the visceral appeal of George Bush—
who, if nothing else, promised to defend Americans—which
defeated the unfocused, pseudointellectual approach of Sen-
ator John Kerry, who appeared to promise only prevarication
and delay in dealing with threats to U.S. security. The U.S.
voters were anxious for a return to certainty, for a leader who
would be iconic and passionate.

The enemies of leadership are sloth and cowardice,

which are hallmarked by short-term self-interest: career over country; safety of position over loyalty to friends or cause or nation. As Clemenceau said, such people are "those men who were always ready to stake everything on the hypothetical effort of the morrow in order to avoid the urgent effort of today."

Of that great mass of society who would avoid risk and shun true leadership, he added: "When men cannot clearly see the future, the weak, in opposition to the demands of the strong, will always postpone action to the morrow, though the strong are seeking, not to rule over them, but to impose on them the effort they need to make for their own liberation."

It is the task of a leader to ensure that he or she creates either unity of action or the effect of unity of action among followers. This is difficult in vibrant democratic societies in which there is a vast array of institutions, often with competing agendas.

Societies prosper through diversity and complexity. They retain, consolidate, and advance their victory through this diversity. But victory is first achieved, and then defended, when the society can be induced to act en bloc. Again, to cite LeBon: "Whatever be the ideas suggested to crowds, they can only exercise effective influence on condition that they assume a very absolute, uncompromising, and simple shape."

Such unity of purpose can be achieved only through unity of leadership, which implies that "collective leadership"—to the extent that this is not an oxymoron—must be exemplified by a single symbol. Leadership, while it may be sought by the individual, is granted by the crowd; therein lies the symbiotic relationship, demanding mutual trust.

The disintegration of the Federal Socialist Republic of Yugoslavia (FSRY) began with the death in 1980 of the country's iconic and determined leader, Marshal Tito. Tito had ensured that there was no clear successor to himself during his lifetime, no one to threaten his personal power. Thus, the FSRY had to resort, on Tito's death, to a collective leadership solution, destined by definition to fail, leading to the disintegration of the state into its smallest components, a process which was continuing a quarter-century later. Tito therefore limited himself to being a transitional figure, and not the father of a victorious society. The crowd had given Tito leadership, but he betrayed the society by robbing it of victory.

Thus we must differentiate between tactical and transitory leadership—the ringleaders and agitators of the hastily formed mob, a "servile flock," a "mass movement" of people who have abandoned individual hope and individual thought—and the victorious leader of a strategically effective, thinking, and capable society. The leaders of mobs are action-oriented; the leaders of victorious societies are driven by thought. Action is easier in the absence of doubt (and is therefore easiest in a state of ignorance).

Nothing, therefore, initiates change better than ignorance; nothing achieves victory better than transforming ignorance through wisdom.

The victorious leader maintains unity of thought while planning and implementing change within visible adherence to established form. But the attainment and sustenance of victory require absolutely that the leader, while appearing to be the custodian of the continuity of society, in fact constantly acts as the agent of change, allowing the society to consolidate that change into stable prosperity and security. The leader bites off the necessary change; the society chews and digests it and transforms it into "the fat of the land."

Given that the task of the victorious leader, then, is to sustain change, and therefore to be in a constant state of risk, and given that the constant desire of a society is to minimize risk and change, a successful leader will make maximum use of legitimacy and tradition to cloak the change and ease his risks. Change is that which is most resisted by society, and yet essential for its well-being and perpetuity: for its victory. The leader, therefore, in order to honestly fulfill the duty of leadership, must at times conceal facts from his society, much as a mother disguises the taste of her child's medicine.

This means that while the victorious leader must retain unity of vision, he or she must embrace complexity of execution. Transitory leaderships, like transitory success, can exist with unity of vision coupled with unity of action. An example would be the leadership of a demagogue who not only dominates the totality of his administration's decision-making, but also oversees the enforcement of policy execution. His is a success which goes with him to the grave. Such was the leadership style of Tito, Saddam Hussein, Ayatollah Ruhollah Khomeini, Hitler, and Hannibal. All believed to a greater or lesser degree that their populations were there to support the greatness of the leader, and not the reverse. And all found their subjects wanting. Their people did not deserve succession.

Dr. Askar Akaev, the former president of the Kyrgyz Republic, noted, in his outstanding philosophical approach to Kyrgyz history, that the theory of *passionarnost'* was first introduced by Russian historian and philosopher Lev Gumilev in his book *Ethnogenesis and the Biosphere.* Akaev wrote: "Gumilev used this term in relation to ethnoses for the purpose of providing an explanation for periods of intense growth in a nation. In such historical periods, a nation under the powerful rule of an impassioned leader becomes conscious of itself and commits to the fulfillment of its 'destiny.'" Akaev goes on: "*Passionaries* or impassioned leaders are individuals whose impulse toward action, according to Gumilev, is stronger than their instinct for self-preservation. For the sake of an illusory idea, these people are willing to sacrifice the lives of others as well as their own."

Passionarnost', then, can be the positive catalyst of leadership, but not without risk. What we saw in leaders such as Hitler, Khomeini, Ahmadi-Nejad, Clinton, Muammar al-Qaddafi, and Saddam Hussein, in the twentieth and early twenty-first centuries, was the willingness to risk the lives of others for the leaders' own ambitions rather than the needs of society, while the leaders maintained their own strong instinct of self-preservation. This is a common expression of "leadership" and revolves around the personal ambition of the "leader" rather than commitment to an ideal and a societal victory.

Increasingly, into the twenty-first century, the management of nations and the threats to nations has become a task in which the separation of political, military, bureaucratic, and economic skills has actually made governing more unwieldy, with the various units of national management competing. Their priorities clash, and sectoral leaders (economic, military, intelligence, and so on) vie for the nod of the supreme leaders. It is for this reason, among others, that the ultimate leadership cannot be apportioned into areas of responsibility.

One individual must always weigh the priorities and be able to make decisions.

It is useless, however, to have leaders able to weigh priorities wisely, and to act decisively and with passion, if the voice of leadership goes unheard, or commands no authority.

PERCEPTIONS OF LEADERSHIP

SEVENTEEN

Leadership, like victory itself, is as it is
perceived and revered to be.

No wonder there is chaos. The phenomenon of globalization—which essentially became viral in the early 1990s—flattened the world's industrial and social hierarchical structures with the leveling effect of a nuclear weapon. This, indeed, is the Nuclear Winter. Not the postapocalyptic gauntness of starving survivors searching for food, but rampant, steroidal, and healthy hordes searching for purpose and leadership.

Toffler hinted at the problem in 1970 in *Future Shock*, when he talked of the role of the computer in transforming decisionmaking hierarchies, but could not have imagined the assault on the value systems of societies by the computer-aided structures of the post–Cold War world, in which technologies created for the very purpose of sustaining opposing power blocs became—with the collapse of the Warsaw Treaty bloc—the technologies of societal integration.

Hierarchies, social frameworks, all fell before the shock wave of globalization. And yet many of us are still in denial of this, still seeking the stability of the pole stars of old orders, or wandering aimlessly in the well-fed freedom of our superindustrial society. In the hope of imposing order, those in denial attempt to compensate for the growing pace, scale, and seemingly unmanageable nature of change by the creation

of more and more legislation and the imposition of greater political correctness.

We have seen the phenomenon before, with every
sweeping, rapid surge of history, from the invasions of
Genghis Khan to the Industrial Revolution. But if our hierarchies of power have again been shattered, and on a
larger scale than ever before, does that "democratization"—
the temporary removal of the authority of our kings, presidents, earls, and barons—diminish the underlying need of
societies for leaders?

On the contrary, it increases the urgency of the search
for strong leadership. And it gives us the chance to see
where "natural democracy" can play a role in developing
such leaders.

The flattening of hierarchical lines is an inevitability of
globalization and the surge of wealth- and technology-
empowered individuals, but this lack of social structure—
which is akin to a postapocalyptic landscape, in that
traditional power structures have been eliminated or damaged—adds to the anxiety people feel as they search for
guidance and horizons. It all adds to the genetic impulse of
humankind to accept and assign responsibilities for individual and societal survival and victory. And stress mounts
when the patterns of assigned responsibilities are changed.

Such periods always generate an urgent search for clear
lines of social responsibility and obligation. Strong leadership is demanded; political correctness and clear, simple,
and formal lines of conduct are embraced.

At all times, but especially in times of chaos, if society
is in some ways *less* than the sum of its parts, a true leader
may be seen as an individual who is greater than the sum
of one.

Because of our primal origins and basic requirements,
all leadership must appear to be—in many senses it also
must be—heroic. This, today, does not necessarily imply

bravado or physical courage, but it implies courage of heart and mind, nonetheless. The leader must embody the courage of the nation.

Clemenceau noted: "Nations have never cheerfully followed any leaders except those who have asked them to shed their blood." But he also said: "Every man is quick to offer himself as leader and the crowd sooner or later is quick to take its revenge on the one who chances to be chosen." Even so, he said, "great lives open for us avenues of light in all directions."

Systems of leadership and societal management exist specifically to smooth the transition of leadership down the generations. Republics favor emphasis on structure and laws to manage this process; monarchies have favored the evolution of a hereditary class of leaders. Constitutional monarchies have combined the two approaches. The key consideration for all systems remains the continuity of transition, the factor which eludes the obsessive selfishness of single-generation systems, such as dictatorships. But then dictatorships—unless under the temporary expedient of urgent need—are not about leadership; they are about control.

In all forms of leadership it is apparent that great acts of intellectual courage are achieved alone. They are rarely the result of collective thinking among equals. These acts of intellectual courage—the essence of leadership—may be passed on to the crowd as inspiration to implement or follow, but the crowd itself, all the while demanding authority for itself, can in no way lead. "Crowd leadership" is chaos and destruction. The normal person—adept, thoughtful, and distinctly individual when alone or in the company of a few people—loses many faculties of reason, and assigns away the most fundamental of rights, on becoming part of a crowd. LeBon notes that "by the mere fact that he forms part of an organized crowd, a man descends several rungs

in the ladder of civilization. Isolated, he may be a culti-
vated individual; in a crowd, he is a barbarian—that is, a
creature acting by instinct. He possesses the spontaneity,
the violence, the ferocity, and also the enthusiasm and
heroism of primitive beings. . . . An individual in a crowd
is a grain of sand amid other grains of sand, which the
wind stirs up at will."

So the leader must achieve a balance between the appropriate degree of separation from the crowd, and the appropriate degree of identification with the crowd. But he can in
no way be subsumed by the crowd. The whole system of hierarchical rankings within societies—civil crowds and military ones—enables the appropriate amount of authority to
ensure leadership appropriate to the task. Hence, corporals
lead few, and generals many, but each has an indispensable
function. Each rank is incrementally further away from the
crowd, for which it must make the rational decisions.

In this process, leaders emerge from the led, having become imbued with the concepts of earlier leaders. Few
leaders emerge full-blown, without the cathartic birthing
process of evolution in the crowd's womb.

All victory depends on the skill of its leaders; indeed,
on the tangible and iconographic function of leadership.
And yet leaders may be voices lost in the wilderness if they
have no society to lead, or if their society chooses not to
listen to them, perhaps being distracted by historical distortions—such as unchallenged prosperity—which cloud
the people's appreciation of their needs. So leadership is essential to victory, but is insufficient on its own. Moreover,
a victorious society, well-grounded over an era, can demon-
strably exist and even prosper for a period *without* great
leadership. In such circumstances, it will rely on overwhelming economic might, or brute military force, to sustain itself in the absence of the delicate precision of good
leadership.

The George W. Bush administration took office in 2001 at a time when the upheaval of globalization had not yet been perceived as unmanageable. The terrorist attacks of September 11, 2001, however, traumatized U.S. society and transformed the Bush administration into a leadership which, at a pivotal time in global history, sought purpose. There was, at the time, little comprehension of the nature of the global upheaval, but President George W. Bush and Vice-President Dick Cheney acted on the two most important fundamentals: to clearly lead the West into the defense of victory and to recognize that the most important element which had emerged when globalization "broke the mold" of the existing social structures was a revival of the natural urge for "democracy" and freedom in mankind— not necessarily the structures of democracy which the West had developed, but the *natural* quest for organization which is innate within the human spirit.

Democracy—as we define it today—is a concept and ideal for social welfare which demands of every participant the exercise of free will in the conscious assignment and division of the roles of governance over the individual and the collective society. Ideally, then, our system of democracy should be balanced between the total assignment of our rights to an absolutist leadership and the retention of all rights and responsibilities within each individual, with no obligations to others. Democracy is a reflection of natural tendencies found throughout humanity; by naming it, the ancient Greeks gave it form.

Democracy represents mankind's need for collective engagement to reproduce and nurture the perpetuation of the species, and for collective action to make that survival triumphant in works which protect and strengthen humanity. And yet it represents the reality of individuality within the species, and the need of the individual for both a personal and a group identity.

Some responsibilities, therefore, are assigned by individuals within the framework of democracy to collective institutions and to other individuals, and some responsibilities are retained within each individual. Each exercise of assignment contains within it specific functions and commitments; each exercise of free will and the assignment of that will, then, also has a price.

The ideal democracy is that in which the individual feels that he has not assigned away more of his rights than he wishes, nor assumed more than is tolerable of the burden for life within society. And given the unique nature of each individual, it is rare that a society can be in agreement as to what represents too much assignment, or too much individual responsibility.

Democratic societies, therefore, are in eternal movement and adjustment of assignments of responsibility. This must be their nature; anything less than constant movement and adjustment would imply a uniformity of thought which would further imply the loss of democracy and the imposition of standards by tacit or express force.

And given that all societies differ in their customs, desires, and logic patterns—which are governed by terrain, climate, and the relative ease or difficulty of human survival—it is natural that the structures and shape of democracy also differ from culture to culture, and from time to time.

Democracy, as practiced in conscious forms from the earliest times until today, reflects that the assignment of responsibilities from an individual to a group, or from individuals to other specific individuals—leaders—varies depending on the transitory needs of societal survival. For example, free will is more happily subordinated to autocratic leadership in times of challenge and conflict. And at all times, the varying nature of individuals reflects a greater or lesser need to assume or assign leadership.

It is this same natural urge toward organization—the fundamental democratic urge—which evolves a body of accepted custom, of moral and ethical codes within society, all of which generates common law. The transformation of historically evolved common law into the codes of society is, therefore, a greater enshrinement of this democratic spirit than, for example, the imposition from above of the wisdom of individuals, such as we saw with the enactment in the French Empire of the Napoleonic Code.

The *natural* fluidity, therefore, of swirling masses of humanity is the beauty of democracy. Ask not how many angels can dance on the head of a pin. Ask how six billion individuals can dance in a choreographed and endlessly moving gavotte. This is the dance which reflects the nature of humanity in search of structure.

Human nature, human desires, and human needs arguably remain unchanged in their basic forms since prehistory. The dimension of the human mind itself has not changed, and the wisdom and intellectual capabilities of the average modern human have also remained unchanged. Man runs but little faster than in the days before history; lifts scarce, if any, more weight; feels no more love, or sorrow. And yet the human *condition* has changed, haltingly, and with violent surges and setbacks, over the millennia.

And this change, when it has been positive, has been due solely to the *tools*—both physical and intellectual—which have been built painstakingly, each better than the last, each tracing its origins to the first rock thrown, the first stick sharpened, and, most important, to the first words formed to provide the abstract representation of things and dreams of things. Progress toward structured societies and civilizations is the accretion or construction of building blocks of lessons.

All progress, then, is fragile and reversible: If mankind forgets, if it loses its will toward inquiry, or if it destroys the framework of lessons and civilizational structures. Dark ages can once again rob mankind of progress, prosperity, and security, if minds turn from learning and permit leaden authority or hysteria to sweep away the facility of individuals to inquire. As with the lessons of progress, this, too, is a lesson we have learned from history, and mankind has not yet recovered from the loss of momentum and civilizational foundations represented by the destroyed or misplaced manuscripts and learning from the times of Zarathustra, of ancient Hellenism, of the Library of Alexandria, or those of Rome. Humanity was robbed of hundreds of years of progress by the Dark Ages which resulted from the triumph of destructive societies over civilizations whose members had forgotten their responsibilities toward their own good governance and survival.

Had we been able to build on the pivotal lessons of Pericles of Athens in a consistent, unbroken line, it is probable that we could have seen such achievements of the mind as movable type and widespread literacy in the ninth century C.E., and supersonic flight and space travel in the fifteenth century. Today, had mankind not, through lapses of human judgment, failed to observe the lessons of history, we could have achieved a greatness which remains still unimaginable to us.

And yet our human failings caused the lessons of Pericles and the great thinkers of Hellenism to be abandoned almost as soon as they were realized. Athens succumbed to corrupt government in the generation after Pericles died of plague; Athenian principles of democracy retreated when Hellenism succumbed to Macedonian absolutism in the fourth century B.C. But the lessons of Pericles and Aristotle, of democracy-shy Plato, and of Demosthenes, still recalled in manuscripts and teachings, remained intact, if but partially applied, through the Roman conquest of Greece and the rise of Roman civilization. And progress in human society continued, albeit often without democracy, until the fall of the Western Roman Empire itself. With the rise of the Dark Ages, human societal achievement faltered and slowed, only fully recovering momentum with the major Renaissance of the fifteenth century. (This is not to discount the significant achievements during the Dark Ages, including the introduction of the three-field agricultural system, which permitted the rise of cities; the development of English jurisprudence, the foundations of the modern scientific method laid by Roger Bacon and Albertus Magnus; the creation of the longbow; and so on. The renaissances of the eighth century and twelfth century paved the way for the pivotal revival of human progress in the fifteenth century.) And even in the Dark Ages, tyranny (monarchical, oligarchical, and clerical) reluctantly allowed a restoration of the freedoms needed by individuals to participate in their own destiny. That reluctance was tempered by the reality that the free exercise of responsibility by individuals also contributed to the creativity, productivity and wealth of the leadership.

We have only to witness how China's wealth has multiplied since tyranny has loosened its reins to allow the more or less free choice of individuals to express their responsibilities to themselves and their society.

It has been assumed that absolutist monarchical government represents a top-down form of societal administration while democracy represents a bottom-up form of government. Neither assumption is completely accurate; both reflect the aggregate of the assignment of responsibilities by the collective will of the people. At different times, or in different segments of society, there will be either a majority or a minority who will *wish* to assign all decision-making to a leader and virtually none at all to themselves. This balance changes with the level of security a society feels—not merely the security from external attack, or from pestilence and starvation, but the security individuals within a society feel about their own identity and sense of self-worth, expressed individually and collectively.

It can be argued that all forms of societal structuring entail the assignment of responsibility, whether that assignment from the individual—the ultimate repository of will—is voluntary or coerced. At one extreme, power is taken consciously in the name of society's individual members by the force of an autocrat or an elite; at the other, it is seized from the individual by the collective hysteria of the mob. In all instances, however, the individual retains the capacity to willingly assign or consciously resist the coercive demands of others that they be allowed to govern in his name. But the exercise of individual will under such coercive circumstances requires courage and introspection. It is when society, at its most rational, understands that its most secure and productive future lies in the judicious balance of assigned responsibilities that democracy is consciously enshrined in commonly agreed laws and constitutions.

It is when insecurity or greed, each a short-term expression of ignorance (and a reflection of Plato's definition of the "appetite" or desire aspect of societal personality), motivates individual and mob action through emotional appeal that laws or constitutions are trammeled, misused, or forgotten, and humanity rushes from the path of progress to the self-destructive path of the lemming.

We could again stumble from the path of progress, if the panic over change now evident in the upheavals of globalism and new social interactions causes individuals to consciously or unconsciously assign away or abandon their responsibilities to mass hysteria or to tyrannical leaders. There remain great portions of the world troubled by the responsibilities and uncertainties of progress and change, fearful of the burden of decisions required of free people to sustain an equitable and productive society. There remain, thus, people who would abolish the technologies which allow and encourage communication between societies and preserve and spread the accumulated learning which stimulates creative and productive thinking and action.

It is fair, then, to say that in this regard the world today is faced with a single great schism: between those who favor learning, inquiry, and progress and those who fear it, and would welcome its cessation. That is a choice between those who welcome the responsibilities of individuals within society and those who are afraid of accepting those responsibilities.

Georges Clemenceau—in his retirement after holding the French presidency—understood the complex and delicate nature of society, and in his study, in 1926, of the great Athenian statesman, Demosthenes, he noted: "The country makes the citizen in the degree that it can establish him in harmonious groups, groups that will become all the finer as men become more intelligent."

A society can be productive and secure into the indefinite future only if there exists the *conscious* commitment and ability of individuals to fulfill their complex duty of assigning and self-imposing responsibilities. Indeed, what Pericles and the Athenian philosophical school gave to us was that single thing: *consciousness*. The gathering of humanity into collective societies is a function of nature, as is the emergence of leadership, and the assignment of rights and responsibilities for the survival, protection, and prosperity of the individual within the framework of society. But the cornerstone of human development is the realization that by conscious reflection and determination, these natural human functions can be assigned proportion and balance.

Since the time of the Athenian city-state, all human progress has been measurable by the extent to which the assignment of responsibilities has been in harmony, and it is *this* that we call democracy.

I have not spoken of how we are to achieve this harmony and this balance of assigned rights and responsibilities. Neither did Pericles define it in absolute terms; nor has it been defined as a universally viable form ever since. Indeed, the shape of democracy—the institutions and forms of leadership, the collective rights and obligations of society, the individual rights and duties of its members, and the forms of expressing their will—vary from society to society. Even in those societies in which the will of individuals is expressed and assigned in a collective ballot—an election—at predetermined times, the *unspoken, unwritten, and informal* expression of will is often more significant in determining the functions of leaders and citizens.

The power of oratory, which was the hallmark of Pericles and which he used sparingly, today shapes collective and individual wills as never before, but often in ways and in iconic shorthand which would have been incomprehensible in the age of Hellenistic formation. Oratory, like song, verse, and theater, helps form individual and collective wills by embedding messages in time and in tune with the pulse and rhythm of humanity.

And the fundamental authority of the individual will remains possible and of paramount significance today, as in the time of Pericles. Clarity of thought, singularity and prestige of image, and the marriage of the message with the target audience all remain key to bringing the consciousness of the democratic process into effective action.

So the process of democracy remains much as it was in the time of Pericles. But the passage of time has alloyed perceptions of it in modern society. For the most part, we take democracy for granted as a mature and finally defined form of governance, which it is not. We have, perhaps, thought little on the meaning of the responsibilities of the individual and the collective within societal management since the great debates which shaped the Constitution and Bill of Rights of the United States of America. We have largely allowed our modern democratic institutions to be modified, burdened, subtracted, and shoved by expedience, until they often scarce resemble the lofty ideals of their formative structure.

We have, in many modern democracies, allowed lust for power to broaden the enfranchisement of the mass at the expense of the individual. And ultimately, mass is the enemy of identity, and identity is the core of individual will. And individual will, we must recall, is the foundation of the assignment of the duties which represent democracy.

Democracy, then, has become seen, and proclaimed, and waved as a banner with the name Excelsior! emblazoned fair upon it. But democracy is not this light pennant blowing scarlet in the wind; rather, it is the tidal surging of individuals in the mass of society, whose will is expressed through complex and changing communications and expression, as well as in the simplistic superficiality of ballots.

So the role of society in placing leaders into power, whether through ballots or acclamation, is an incomplete action. Society then has an innate requirement to honor and revere its leaders, so that the command structure of society functions efficiently and harmoniously, and so that the authority of the society and its leader are unquestioned by external allies and rivals alike. What we have seen in the current hierarchical revolution in the West, and particularly in the United States, is that although the process of electing leaders remains intact, the new and temporarily flattened social structure means that the society does not then respect or honor its leaders.

And this absence of cohesion or respect for hierarchy in Western societies is what is most evident to outside observers, who correctly perceive this to be a sign of weakness.

How we address the relationship between leaders and led will be one of the determining factors of our success with this Age of Global Transformation.

THE GREAT SYMBIOSIS OF
LEADER AND LED

EIGHTEEN

All victory is the responsibility of the leader, and
the leader is the fruit of the society. A single
poor leader damages victory, just as a single
great leader may advance its cause.

No office in the world has held more power in the past
half-century than that of the U.S. president. And the
U.S. public, at the time of this writing, is pondering
whom to select as its 44th president. Despite the apparent
awe, however, in which the office is held, few Americans
can name all of their nation's presidents. Few could even
name all of the presidents of the twentieth and twenty-first
centuries. But most could name a select few U.S. presidents, because these men who captured imaginations
through the decades transcended their peers to advance the
cause of their country.

For all their qualities and political savvy, van Buren,
Millard Fillmore, Jimmy Carter, and the like were all just
marking time, failing to raise the median of American society, and often damaging it until more visionary leadership
could be elected. But, as eighteenth-century Piedmontese
philosophical writer Joseph-Marie, the Comte de Maistre,
put it, every country gets the government it deserves. This is
not always true, but generally so, largely because leadership—and government—is a reflection of its society.

So the masses are vital to victory; numbers are required for many aspects of life, including the perpetuation of the species, the diversification of tasks, and the creation of that complex soup from which a leader must emerge. But the victory of the crowd cannot exist for long without a victory-oriented leader. True civilizational development became feasible only when human society divided its functions among its members, enabling specialization and the focused development of skills and ideas. This process automatically creates hierarchy. The activities of crowds and committees alike—committees, in fact, are a type of crowd—demonstrate that mankind is in many ways less than the sum of its parts.

The balance of a complex society and a clear and unified leadership vision is the most difficult to sustain. The complex society—necessary to safeguard and consolidate gains—resists automatically the agent of change represented by the leader. And unless the leadership becomes more than the individual (in other words, unless it becomes a symbolism and office greater than the individual by force of law, myth, tradition, and ceremony), the complex society will overwhelm and neutralize the leadership function upon the passing of the leader.

Thus, in the embrace of complexity, the visionary or victorious leader must allow for his or her succession in such a way that a new leader will be able to assume the authority of power and yet still automatically institute change necessary to ensure control of the process. The new leader must have an orderly transition, but the orderliness of the transition must not allow the complex bureaucracy—which has been constantly pressing at the freedoms of the leadership—to impose its curb upon the process of change.

That does not mean, however, that the institutions which safeguard the transitions of leadership can be entirely formulaic. The office of leadership does not make the leader, contrary to popular myth. The office of leadership can only be viewed as a tool of leaders. The character of leaders is not formed by the institution of leadership; rather, it is the other way around.

Equally, the character of a society is what shapes how it will respond to leadership. Not all societies respond to the same stimuli (nor does the nature of societies remain constant), which is why the imposition of an alien political structure on society—because of colonial or other external pressures, or merely because it is alien to the time and mood of the populace—so often fails. French historian Ernest Lavisse is quoted as saying: "No form of government was founded in a day. Political and social organizations are works that demand centuries. The feudal system existed for centuries in a shapeless, chaotic state before it found its laws; absolute monarchy also existed for centuries before arriving at regular methods of government, and these periods of expectancy were extremely troubled."

LeBon also noted: "Peoples are not governed in accordance with their caprices of the moment, but as their character determines they shall be governed."

Leadership axiomatically cannot occur within a vacuum. It must be matched to the nature and condition of the society (whether that society is a company of troops or the population of a nation-state), as well as to the threats and opportunities facing it.

Leadership always requires the consent of the led. But how that consent is obtained is crucial; winning approval without compromising the responsibilities of leadership is the acme of skill.

The shallowest form of leadership is when a leader, seeking or assuming command of a society, accepts its existing condition and merely adapts to the society to win its support, conforming with its base contentment and traditional practices. This is the manager, who allows the society to slumber, not materially furthering its interests and, at best, not allowing its interests to be eroded by a more wakeful world. And yet, by merely feeding the short-term desires of a smug society, the manager is already allowing that society's strength to evaporate as the world moves on without it, or consciously maneuvers against it.

Of equal failing is the leader who merely imposes his desires without understanding either his own society or the historical realities. He will be ignored, bypassed, and misunderstood, and in times of great national threat can be disastrous.

Of greater failing is the leader who sees the society as merely a tool for his personal ambition. This leader's historical damage is compounded when he actually understands the means of motivating his society, but does so solely for personal ends. This is the leader most prone to create or use "mass movements," knowing that such movements can be manipulated to suppress logical inquiry and debate.

Failure to understand the relationship between leader and led—the responsibilities of loyalty—could cost us our victory.

LOYALTY AND SURVIVAL

NINETEEN

Mutual loyalty exists only between equals.
In all other instances, loyalty flows only in any
durable form from the weaker to the more
powerful.

M any in the U.S. political arena are, in the wake of the now-ended "post–Cold War era," disheartened by the seeming lack of loyalty from many of America's erstwhile allies of the past century. Those former allies, at the same time, feel anger and frustration toward the United States. But it was not the matter of the Iraq War which was at the core of this anger and frustration; that was merely a convenient symptom to which transient public sentiment could attach itself. More importantly, the mutual threats the West faced during the Cold War were no longer there.

It had, from about 1991 to 2001, become a squabble over spoils.

It was after that period that the United States decided that the time had come to resume the defense and advancement of victory. Europe, however, did not see the threat, and wished to continue the revelry.

In reality, neither side understands the other. The present disquiet is the result of natural conditions, which must be understood if they are to be addressed, and if mutual needs are to be satisfied. This is not an issue which affects only the long-term victory of the West; it also directly affects the economic success of all businesses and careers dependent on global trade.

Human survival—indeed all species' survival—is based upon interdependence of individuals and groups, primarily to ensure reproduction, but, in the case of humans, also for productivity, protection, prosperity, and progress. This necessity for interaction determines hierarchy, which is defined by the question of who needs whom most at any particular time and in a particular circumstance. There is always a mutuality of need between individuals, between men and women, between leaders and led, friends and enemies, but it is the *degree* of that need which determines its nature and strength.

This differentiation in levels of need (by individuals as well as societies) is one of the factors at the heart of the quest for, and sustenance of, victory.

Loyalty is espoused as the nobility of the primal need of one human for another, of one society for another. The powerful ennoble the concept of loyalty because they need the weaker to acquiesce to their power. The weak ennoble the concept of loyalty because it dignifies their aspirations as well as their stature—and security—as junior partners.

The weak talk often in terms of their loyalty and fealty to their leaders; the strong talk not in terms of loyalty to their weaker dependents, but of their "duty" to their subject partners. And as the urgency of the need of the stronger for the weaker lessens, even the concept of "duty" of leaders toward the led becomes less. The task becomes more onerous, until the lesser partner is ultimately viewed as burdensome, troublesome, and worthless, or in need of discipline.

Loyalty, in other words, is essentially a one-way traffic except between powers (or individuals) of equal stature and therefore equal and symmetric need. Even under such circumstances, the "mutual loyalty" might better be described as a "mutual hostage" situation, where the survival of each partner is held at risk by the other.

The realization that loyalty is not mutual has never denied its necessity, or appeal, as a behavioral mode, either between states, within societies, or between individuals. The weak must seek tactical advantage by association with the strong; the strong, when it is not threatening to their interests and where gain can be achieved for little cost, also benefit from such associations. Without such associations and without attracting the fealty of the weak, the strong cannot remain strong.

In many relationships, however, loyalty is a matter of life and death. Duty, on the other hand, is a matter of discretion and honor, and these are emotional and subjective qualities. In the case of individuals, loyalty is often also a matter of life and death between equals, as in military units and firefighting teams, or marriages. But, stripped of the passion, even this mutual loyalty is also a "mutual hostage" situation, often with lingering emotional bonding after the need for the loyalty has passed.

Societies, too, can, in times of shared danger, transcend their peacetime hierarchical separation, in situations in which the weaker can be in a position to save the stronger through joint or supportive actions.

But the "mutual loyalty" between societies rarely outlives the crisis for long, and soon reverts to the old structure of "duty" and "loyalty." Or perhaps the crisis itself reverses the role of stronger and weaker partner. The weaker party is the one which still feels loyalty; the stronger the one that now relegates the obligation to "duty."

The truly sovereign state, or individual, understands that part of loyalty which is of tactical necessity, and that part which is on the basis of emotional commitment and shared love of ideals and culture. And by understanding the difference, a state or person can act appropriately in the protection of its own interests.

There is, ultimately, no loyalty from the strong to the weak. There is sometimes the transitory and conscious need of the strong for the weak. There is sometimes friendship on the basis of a deeply inculcated set of moral standards or laws, and more often on the basis of recognition of the fact that public betrayal of formalized alliances in one instance will discourage the loyalty of other subject or weaker allies.

The United States, having worked with the Republic of China (ROC) in World War II to defeat Japan, and having used the great-power status of the ROC to bring about the Allies' creation in 1946 of the United Nations, then innately began to see the weakness and dependence of the ROC. By this time, however, the United States was bound in a series of treaties with the ROC, which continued to hold value for the United States in the battle against the communists in China. And when the ROC entity—with which the United States had treaty obligations and a common cause against the communists—was forced by the Chinese civil war to retreat onto Taiwan and a few other islands, the U.S.-ROC relationship began its inevitable slide from mutuality of interests to the "duty-loyalty" matrix.

By the 1970s, the United States, under the presidency of Jimmy Carter, abandoned all pretense of mutual loyalty and even its description of its "duty" toward its ROC obligations had been reduced to the position where the ROC's expressions of loyalty to the United States were regarded as the blackmail of a former lover. Carter reduced all recognition and privilege for the ROC in bilateral relations, including removal of full diplomatic recognition and support for the ROC's standing in the United Nations as one of its primary founders. Carter stopped short of abandoning U.S. mutual defense obligations to the ROC only out of fear that other states with treaty relationships with the United States would balk at the lack of U.S. respect for its legal undertakings.

The need of the United States to develop effective relations with the People's Republic of China (PRC) was unquestioned once it became clear after the 1960s that Nationalists in the ROC would not be able to regain power on the Chinese mainland. How the transition was handled by the United States became the issue, and how the ROC on Taiwan handled the transformation of relations with the United States was a matter of survival for the ROC and Taiwanese leadership.

By the early twenty-first century, the process of abandoning the pretense of mutual loyalty was, for the United States, accelerated, like almost all other aspects of life. In 2005, the State Department readily abandoned established partners, placing expediency above even the pretense of loyalty or respect for its own tenets (such as democracy). There was no apology, or even explanation, for the fact that the State Department encouraged and assisted in the overthrow of its democratically elected ally, President Askar Akaev, of the Kyrgyz Republic, despite Dr. Akaev's unquestioned and strenuous support for U.S. objectives and ideals.

The Akaev administration was unique in Central Asia in the degree to which it had built a government, a state, and a society which were open, democratic, and committed to market economics; meeting and exceeding the stated goals of the United States. Moreover, without President Akaev's commitment of base facilities for the United States and other allied defense forces, the United States could not have effectively prosecuted its war against terrorism and against the Taliban in Afghanistan. As well, President Akaev created the only counternarcotics agency in Central Asia to be funded entirely by a local government, and with this and a dedicated militia he effectively curtailed the narcotics trade, which was running heroin from Afghanistan—where the U.S. efforts to stop opium poppy cultivation had entirely failed—up through the Ferghana Valley and on through Russia and East Asia to the world markets.

But the State Department was indifferent to this; it wanted to ensure that the United States, not Russia, dominated Central Asia. So it threw away the strenuous and valuable loyalty of the Akaev government. The results were, by 2006, manifold, but not what the State Department wanted: the narcotics trade once again flourishes through Kyrgyzstan; Central Asia has lost its one stable and transparent economic-legal-political entity, which in turn had promised to enable the viable development of the region and the revival of the Great Silk Road overland trade route.

President Akaev paid the price for having attempted to retain—as he was bound by logic and common sense to do—essential relationships with the great powers of the region, Russia and the People's Republic of China. But more important, he believed that mutual expressions of respect and shared expressions on freedom, democracy, economics, and geopolitics between his government and that of the United States were expressions of mutual loyalty.

The peremptory treatment which he received has already come to haunt the strategic posture of the United States, though few in Washington will talk of it. Dr. Akaev's unrequited loyalty was not the first instance in which the United States had abandoned those who had undergone great risk and cost to support it.

Few, if any, of those states which supported the United States in the 2003 Gulf War, or in the war in Afghanistan and the subsequent policing operations, can say that they have been truly recognized for their efforts by the United States. Those few that have been invited to "sit at the head table" with the United States after their efforts in Iraq and Afghanistan have not found a place "above the salt." What have the governments of the Dominican Republic, El Salvador, and Australia really gained from their loyalty to the United States? And yet it would have cost the United States little to have paid some attention to its allies.

This is the reality of unequal relationships. Loyalty is always unrequited. It is merely a matter of *when* the "duty" of the greater power diminishes, is diverted, or is attended to with only token effect. But it is equally true that it is the responsibility of the weaker power to understand the nature of this equation, and to act accordingly.

Because the strong do not remain strong without the support of the weak.

THE USE OF AD HOC COALITIONS TO PRESERVE VICTORY

Nineteenth-century British prime minister Lord Palmerston said that Britain "has no permanent friends, has no permanent enemies, but has permanent interests." The phrase expressed realism forged through the fires of cynicism, but it is true that the sole permanent interest of a society is in its own victory. That does not deny, however, the existence of natural friends and allies, as well as those which must or can be created along the path to victory.

"Natural allies" will always be perceived among those whose strength and resources are vital to, or supportive of, our own interests. They are likely also to be countries which share some or most of our own values, the essential ingredient in the construction of bonds of mutual trust. It is generally from among those states which have historically been trusted kinsmen that core alliances are formed. But even these core alliances can be displaced by tactical needs or strategic expediencies.

It is also said that "politics makes strange bedfellows,"

but there is nothing strange about any workable coalition if the factors are analyzed. These invariably include one or more of the following: common enemies, common objectives, common needs, or shared geography and spatial factors, or common ideals, language, religion, and shared historical experience. (Australia and Turkey, for example, both took part in the conflict in the Dardanelles in 1915, though on opposite sides, an experience which brought about mutual respect.)

Modern society assumes in its collective actions common sets of values, and implicitly believes that the overarching commonalities will preserve the status quo, or remedy any minor ills. Globalization and the power of the victorious societies to impose their values—at least superficially—mean that most elites will pay lip service to the supposedly common ideals: peace, order, mutual respect, "human rights," and so on. However, the superficial layer of mutual ideals covers the necessary divergence of interests among various societies.

The "peace" of the victorious may be perceived as the enslavement of another society. The USSR, in its use of dialectics (and "dialectical legerdemain," or verbal sleight of hand) to pursue its objectives, often spoke of "peaceful coexistence." The USSR's opponents in the West interpreted this as "getting along peacefully," but the textbook definition in Soviet circles was "maintaining state-to-state relations while continuing the struggle by means less than formal war." Similarly, "one man's terrorist is another man's freedom fighter": more "dialectical legerdemain"; mumbo jumbo. The fact is that the overarching attempts to bind all societies to a single interpretation of values denies the reality of differing requirements and aspirations, and indeed makes impossible the dialogue needed in attempting to find viable modi vivendi among the competing societies.

The creation of the United Nations after World War II

attempted to impose the peace of the victorious upon the world, affording paternalistic protection to the defeated and the smaller nations. In reality, it attempted, de facto, to freeze the world into an acceptance of the status quo, containing the natural aspirations of peoples as a means of constraining war. The world's response was to flow around this pseudo–status quo by paying only lip service to borders. Globalization, meanwhile, has reduced the sovereign powers of states; sovereignty *can* be preserved in fairly absolute terms, as the Democratic People's Republic of Korea (North Korea) has attempted, but only at the cost of true victory.

As a result, the construction of alliances to achieve victory is today a more abstract and subtle process than at any other time in history. Core, natural, and essential alliances must, of necessity, allow greater flexibility in their application, reducing wherever possible the rigidity and brittleness of codified, formal alliances. The usefulness of absolutely defined and overt alliances is of a short-term or expedient nature, to address specific threats or needs on the path to victory. Core alliances therefore are often unspoken and instinctive, growing and flowing with the changes in society, but based on common understandings, bred of trust engendered over time.

PEACEKEEPING AND PEACE ENFORCEMENT TO PRESERVE THE STATUS QUO OF VICTORY

The initial result of triumph is usually the stimulation of the ego. The adrenaline of confrontation continues beyond triumph and then becomes a threat to victory. Not only does it cause the unwise treatment of foes; it also causes impatience with allies. Inevitably, however, there is a need for stable, victorious societies to move with force of arms to quell problems and conflicts which, if left unattended, jeopardize the well-being of those victorious societies.

In any event, the maintenance of the status quo is the victor's way of staving off challenges to victory. However, it is essential that the status quo be maintained only vis-à-vis the adversary or potential adversary societies, because the status quo of the victor—that is, the peace of unchallenged superiority and wealth—can only be preserved by constant progress. "Peace" and "status quo" have very different meanings to the vanquished. To the disenfranchised, the status quo is totally unacceptable, and is something which, in many instances, can be transformed only by struggle, very often by armed struggle.

Modern society, represented largely by the victorious, has developed modalities to avoid structural changes which threaten its victory, or, failing that, to minimize or slow the impact of change. (See Chapter Eight.) As a result, when unrest breaks into violence, the great momentum is not toward conflict resolution, but rather toward conflict *containment*. Containment is most often misused as a tool of the "managers" and squanderers of victory; it fails to resolve the problem, merely putting it aside for future handling. Inevitably, containment worsens the problem, so that when it does erupt it presents a far greater challenge than would have been the case if appropriate effort had been expended in resolving the original problem.

Thus, peacekeeping and peace enforcement often create more enemies than they should, building hostilities and placing entire societies in limbo, delaying and often preventing their embrace into the process of victory.

Conflicts suppressed should not be confused with conflicts resolved, and while it may be desirable and necessary to contain what would otherwise be unrestrained conflict and chaos, to do so at the expense of *resolution* merely threatens victory.

KNOW WHEN TO HOLD 'EM;
KNOW WHEN TO FOLD 'EM

In the words of the popular song about card-playing: "Know when to hold 'em; know when to fold 'em; know when to walk away; know when to run." This Age of Global Transformation has placed the matter of loyalty to the fore, and the many strategic alliances will either hold, fold, transform into rivalries, or be replaced by new ones. What can we expect over the coming decade?

First, alliances will often overlap and sometimes contradict each other, as governments attempt to deal with new realities while retaining many of their old "safety net" alliances. And, of course, many alliance structures will depend, for example, on whether Iran transforms into a secular state, or whether the People's Republic of China runs into internal problems, and whether it goes to war over Taiwan, or whether the European Union (EU) starts to run into trouble as Turkey goes its own way and begins its attempt to rebuild a pan-Turkist empire. And so on. The variables are many.

What is critical, however, is that trade will follow alliances. But many alliances and treaties will be transitory and tactical.

* Watch for the rise of tacit alliances, or "understandings," the prime example of which could well be the so-called "Anglosphere" of English-speaking countries, building around common language and relative harmony among cultures and values. This would involve, at the very least, the United States, Canada, Britain, Australia, New Zealand, and possibly India, Israel, and some of the African states, such as South Africa and Nigeria, Ghana and Sierra Leone. Japan and South

Korea could well be regarded as part of this "West without Europe," and, if the dinosaur thinking within the State Department abates, it could also include Russia.

- NATO will increasingly be a dazzling, but unproductive, jewel, used to distract, but is already less and less capable of achieving meaningful goals. It is fraught with mutual antagonisms, and this will worsen over the coming two decades.

- The EU will continue to falter. Turkey will continue to engage in dialogue and posturing on participation in the Union, but its leadership is already aware that it will not sacrifice Turkish prerogatives and approaches to government (military control over the elected government) in order to participate. The only governments unaware of this are those of the United States and Britain, which persist in promoting Turkish membership in the EU. But the concern of most inside thinkers is the possible conflict and chaos which will occur when Turkey and the EU on the one hand, and Turkey and the United States on the other, realize that the game is over, and that Turkey will go its own way. And with a weakened EU, will this cause the next stage of the Turkish invasion of Cyprus, with Ankara seizing the remaining two-thirds of the island? Probably only Greece, as a guarantor power for Cyprus, would react. Britain, another guarantor power for the island, would continue to abandon its obligations and—through lack of military capacity—prove less than helpful in resolving the situation. A Greek-Turkish war would probably occur, with, at this stage, an unpredictable outcome. Meanwhile, the EU will progressively become unworkable as a superstate, but will remain somewhat effective as a market area.

• New, informal alliance structures will govern the oil market, and these will be critical over the coming three decades, when oil will remain a vital commodity. OPEC, the Organization of Petroleum Exporting Countries, will continue to be relatively unimportant, but China, Iran, and France, at a bare minimum, will begin to work together to create a new market mechanism for oil, based not on the dollar but—as long as the currency holds—on the euro. This process is already underway. The unknown is what damage this could do to the U.S. economy, if any. Certainly, the trend is now to wrest control of oil markets away from the United States, just as the United States itself attempts to consolidate its control over the oil sector. But the new informal alliance structure is about more than just controlling an oil exchange and the currencies used by it. It is about removing the control over pipelines from U.S. domination, and this process is already showing signs of bringing about strange bedfellows: the Turks working with the Armenians and China; China and Israel working to bypass any Arab control over oil pipelines critical to them. Iran may soon find itself working with Turkey and with some of the Central Asian states, including its old nemesis in the Caucasus, Azerbaijan. This is far from the headlines of the Western media, but this process—reflecting the anger and displeasure at the United States—will have profound affects on the U.S. and Western economies.

• Australia, as an emerging middle power, unable to count on any single ally for its survival in the future—even as part of an "Anglosphere" of states with the United States as first among equals—is already thinking in terms of expanding its geopolitical influence through participation in a possible South Pacific alliance. This could extend geographic security over vast areas of maritime resources, and could include Australia, New Zealand, Papua New Guinea, and many of the smaller South Pacific states (including Fiji as one of the more important). Such an alliance could well continue to look eastward and include Chile as the critical and compatible South Pacific partner in the Americas. It would link with the United States, which itself extends its reach deep into the Central and South Pacific. And westward, such an alliance, even if a combination of formal and informal relationships, could well embrace closer ties with South Africa and other states.

- China has already been developing its alliance structures on a discreet and informal basis. There can be no doubt that, even at this stage, it is in committed and strategically significant relationships with North Korea and Iran, and, in a different way, with Australia. But as China's power and economy grow, the Chinese sphere of influence will pointedly include attempts to penetrate the Americas more thoroughly from the Pacific and Atlantic. Already, Panama is heavily engaged with China, as are Venezuela and Brazil.

These are but a handful of examples of how changing relationships can affect global security and trade—particularly the interests of the status quo powers, notably the United States—over the coming two to three decades.

Given the profound impact of the flux of the current alliance structures, it is critical to understand the nature of loyalty, duty, and maneuver.

But we do not expect the quest for victory to have a finite goal. We have embarked on a never-ending quest which embodies the essence of human progress.

THE NEVER-ENDING CHALLENGE

TWENTY

Victory can never be total, and this is its beauty.
Victory is always relative and will ultimately fail
if it attempts to be absolute.

It is tempting to think that the task of securing victory can be completed. That would imply that a single power, a single government, a single entity could reign supreme and perfect, free from challenge. The groans of fear and anguish which arose in parts of the world when the United States was viewed as the "sole global superpower" were unwarranted and unrealistic. The utopian belief in the eventual creation of a single "world government" is equally unrealistic, and yet many seemingly intelligent people hold the hope that the United Nations could fulfill such a function.

All things in nature die when they no longer share the planet with others of their species. And yet to share space is to compete for it, and the resources of that space. The late European businessman Sir James Goldsmith once said: "When you marry your mistress, you automatically create a job vacancy." Facetious or not, the parallel applies to many aspects of life: When your adversary is destroyed or disappears, another will rise to take its place. Interaction—and therefore competition—is the reality, and joy, of life. The same applies in the intellectual environment: Without debate, there is no intellectual progress.

Competition stirs productivity and growth. The total elimination of competition—either by state decree, the destruction of rivals, or merger—stirs complacency, sloth, and decline.

In Britain, socialist prime minister Harold Wilson (1964–1970 and 1974–76) conceived of nationalizing the shipbuilding industry, and the government executed the forced seizure of an entire industry under his successor, Prime Minister James Callaghan (1976–79). Callaghan, in 1977, created British Shipbuilders. This brought all of the once-famous, innovative, and globally competitive shipbuilders into a single institution. But the driving force of this move was not economic success but sustained employment levels, something which, cynically, in the short term would bolster the Labour Party's chances for re-election. It was under this governance, in which competition was ended by fiat, that Britain ceased to be a maritime power.

The takeover did not even achieve its initial purpose. As British Labour Party parliamentarian John Robertson put it: "As recently as 1960, nearly 200,000 workers were employed in British shipyards, but by 2000 that figure had declined to some 30,000." By 2006, the figure employed in building oceangoing ships in the UK was much lower, and only a handful of shipyards remained viable. The UK Labour Party, again in power in the beginnings of the twenty-first century, continued to penalize local manufacturing, seeking to complete the transformation of Britain into a "service economy." Ironically, by attempting to legislate the marketplace in shipbuilding, for example, the socialist government had destroyed an industry and ultimately most of the jobs of the workers it had claimed to champion. Destruction of British shipbuilding, aerospace, and defense industries—through nationalization and forced mergers—reduced Britain to the status of a third-rate power, something two world wars had failed to achieve.

In the United States, since the end of the Cold War, the "rationalization" of the aerospace industry—with the forced mergers of many companies—has begun to have similar effects. It reduced competition and innovation, and ultimately, then, forced up the cost of technology.

The point, clearly, is that competition—even wars—promotes ingenuity and efficiencies. Flowers thrive, people blossom, only when there is pollination over a wide swath of the species.

The very existence of multiple societies and multitudes of individual aspirations guarantees that there will always be challenges to total control. At most, comprehensive control can only briefly, tenuously sustain the apex of power, like an aircraft poised at the balance of its thrust and lift in a climb, hanging on its energy before a stall causes its nose to fall away to regain momentum, energy, and lift.

And just as normal flight in an aircraft eschews the wasteful stall at the apex of an energy-expending climb, so victory—meaningful victory—avoids the meaningless drive for "total victory." True victory must expect and welcome challenge and focus on dealing with it and using it to hone introspection and improvement through competition, rather than on attempting to eliminate it.

In reality, there was *never* a prospect of a unipolar world (a totally dominant global power), even when the Soviet Union—which was only a mythical or illusory superpower—imploded. The global power structure merely reverted after the Cold War from bipolarism to multipolarism. The pivotal point of the implosion of bipolarism should in itself have reminded us that there is no predetermined movement toward either victory or vanquishment in which we do not—or cannot—write a part.

Rome, Britain, and the Hellenic and Persian empires—not to mention Mongolia and China—have all achieved peaks and troughs in their march to victory. It is never over for a society until the last member of the society abandons either the will to victory or the memory of it.

Gavin Menzies, in his 2002 book *1421: The Year China Discovered the World*, noted: "On the 8th of March, 1421, the largest fleet the world had ever seen sailed from its base in China. The ships, huge junks nearly five hundred feet long and built from the finest teak, were under the command of Emperor Zhu Di's loyal eunuch admirals including Zheng He]. Their mission was 'to proceed all the way to the end of the earth to collect tribute from the barbarians beyond the seas' and unite the whole world in Confucian harmony. The journey would last over two years and circle the globe." Are we to think that China has forgotten that it nearly controlled the world? The fact that Emperor Zhu Di lost power, just as the fleet was returning to China, meant that the dramatic surge for global influence was lost before it could be consolidated. As a result, China's surge toward victory was essentially suppressed—or held in the dark recesses of memory—for some five hundred years.

At the same time, Iranians are aware that today—despite the inefficient and paranoid grasping of the clerics—they are closer than they have been for more than two millennia to returning to direct land access, via Iraqi and Syrian Shi'a allies, to the Mediterranean and Europe. There is, however, a revived consciousness in Iran that, without the clerical government, Iran could—as the late shah envisaged—become an integral part of the West, not so much through domination of Shi'a territory in Iraq and Syria, but through gaining dominance, stature, and viability as the great power at the nexus of Asia, Europe, and the Middle East.

The Iranian clerics, having failed to think through a grand strategy, are gambling all on the toss of the dice, preparing to risk all by threatening to engage in a major war with their neighbors and the West. Do they think that such a war, even if they were to win it (whatever that means), would end the challenges to their rule? The reality is that they have not thought beyond "winning" or "losing" such a war. War, as we have discussed, is only part of the equation in securing victory.

Failure in such a war by the clerics would certainly have dramatic ramifications, and could forestall or permanently end Iran's hopes for a revived victory. The country could be broken up into the empire's constituent parts, with Baluchistan falling off to unite or compete with Pakistani or Afghani Baluchistan; parts of the north falling under Kurdish, or Armenian, or Azeri control; perhaps parts of ethnically Arab Khuzestan coming under Iraqi control. By thinking—like General Galtieri in Argentina, when he invaded the Falklands—that they can pluck victory out of the air with a deft stroke, the Iranian clerics have failed to realize that victory is a constant checkerboard of maneuver. It cannot be decided at a single gesture.

HAS THE WEST WALKED AWAY FROM THE CHALLENGE?

Many of Iran's clerics, and many within the jihadist movement and in Pyongyang and even Beijing, feel that perhaps just one big push can topple the West; that its house of cards will collapse, its bloated and lazy populace too frightened to fight in their own defense. But as we have discussed earlier, the long victory of the West has made it complex and flexible, which means that it would be unlikely to collapse with a single push. Nonetheless, there is ample evidence that the West has proven reluctant to fight for its own victory.

Perhaps the single most important message to the opponents of the West was the U.S. decision to invade Iraq and remove Saddam Hussein from power, in 2002–03. Forget about the rationales offered for the war, or even the arguments about the tactics employed. The George W. Bush administration showed that it would fight for the U.S. and Western position. But equally, the response of many in other parts of the West, and in the U.S. mainstream media and parts of the U.S. Congress, in opposing the Bush initiative on Iraq, supported the belief among the anti-Western camps that the West really lacked the stomach to fight in its own defense.

But there are signs of stirring in the West; significant people in France, Italy, the UK, Germany, Poland, Japan, and other states, but particularly in the United States, are talking about the potential for cataclysmic change and the loss of Western victory. President George W. Bush galvanized much of that sentiment when he refused to stand by while a combination of religious extremists and ideologues began working against the West and the United States.

The late shah of Iran told me that his greatest fear—in the 1970s—was the "vicious and unholy alliance of red and black": the clerics and the political extremists (at that time Soviet-backed communists). It was this combination which cost Iran years in the march toward a resumption of Persia's historic victory.

President George W. Bush's approach to responding to the challenges to the U.S. and Western victory may have been open to criticism and debate; not all need agree with his methods or priorities. But the sharp, shrill, visceral attacks on him and his policies were, and are, from those who wish to continue "the good life," living off the fruits of the aggressive battle for victory undertaken by earlier generations within the West, without wishing to recognize that their way of life, and their wealth, were being challenged and that the fate of their grandchildren was at stake.

There was never a chance that the world would see, for more than a handful of years, a truly capable, sole global power. Or a world government. Or the total, undefeatable victory of one society over another.

In the meantime, the warm glow which we see on this eve before the dawn of the Age of Global Transformation is not the gentle sunset. It is the fires of burning homes at the city gates. It is the West's victory which is afire. And those who are awake in the West may find strength and revived companionship stemming the flames.

We must look at what this means in the life cycle of human societies, the pattern of life and death among nations.

WELCOME TO AN INTERREGNUM OF CRATOCIDE AND CRATOGENESIS

TWENTY-ONE

The enemy of "identity" is "mass." Where
identity is sacrificed to mass, victory suffers.

D eath is our inevitable fate; our birth was not. It was
the result of the survival and triumph of our forebears; their victory shared with us. Individuals, societies, organizations, and states will all ultimately die,
transforming, in many instances, into something which
will use the legacy, genetics, or wisdom of their ancestral
experience. The birth of any life is a cause of joy and hope
for many; the death of life—even a corporation's—is a time
for reflection and, most often, sadness. Some lives—
human, corporate, or national—die in "mercy killings,"
some by malice, some naturally.

Our current system of modern nation-states began,
after the Industrial Revolution (but particularly with the
"great reorganization" of World War I, which was part of
the global social upheaval), a process which was frozen in
some kind of time warp by the United Nations after World
War II. There was little about the creation of the modern
state system from the beginning of the twentieth century
until the beginning of the twenty-first which was "natural."
New states were created for geopolitical and expedient reasons, such as colonialism or triumph in war. And the

United Nations then confirmed the specifications and legitimacy of each state, essentially guaranteeing its existence.

It was a glass-house environment, often threatened, but ultimately one which attempted to deny the natural urges of some societies for growth, or the aspirations for independence of others. It kept on life support societies which otherwise would have died or transformed, and suppressed others which sought life. There were "failed states" which could not even transition through bankruptcy—financial or spiritual—to death. And societies which were aspirant "new states" were mostly killed at birth or aborted before they could gasp the oxygen of creation. The United Nations was created to slow or stop the processes of change and natural societal evolution.

As we discussed earlier, the UN experiment ultimately failed because it attempted to freeze the sovereignty of states and the movement of peoples into a specific pattern, ignoring the reality of the inevitability of growth of the global population and its wealth, and the prospect that evolving technology would—as had occurred many times in history—change the definitions of statehood. The failure of the UN after it had achieved its brief mission to stabilize society after World War II was a sign of the triumph of the human spirit.

The process of attempting to regulate and constrain the life cycles of societies began to crumble with the end of the Cold War and drifted into confusion in the decade after. The 1990s and early years of the twenty-first century were a chaos of destruction and creation. Attempts by some societies to form states were strangled through infanticide; others were born out of the impotence of their parent societies. And while the period created the upheaval which contributed to terrorism, it also created the reactive age of political correctness and efforts to hold back the tide through obeisance to a new artificial god, "international law."

I discussed this phenomenon of the end of the sclerotic

state system and the new transitional period of the creation of new states and new modalities with Dr. Marios Evriviades, a brilliant friend and professor of political science from Athens. "I have devised a name for this process of the murder of states," he said. "It is cratocide": the death of the *cratos* (or *kratos*), the structure of a society. "What, then, is the process of national creation?" I asked. Marios pondered briefly and said: "I suppose it would have to be cratogenesis."

This, then, is the hallmark of our brief new era, as we make the transitional voyage through heavy seas to a new stability: cratocide and cratogenesis. We will continue to see existing societies of great and small powers approaching their death through cratocide over the coming decade or two. For some, the rump state structures will remain, possibly preserving an ancient name. For others, feeble through the abandonment of victory—the lifeblood—little will remain as new societies hive off portions of the territorial flesh to create new states or entities. Always, something will precipitate the death and birth of states. Some will die by their own hand, but most will die at the hand of a lover: A part of the state will turn on another part; a former ally will administer the hemlock.

It was easy, by 2005, to see the gathering of cratocidal diplomats around the debilitated remains of the ancient kingdom of Serbia—once grown to maturity as Yugoslavia, now reduced to "Serbia & Montenegro," and then, by 2006, just to Serbia, as Montenegro left the loose federation—determining where next to drive home the blade. But less visible was the process of cratosuicide engaged in by the United Kingdom, or Germany. This could result in the cratoregenesis (in fact, rebirth) of sovereign states Scotland, Wales, and the like; or Bavaria, Prussia, or Thuringia. Turkey, too, preserved in 1921 as a rump of the Ottoman Empire, faced the threat of cratocide from an army of minorities, tearing at its flesh.

The difference between Turkey and Britain and Germany, however, is the fact that the Turkish General Staff can be expected to fight for the preservation of the national entity. Britain, consciously, and Germany, unconsciously, have acquiesced in the process of their own drawing and quartering. But they are not yet dead.

The concept begs the question as to whether a society when it has achieved pre-eminence must inevitably and immediately begin its decline, whether, in fact, the achievement of sole hyperpower status by the United States with the end of the Cold War spelled the beginning of U.S. decline and the inevitable end to its pre-eminent victory, or whether, after consolidation and a health cure, the United States can begin the process of rebuilding its victory.

It also raises again the question upon which we touched previously: Can a victorious society expand to embrace all other societies? Can there be, for example, a universal power, or a universal government? The question is relevant in the face of concerns over, or even hopes for, globalization. Is a global society merely a reflection of a unipolar global domination? Or do societies, particularly victorious societies, become so large that they are forced to split, cell-like, into coherent subunits (cratogenesis), some of which become rivals of the parent victory? That was how the United States began its life. In other words, regardless of hopes or fears, a "global society" or "total victory" is ultimately infeasible.

Vanquished, threatened, and impoverished societies rarely face this challenge. While the maw of defeat may reach out to overwhelm them, once embraced into dispossession they are, in effect, isolated and ignored. They are of little worth, and are not bound by the expensive technology of the wealthy, victorious societies into the common weal. They become the "free radicals" of the global structure, free to attach themselves to whatever patron they choose, but more often remaining inert and sterile. Their only opportunity for change rests in destruction or disruption of the wealthy, in attempting, even at the risk of their own existence, to blackmail the victorious into recognizing their needs.

But each great, embracing victory of a hyperpower—in Alexander's Hellenism, in the *Pax Romana*, in Mongolia's khanate empire, in the *Pax Britannica*, and in the *Pax Americana*—has always split or hived with giddy fecundity into fragments before it could achieve absolute domination. There are many reasons for this, and many reasons why the "global empires"—the superpowers—have, because of increases in population and the use of new technologies, progressively become larger and larger through history before the inevitable split has occurred.

Technology has enabled progressively greater control of strategic mass, but the ultimate enemy of mass has always been *identity*.

Identity relates to the logic of survival. We know who we are because we can recognize the boundaries of our existence, just as a sailor's sight of the horizon prevents disorientation, the cause of seasickness.

Our sense of identity is intertwined with the logic patterns which tell us what is necessary for our survival. To be moved away from our known environment and community, where we are familiar with the paths and byways of feeding, mating, and dwelling, is disorienting. This accounts for the success of the British Army's regimental system, which allowed military careers to be built in a context of "familial" attachments to fellow warriors, often recruited from the same county background. The Spartans took this approach to an even more extreme level.

To be enveloped in a broad and featureless society without sight of the horizons and boundaries which we recognize as our own is so unsettling that we seek to redefine ourselves. And we generally do this by reverting to an old and familiar—or pseudofamiliar—identity, sometimes constructed out of myths. Thus, the British Empire split into cells which ultimately created new identities. And the unipolar post–Cold War Western victory soon reverted to multipolar status, just when the *Pax Americana* seemed to threaten to embrace all within its disorienting wealth.

THE NEW, AND BRIEFLY MULTIPOLAR, GLOBAL POWER STRUCTURE

Brace yourself, then, for the disappearance of whole nations and the appearance of new ones. In large part that is what the creation of the European Union (EU) is—albeit somewhat unintentionally—all about: the evolution of a semisuperstate in which the identities of old societies re-emerge. Scotland, Wales, Bavaria, Normandy, Brittany, Catalonia, the Basque, and other societies may rediscover their identities.

Watch also for a briefly independent Montenegro, before it succumbs to absorption into an Albanian morass, and an independent Kosovo as the basis for a state with only one aim—to absorb all of its neighbors (including Albania), yet without any of the goals of a normal modern state to create stable structures for the welfare of its citizens. This will be a state driven purely by the visceral lust for victory in its most base form: acquiring the substance of survival solely through conquest and intimidation, moving without moral constraint among the carefully tended modalities of Europe.

Watch, too, for a de facto breakdown in the African Union's strict ban on the reversion by African societies to precolonial boundaries. We have already seen the chaos created by the secession of Eritrea from Ethiopia, bringing back to the surface age-old animosities and seemingly irreconcilable goals between the two successor states to the old union. As the older generation of African leaders, steeped in Westernism and the concepts of the Westphalian model of modern nation-states, pass from the scene, and as the Westphalian model of the nation-state itself becomes vitiated by "globalism," we will see the real challenge to Africa's existing structure of borders and national identities. This will not all be bad, nor will it all result in chaos.

The question is: Will that end the age of inefficiencies in African governmental models and allow more "natural" states to form around ethnically, culturally, and linguistically cohesive groups? Already we see the tendencies of areas of African states toward new state creation (as we saw with the attempted secession of Biafra from Nigeria on May 30, 1967), in Nigeria (the Niger Delta oil-producing states), parts of Cameroon, Côte d'Ivoire, and so on. The attempted union of Italian Somaliland and British Somaliland failed in 1960 as soon as it was created, and yet even today we have not seen a final resolution of that, although the former British Somaliland has totally withdrawn from "Somalia" and functions in all respects as a sovereign state of some importance, dominating the egress of the Red Sea into the Indian Ocean.

So the great promise of African economic progress will be accompanied to some degree over the coming decades by new acts of secession. This time, some will succeed. In the United States, more than a century after the Civil War and attempted secession of the Southern Confederacy, the paranoia about separatism also remains heightened, albeit simmering below the surface. (Given the U.S. experience with attempted secession, why, then, does the United States encourage the breakup of other states, such as Serbia?)

Yet within all of this, we will see re-emerge several great centers of global power during the coming few decades, with the United States the most powerful. If tensions persist, as historically they do, then ultimately two main, loose blocs of power will emerge. But they may not be immediately recognizable to us today. If, as we discussed earlier, China is fighting a battle with itself for survival, then so, too, is the West, and, quite separately, the United States.

The United States will, as it inevitably becomes less dominant than it is today in the global power structure—when other contenders (China, India, Iran, and so on) emerge—need to establish a new framework of core alliance partners. Because the entire concept and delineation of nation-states and governments is becoming vitiated by global economic modalities, there will be a necessity within the United States to reassert a sense of U.S. identity and cultural values. It seems logical, then, that to avoid its own political fratricide the United States will seek to build bonds with culturally similar states. One body of thought calls this new multinational grouping the "Anglosphere," not specifically to delineate an Anglo-Saxon ethnicity, but to define an identity based on English-speaking states with a Judeo-Christian ethical base.

To achieve that cohesiveness, however, the United States and its partner states would embrace the reaction to the chaos and anomie of the world as it is developing. This reaction, the natural urge, would be to create a more ordered, almost militant, society, perhaps more like the United States of the 1950s. In some respects, failure to follow this path could see the United States decline in productivity, societal cohesiveness, and national will to survive and assert its rights to victory.

The process of cratocide and cratogenesis is much like death and birth of solar systems: the fiery or silent end of planets and stars; the amorphous gases coalescing into shapes that gradually assume, under the right circumstances, atmospheres and life. Seen in the context of our own period, we can expect the phenomenon to affect our economic condition and the security of life, if we live or invest, or trade, in areas where the fires are consuming or creating societal life. If a country such as Turkey, for example, or Britain, was to break up—or a country like Germany, which has only so recently expanded through the union of two older parts—then whole patterns of legal structures and legislations would change. But, in all likelihood, mechanisms would protect the value of most investments and property title. Most lives would change only to a degree, as component parts (Anatolia, Scotland, Bavaria, Kurdistan) sought new independent life.

But some processes, such as the creation of Kosovo as an independent state, or the possible cratocide of Republica Srpska (the Bosnian Serb republic established in 1995 within Bosnia-Herzegovina), will be attended with great personal, economic, and human pain. True, some opportunities will be found in the chaos, but the process of the search for victory of entire societies will be threatened in many areas where the process occurs.

All societies, like the individuals who compose them, have their unique DNA. All are born, live, and die, in circumstances particular to them. So all societies must address victory each in their own way.

VICTORY'S UNIQUE DNA

TWENTY-TWO

Victory is an art beyond science, but embracing science, and each society must pursue victory in accord with the needs and character of that society.

Venture capitalists and entrepreneurs continually ask: "What is the next big thing?" But perhaps the question should be: "What is needed?" Blake Ross, the cocreator of Firefox software, in December 2005 told *Business 2.0* magazine that "the next big thing is whatever makes the last big thing usable," noting: "We focus on the everyday problems that nag at everyday people. There are more than enough to go around without imagining new ones."

Some things are right for the time; some things are right for the long haul. Our obsession with novelty and the future makes us forget that some things are of enduring value. And we forget that at our peril. Why, when the survival of Britain's victory depends on trade, and particularly maritime trade, does the UK no longer build ships on a scale commensurate with its needs? Because it *trusts* that it does not ever again have to assert or protect (or project) its victory, that there will never again be a crisis in which someone else will not help protect it.

And yet the alliance structures which have protected Britain for the past six decades or so—the West, NATO, the EU—are crumbling and changing.

Why do the aspirant powers breed people who still see the obvious: that they need ships, steel, cement, cars, basic military platforms of all types, and so on? That does not imply that they also neglect "the next big thing." These aspirant nations also graduate more scientists and engineers by far each year than the United States and Europe. The world's biggest steel producer in the early twenty-first century was not a U.S. company; it was LNM Group, controlled by an Indian entrepreneur, Lakshmi Mittal. In 1995, he moved his headquarters to London, but the UK is not where he produces his steel; he produces it in India, Ukraine, Indonesia, and a string of steel mills worldwide. He had for some time based his empire in Indonesia, which, problems notwithstanding, he still regards as a major world finance center.

The difference between corporate life and death is often a matter of belief; of willpower. A lack of belief—a weakness of commitment—sees self-protection only in immediate gratification and clings to the hope that "the next big thing" will be what saves it. Argentine president Leopoldo Galtieri, after mismanaging his country as military leader, took a desperate gamble on the invasion of the Falkland Islands as the "big thing" which would give him a new lease on political life. He failed, and fell from power, but in so doing did enormous damage to Argentina.

A seemingly unassailable victor company, IBM, in the 1980s and 1990s faced the assault of new, more flexible, and more economical computer hardware and software technologies, and start-up companies such as Hewlett-Packard and Microsoft, which could take these products directly to the marketplace. At first, from its fixed fortress, IBM was slow to respond, and its very existence seemed threatened. But, with determination and wealth, bolstered by inherent pride, IBM changed its fundamental philosophy and regained its stature. It gave up thinking of itself as merely the leader in the large computer mainframe market and concentrated on diversity and corporate health, rather than on a monopolistic and proprietorial concept of the marketplace.

Pan American World Airways, faced with the same type of market transformation, failed to recognize the changes. At its peak, in January 1980, Pan Am acquired National Airways as a means of taking over domestic route licenses. The move meant acquiring National's debt and aircraft fleet. But even as the takeover was being consolidated, a long-gestating change in the political environment was consummated, and air routes were deregulated. Lack of foresight had caused Pan Am to be submerged with debt and with duplicated and incompatible equipment; it was unable to compete with newer airlines which were not burdened with acquiring expensive route licenses. Pan Am thus could not muster the same adaptability as IBM; it had already expended its financial and intellectual strengths. When the terrorist bombing of 1988, over Lockerbie, Scotland, took down only one of its large fleet of Boeing 747s, it lacked the energy to survive, and perished.

It is one thing for entrepreneurs to see needs and to fill them. But it also takes society to understand the need for strength in the basic underpinnings of victory, and to elect leaders who will not be seduced into thinking that they can transform entire economies into "service economies" and yet still expect to deliver and protect long-term victory. Teddy Roosevelt, even before he became president in 1901, recognized that the United States needed the physical capacity to build the infrastructure required for a U.S. victory and U.S. world leadership. He not only built the technological base for the U.S. Navy, he later, as president, ensured, by whatever means, that the Panama Canal could be built to enable the United States to function effectively as a maritime power in the Pacific and the Atlantic.

Even when the United States remained under threat during the Cold War, another president—Jimmy Carter—came along and threw away the great and vital advantages which had been built up by Teddy Roosevelt and others over the previous 150 or more years. He gave away the Panama Canal. Ultimately, day-to-day control went to the People's Republic of China, which knows exactly how valuable this asset is to global power projection and trade. Carter also abandoned the U.S. capacity in intelligence collection, dispensing with a human process vital to understanding the world. He believed that U.S. understanding of the world could be achieved by "technical means": satellites, computers, and the like. "The next big thing."

Few U.S. presidents have been as damaging to U.S. victory as Jimmy Carter, and despite the revival of U.S. fortunes which later President Ronald Reagan achieved, the legacy of the Carter voyage of destruction in the U.S. intelligence community and Department of State still greatly damages the nation's ability to interact with the world.

The principal underpinnings of victory remain the same for every state, and can only be appreciated by a continual study of history. The application of the lessons of history must, however, be in tune with the character and needs at the time of the society which pursues victory.

At present, there are many analysts in the West who look with bemusement at China's struggle to build indigenous combat aircraft and advanced ships. In the United States, for example, access to these basic "platforms" is taken for granted; today, the West is focused on the advanced systems and software which will extend the power and capabilities of its existing platforms. But in this focus, the West has forgotten that the platforms—ships, aircraft, rockets and missiles, ground vehicles—remain necessities of strategic and economic life. And yet they are regarded as "old technologies," and "sunset industries," and, where possible (despite the enormous budgets involved), aerospace companies, shipbuilders, and vehicle makers are urged to "consolidate" into tidy pockets to be placed in the corners of society so that we can focus on "the next big thing," which may be bioengineering, or the internet.

This process—which is not the way China, India, or even Russia sees things—neglects the fact that the traditional capabilities to build basic "platforms" are still vital and that they need to be integrated into a competitive framework *with* the advanced sciences. Traditional capabilities are, in fact, a linear part of the push toward "the next big thing," and these sectors of society often perform at their best when *not* consolidated into vast and inefficient clusters, but when they operate in a competitive, innovative climate.

At one time in my career, I took over some British shipyards which the UK government of Margaret Thatcher rightly wanted removed from government ownership. The earlier Labour Party government had (as we discussed in Chapter Twenty) nationalized all the highly successful and competitive shipyards and turned them merely into places where the socialist government could guarantee jobs (and therefore votes). They quickly became inefficient and uninspired.

And even when the Thatcher (Conservative) government came to power, the obsession, apart from ending the socialist malaise, was with "the next big thing." Heavy engineering, with its unfortunate byproduct of grime and pollution, was regarded as a "sunset industry." Shipyards were no longer seen as necessary. And this at a time when Britain was importing even more of its necessities by sea even than during World War II, because it had stopped much of its domestic manufacturing capability.

My goal at the time was to restore British shipbuilding to competitiveness. I created a concept of "sunrise engi-

neering," to marry the high skills of the engineering workforce to modern technologies: not to replace skilled workers, but to enhance them, by making them more efficient
and capable through the use of "next big thing" technologies and systems. Eventually, however, it became clear that
the European governments—the British included—were in
thrall to the "service economy" mentality which allowed
the infrastructure of victory to wither away.

Unless society understands, and takes pride in, the historically compounding and accreting development of its
tools of victory, it can never be expected to elect governments which will reflect that same understanding.

Society and governments understand consumables,
however. And energy is the most significant consumable,
the fuel for our life, for our ability to process food, to move
around, to stay warm in winter, to read and educate ourselves through the use of electric light and computers, to
project power. This we understand. And yet we do not
wish to build new refineries to process oil, or to transform
our energy process from fossil fuels to biomass. Or to build
new nuclear power plants.

The production of oil by countries which are not
members of OPEC is expected to peak by about 2010 or
2015, if present indications are correct. After that, once
again, and assuming a continuation of present trends, the
West and the world would once again be under the power
of OPEC states to set oil prices and conditions of sale. This
will not be a repeat of the 1973 oil embargo period; OPEC
is unlikely to regain that degree of power, even if it wished
to do so.

There is no question, however, of the world marketplace being ready within that time frame to produce alternative forms of energy in the quantities required to stave
off dependence on OPEC-produced oil and gas. Indeed, by
2015, it is probable that the United States will be import-

ing some 25 percent of its oil from Nigeria, not from the Middle East.

What does this portend? Quite apart from the move of considerable economic power to Africa, it will help drive the West—and the United States in particular—toward the "crunch point" when it must invest heavily and rapidly in alternative energy. Already the trend is obvious: more and more cars are being produced which can run on combinations of refined gasoline or diesel with biomass fuels (ethanol). This trend will continue even more rapidly, to vehicles built or converted to run solely on ethanol. This is not "the next big thing"; this is a technology which has been around for more than a century. (Biomass energy production, in the form of burning wood and wax for heat, light, and engineering power, even motive power in steam engines, has, of course, been with us in various forms since human society formed.)

But "the next big thing" will be making biomass refining—and the processes of delivering agriculturally produced material—increasingly more economical. And the increasing price of fossil fuels is making such investments attractive for the banking and entrepreneurial communities, just as the increasing cost of whale oil (the principal fuel for lighting in the nineteenth century) made petroleum economically attractive.

The marketplace responses to the changing fuel situation are already profound; the problem remains the political elements of society. The political perception is that no one wants a refinery in his or her backyard. And governments respond accordingly. Environmentalists, rather than attempting to find ways to make ethanol refining work, have yet to become part of the solution, and continue to promote a legislative framework which tends to make delivering energy solutions difficult.

The reality is, however, that change must occur. Delay

in bringing renewable and sustainable energy technologies into dominance has only meant that, for example, old-style petroleum refineries are kept in operation, but no one wants to invest in new ones, knowing that change in energy patterns is coming. This means that coal-fired energy production is sustained, even though it has been polluting and inefficient (and rising economic patterns have thus made new "ultraclean coal" technologies feasible).

Two major areas of energy production will emerge over the coming half-century, beginning right now. The fastest will be ethanol production, because it can, within the five- to ten-year timeframe, reduce requirements for conventional fossil fuels for automotive use. But it will expand in sophistication rapidly as an industrial sector, bringing with it new life to the agricultural community. The second will be new nuclear technologies.

With biomass, within fifty years, then, major agricultural states will also be energy powers, although within that timeframe also other forms of energy production will become feasible, and nanotechnologies will make energy use more efficient. This assumes that Western society does not move into a period of intellectual and scientific decline, stifling capital accumulation and market demand.

The Roman Empire, which pioneered many advanced technologies, including the movement of water and hydropower to enable the foundation and growth of cities, fell through lack of political cohesion. All scientific progress was disrupted, to say the least, by the political collapse of Rome. The processes of city-building and nation-building were halted by dark ages which for centuries skewed and narrowed the processes of education and scientific advance. This could easily happen again. So linear projections of where science can and will take us must be tempered with the realization that a failure to attend to the basic requirements of victory can destroy everything.

Remember the boast of Ozymandias: "Look on my works ye mighty, and despair." And yet nothing of his empire remains.

Building a national will to move from a fossil-fuel-based society to renewable energy (and biomass ethanol is just one aspect) and to safe, new nuclear technologies is clearly critical. The new nuclear forms—ultimately leading to cold fusion—will do many things for society, and the production of electricity is only one of them. Getting the new nuclear technologies, particularly the low-cost, low-temperature and small (say fifty megawatt) thorium reactors, out into the marketplace will mean that desalination of seawater on a large scale will become economically viable. That means, too, with small reactors dispersed around the countryside, that the "national grid" of heavy power lines will be partially replaced by a new grid: water pipelines.

Western Australia's great exploitation of its vast mineral wealth began because of just such a capacity. Engineering genius C. Y. O'Connor built dams near the Western Australian coast, and then a pipeline hundreds of kilometers into the interior, to the town of Kalgoorlie, in the desert, where gold had been discovered. The delivery of water to Kalgoorlie in the 1890s began the enormous mineral boom which continues to fuel Australia's economic power in the twenty-first century. (And, by the way, Kalgoorlie's boom also gave a start to mining engineer Herbert Hoover, who was to become the thirty-first U.S. president in 1929.)

We have long been aware that the pace of these changes has been accelerating, and that change generates anxiety. Significantly, societies which grasp change rapidly—or are more accustomed to facing it—are the ones best equipped to cope with the level of changes we can expect in the coming decades. Societies composed mostly of immigrant states—the United States, Australia, Canada, New Zealand, and so on— flourished because change was what these immigrant societies expected and sought. But, a century or more into their new societies, Americans, Canadians, and the like have become contented with their historically recent status quo and are now more resistant to change. In these Western societies, and increasingly in Western Europe and Japan, then, we readily embrace transience in superficial areas of our life (faster cars, new computer or entertainment gadgets, telecommuting, and so on)—perhaps we could call it "pseudochange"—but find substantive change in the fundamentals of our infrastructure increasingly difficult to address.

In this respect, despite the reality of the growing transience of society which Alvin Toffler highlighted so well in 1970 in *Future Shock*, the reality is that human society needs a mix of permanence (or pseudopermanence) in terms of identification with historical identity, geography, and culture, while adapting to the societal changes made inevitable by human population growth and the speed of scientific change. The key in achieving and sustaining victory is knowing and managing the balance between "traditions" and "breaking traditions"; between what is appropriate to keep in our set of circumstances and age, and what is appropriate to change.

We talked about the fact that we face the need for a shift in energy technology, and that, as part of this, we can use the change to address a change of infrastructure distribution nets from electricity to water. Water remains the problem today, not only for China—for which it is almost a life-and-death matter in the national quest for cohesion and victory—but also for societies such as Phoenix, Arizona, where shortage of local water threatens the viability of the great urban populations. The new mininuclear refineries, using safe and cheap thorium power, can breathe new life into Phoenix and other such communities worldwide.

So new energy thinking can revitalize entire societies. But it can change more things than just whether we have energy for our cars, light at the flick of a switch, or water when we thirst for it. The "next big thing" may well be extrapolations of "the last big thing": creating new water technologies and distribution patterns, new nuclear power approaches and disbursement, and a switch to ethanol (and later hydrogen) for motive power. But these developments will need to be coupled with the great new advances we expect from nanotechnology and other scientific advances.

And in so doing, we will, with some of these capabilities, be moving energy production back into the hands of agricultural states, which will produce the crops to create ethanol, and, with disbursed patterns of mini thorium-based reactors, will be creating electrical power and potable water for that agriculture as well as for human sustenance. This alone will dramatically change the total pattern of worldwide trade. And if oil does not fuel the world economy in, say, fifty years, then what will that do to the present oil-based economies which fund the jihadist-based challenge to Western societies?

The question is, can the West keep its victory alive during this time, or will it merely continue to fund the jihadist movement through continued Western dependence on oil until that oil is no longer available?

With the consciousness of our unique requirements, why, then, should we expect others to understand and cater to us? It is up to each of us, and to each society, to pursue our own victory. We can neither give victory to another, nor expect to be given it.

THE GIFT THAT
CANNOT BE GIVEN

TWENTY-THREE

Victory cannot be bought or sold; it can only
be won.

The way victory is achieved changes in style throughout history, but the fundamentals remain constant.
Each society and individual is responsible for its own
victory. Victory cannot be given to another society or individual outside the victorious society or family line, for victory which is unearned is not victory but a resented
paternalism.

It is unnatural and counterproductive to expect a society to be responsible for any victory other than its own.
Such hopes only lead to disappointment. That is not to say
that victories cannot be achieved jointly or cooperatively.
Cooperative evolution is the essence of human society, and
one of the keys to victory is to enlarge the framework of
cooperation as broadly as possible.

But just as the achievement of victory must, to begin
with, be based on the responsibility of each individual,
each single society, or each alliance, so victorious societies
cannot allow themselves to be forced to believe that the
victory of others is their responsibility. Assisting competitors, enemies, or dependents to achieve their own separate
victory neither assures peace nor enhances security; it
achieves only the reverse. Equally, it must be expected that

each society (or individual) is compelled by nature to seek its own victory: Each must do what nature compels it to do. Only by recognizing the impulse to victory in our adversaries as well as ourselves can we comprehend what is reasonable behavior on their part. Such comprehension leads to a greater possibility that competition can be resolved amicably, or that competition may be transformed to cooperation.

Victories may exist side by side, competitive but not necessarily uncooperative. However, resentment will arise and cooperation will be marred when one victory falters and the other surges. The less successful will attempt to diminish the success of the greater, and the greater will scorn the lesser; envy and arrogance thus diminish both societies.

Demosthenes, as Clemenceau recorded, would have "saved his country had it consented to be saved. Man does not suffer salvation; he makes it. He must know how to forge it with his own hands. When the enthusiasm of the moment is past, unending endurance is the virtue that crowns the success of the day with the confirmation of the morrow."

Modern colonialism—largely from the seventeenth to twentieth centuries—conquered and absorbed traditional, tribally based nations, particularly in Africa, the Americas, and Asia. Old nations were divided, artificial new boundaries were drawn, and "modern" (post-Westphalian) nation-states were created. But the colonial overlordships continued, overlaying the local cultures and languages with those of the former colonial powers. The only victories which were possible were those which were part of the occupying powers' own victories.

When, most prolifically in the post–World War II period, the colonial powers, largely for economic reasons, abandoned their colonies, the "modern nation-states" they had created were left rootless. The entire society of such an artificial state—which in most instances had no unifying victories or searing events to bond together its varied peoples—was left as a gift to a new neocolonial overlord, the leader of the most dominant subgroup, usually the one which controlled the military.

Given that international acceptance required the preservation of the modern nation-state boundaries which these entities had inherited (no matter how irrational or unviable they might be), the military-backed postcolonial administrations still lacked the tools to create the common bonds of victory. Europe, at the time of the Treaty of Westphalia, had seen the natural growth of societies toward what was now accepted as the modern nation-state. The treaty merely ratified and codified it. Thus, in many ways, the first "modern nation-states" were a natural evolution. Colonially created modern states did not have the same chance to evolve, and, following the colonial powers' departures, could be held together only by force and by the laws which had been imposed by the occupying outsiders.

The "victory" of independence was therefore no victory. Natural societal evolution had been disrupted forever. The countries given to their inhabitants were therefore unnatural and alien to them, as were the laws and instruments they had inherited from their former conquerors.

The aching void left by the missing victories could not be filled. To retain the new nations, their inhabitants had to retain the alien power structures they had been "given" at independence. To achieve the victories needed to enable them to seize life on their own terms required—and still requires in most cases—that the mold they inherited be broken. The conundrum was how this could be achieved without also irrevocably destroying the country. As Omar Khayyám, said, *"Could thou and I with Fate conspire / To grasp this sorry Scheme of Things entire, / Would we not shatter it to bits—and then / Re-mold it nearer to the Heart's Desire!"*

But the great Persian poet, mathematician, astronomer, and philosopher also said, *"The moving finger writes; and having writ, / Moves on: nor all thy Piety nor Wit / Shall lure it back to cancel half a Line, / Nor all thy Tears wash out a Word of it."*

The shackles of colonial bondage still therefore bind the steps of the modern postcolonial nation-states. How can they find their requisite victories without first destroying themselves? It is critical, therefore, that the leaders of these postcolonial modern states recognize the true nature not only of their constituent peoples, but also of their historical institutions, including the accepted myths of those institutions. What will be successful in the postcolonial context, then, is either the reintroduction of structures which truly reflect the character of the society or the transformation of colonial legacy structures so that they absorb some of the character of the indigenous society. To continue using the imposed foreign structures of government merely postpones the reckoning to which a society must come with itself; it must ultimately shed the borrowed garment of foreign institutions before it can once again assume its natural state.

This is more easily said than done. In Nigeria, for example, 1960 saw the "independence" of a new, modern nation-state with artificial boundaries encompassing scores of different peoples and hundreds of languages and traditions. How could it be possible to "return" to institutions which mirrored the character of the people? The challenge, then, was to imbue the foreign structures with a "Nigerianness" which would borrow from the great historical institutions of the various constituent peoples.

Even the revolution of Britain's American colonies—by colonials who were free to create institutions in their own image—led to a decade of chaos after 1776 before the institutions they devised through "reason" began to be shaped to the sentiment of underlying character. It is a process of shaping and reinforcement which, in the United States of America, continues more than two centuries later.

GIVING VICTORY TO IRAQ?

For those, then, who thought that the United States was giving "victory" to Iraq, with the invasion and removal of Saddam Hussein in 2003, there could only have been disappointment. The gift had, to a large extent, been spurned, or at least accepted with few thanks—not because the Iraqis wished, by and large, to continue under Saddam's harsh rule, but because Iraq was not the gift of Washington to give. Those more realistic in Washington recognized this and attempted merely to support the Iraqis in seizing their moment and making the country their own. Given Iraq's complex history, and its creation as a modern nation-state in 1923—again the gift of outside powers—the eventual shape and substance of the country remains an open question.

The fact that outside powers continue to attempt to define Iraq may well cause Iraqis of all origins and cultures to ultimately embrace each other in defense of their common state. Indeed, the United States, having broken the artificial construct of Saddam Hussein's control of Iraq, had already been overtaken in 2006 by Iranian involvement in the country. Iran, which once had been able to call Baghdad a Persian city, was now remolding the clay of Mesopotamia "nearer to its heart's desire," something which many Iraqis find threatening. U.S. troops, the Iraqis know, will leave their country. But will those of Iran and its surrogates?

Iraqis know that if they want Iraq to exist as a sovereign state, they will have to fight for it. All the United States could do for them was to open the door. History will determine whether, after being brought together only eighty years before as a multisociety nation-state, enough of its citizens had achieved a sense of "Iraqiness" to fight for the entity, or whether they will drift back into more communal divides. There are forces in Washington, Tehran, Riyadh, Damascus, and Ankara all pushing the Iraqi entity in different ways to see whether it can be made into a viable whole, or whether it can be shaken apart.

Although we might cheer for another society to achieve its victory, we see that victory is possible only as a gift to oneself.

THE GIFT TO ONESELF

TWENTY-FOUR

The gift of victory is something that can be
given only by a society to itself.

For Australia and New Zealand, "victory" meaningfully
began in the form of their collective military defeat
early in World War I, ten and seven years respectively
after they were given independence from Britain. In 1915,
the combined Australian and New Zealand Army Corps
(ANZAC), part of a larger British force, invaded Turkey at
Gallipoli, on the Dardanelles. There, faced with overwhelming hardship and titanic odds, they suffered a crushing military defeat. The searing effects of that seven-month
disaster—with some ten thousand ANZAC troops dead
and more than thirty thousand wounded—were such that
the ANZAC states created a bonded set of identities separate from that of Britain, whence their societies had sprung.

It was at the call of Britain, and under its leadership,
that Australia and New Zealand had marched into disaster
at Gallipoli. They had proven their prowess at war, however, and the disaster was Britain's. They could hold their
heads high and face the future with confidence and independence, the first step on the road to victory.

Can pride in country or self—not smug contentment,
but motivating pride—be engendered without victory or
the quest for victory? And can victory be achieved without
the pride or galvanic struggle which generates a sense of
common purpose?

Victory embraces the most fundamental as well as the most abstract aspects of human nature and achievement. It embraces the subjective as well as the objective. It is visceral, emotional, intellectual, and physical. It embraces all of the sciences and disciplines known to mankind. Its mastery, therefore, is beyond science and quantifiable factors alone. The achievement of victory can only be an art, and not a science.

Moreover, what is perceived and desired as victory will evolve in form, but not in substance. It will always entail mastery over the means of survival—food, shelter, and the selection of mates—and the fundamental tools (language, beliefs, movement) of the societal evolution necessary to achieve the competitiveness against nature and other rivals required to guarantee control of those means of perpetuation.

What we seek from victory constantly evolves, both in terms of what is feasible, technologically and scientifically, and in terms of the constraints imposed by such factors as growing (or declining or aging) population and finite resources. Thus, while we may move from societies which were largely agrarian and rural to those which are mostly urban, the fundamental requirements of victory do not change. We must merely recognize the evolving context and adapt our victory instincts to match the changes. Those most attuned to changing patterns will dominate the race to victory.

This may include recognizing the fact that "our" society has transformed, or must transform, to achieve or sustain victory. There comes a time when children leave the nest, thus changing the shape of the family. So it is with societies. The art lies in achieving the right balance of what is retained, and what is made new.

Geopolitics, for example, remains a seemingly immutable factor in strategic life. But the human factor—the way we use geography—is changed daily by our technology and our needs. Thus the "politics" in geopolitics changes. To illustrate the evolution: In the eighteenth century, labor was cheap and silver expensive, so massive artisanal efforts were expended to make the most beautiful silver objects from the thinnest possible plate. By the late twentieth century, labor was expensive and silver relatively cheap, so more easily worked thicker silver plate was used to compensate for lower skill levels and the need to use less labor time.

Victories are rarely achieved or sustained unconsciously. Not only does victory represent the mastery of challenges that arise to confront society (and therefore the individual), but, indeed, its hallmark is that it requires the conscious seeking out of challenges. And yet victory lies not only in achieving the goals which may be devised by man, but in seeking to expand success beyond those goals. In other words, the goal should not be attaining one's goal, but rather surpassing and thinking beyond all goals.

In 1989 it was valid to ask the Western leadership: "After you have seen the collapse of the Soviet Union, how will your victory be realized?" In 2006, in the period after the death of Palestinian Authority chairman Yasir Arafat and new elections, the question could be asked of the Palestinians: "How would the destruction of Israel bring victory to the Palestinian society?" Too often a fixation on the elimination of a rival for victory distracts a society from the true goal of victory itself.

Victory is built in some key respects on what we may call "love of nation"—the collective expression of the desire for the security and success of the society—and if the nation is ill-defined, then the victory is assembled on vague, unstable foundations. The Peace of Westphalia in 1648 moved the understanding of "nation" from a tribal and dynastically based sense of society to one which was geographically and legally defined above all else. Various cultures and languages found haven within this new structure, becoming increasingly viable as a force for victory as the sense of common identity gradually transcended and subsumed the different characters of the various "classical" nations which had been molded into the modern nation-state.

The achievement of true victory, indigenous and heart-felt, in the states created after World War II, will depend as much on art as on science. For them, the Art of Victory will entail the conscious creation of imagery to make the institutions of state their own, and not merely the property of the dominant groups within the state (or, worse, the alien remnants of a departed conqueror).

There will need to be a great and conscious construction of nationalism which must still coexist with international society. These states' victories must fit into the context of the surrounding world, with which they must trade and interact, and yet be individual enough to bind the people of the new state into a common love of country.

Those states which have wrested independence from their overlords through unity and resolve, in the crucible of conflict, usually fare best. The only victory which holds is the victory self-grasped and hard-won.

Despite this, we see societies grow blind to victory and, lost in the luxury of it, let it slip away.

Ralph Sawyer, in the introduction to his indispensable translation of *The Seven Military Classics of Ancient China*, noted: "Military thought, the complex product of both violent war and intellectual analysis, suffered from disparagement and disrepute during almost all of the past two millennia in Imperial China." Other societies, such as Sparta's, were, on the other hand, so conscious of the need to preserve their instruments of victory that they eschewed comforts and the fruits of victory in order that the embellishments of civilized life would not enervate and undermine their defenses.

WHO, TODAY, SEEKS TO GIVE THEMSELVES THE GIFT OF VICTORY?

Almost all individuals and societies seek to improve their lives. The difference, however, lies in which individuals and societies seek to preserve, protect, and expand their long-term victory, or to achieve victory to take them permanently from a place of great emotional discontent, and which individuals and societies do not wish to face these thoughts.

We see in Western Europe and most of Latin America no great thoughts toward preserving or acquiring victory; both areas are preoccupied with short-term gratification, but each in different ways. The dynamics of unrest and self-assertion we see in Venezuela and Bolivia are not the stirring of the hemisphere to greatness, but are fairly reactionary responses of elements of societies seeking immediate gratification or redress for long-standing grievances.

We see conscious striving for victory in the longer-term sense in places such as the People's Republic of China, Croatia, Albania, and among the procaliphate jihadists. In these societies we see a sense of destiny, albeit—with the exception of China—reflected in an emotional "sense" rather than any depth of understanding. Croatia, Albania, and the jihadists will need to do a lot more thinking if they are to see victory inure to their societies. We see the stirrings of a sense of the multigenerational impetus toward victory also in India and Australia, but only the stirrings.

If we think of the will toward victory in the context of the analogy of "the gift which a society gives to itself," then we can divide the societies into those that are preparing their lists and doing their early shopping for the big gift-giving day and those that are shopping ad hoc at the last minute, hoping to stumble across "just the right thing." For the most part, societies in Europe, Africa, the Middle East, and South

America are not even shopping. Arguably, the United States itself began "shopping" to save the victory of the West only when the George W. Bush administration responded so vigorously to the September 11, 2001, terrorist attacks. But given the decade of frittering away the "peace dividend" which preceded that catalyst, the United States still has not been able to galvanize its society into compiling the "shopping list" for its revived victory.

PLANNING THE GIFT OF VICTORY

The shopping list of the gift of victory is, in fact, the grand strategy we discussed earlier. Victory is the comprehensive and total gift, which a society, or an individual, must struggle to afford. It is not just the "little extra," such as a short-term improvement in the standard of living of a society; something which could disappear within an economic cycle. It is the gift of an heirloom, to be passed down the generations. Therefore, in planning the gift, we must consider all of its elements.

As economies become more abstract and sophisticated—that is, as they move away from being simple direct cash or barter economies into the use of multiple forms of credit, values, and transactional possibilities—and move toward the framework which we are now calling "service economies," we find that classical industry is increasingly relegated to the more basic and primitive economies. Indeed, the populations in "service economies" begin to lose their understanding of manufacturing and producing industries, stop training for them, and begin viewing them with disdain.

In *Future Shock*, Alvin Toffler articulated what many people in modern societies feel: that "white collar" workers are superior to "blue collar"; that talking about things is superior to doing things or making things. It is true that in modern societies, the computer and associated technologies have "flattened" the hierarchical structure of societies; we feel sufficiently well-informed—through our modern technologies—to criticize and maul our leaders. But in fact, we have already replaced the old hierarchy with a makeshift, fragile, unfinished one, in which societies living off the fruits of hard-won victory can look down at societies still struggling to achieve their secure futures.

This works well in times of relative harmony: the rich, through the prestige created by their historically developed power, can give work to the aspiring, who are grateful for it. But when survival is at stake, a "real" economy is critical. A "real" economy needs a comprehensive balance of intellectual and physical capabilities to provide the means of defense, food, energy, water—the staples of victory—in a manner which cannot be assailed by problems or threats from elsewhere.

The new hierarchy in which the world is now operating—the world of outsourcing by wealthy "service economies" to foreign providers of manufactured goods, services, raw materials, and the like—is inherently unstable, and is unsuited for periods of crisis or threat. And we are now entering a period of great instability and threat to established modern societies. But that is not to deny the importance of the abstract "service economy" functions and thus call for the restoration of the primacy of physical industry. On the contrary: Both are vital to victory. One is the engine of survival; the other is the engine of wealth and progress.

Let me put the example in more basic terms. As we engineer biology, do we do away with the basic biological urges or tendencies? We have in many ways—through artificial insemination and cloning—been able to disassociate sex from human or animal reproduction, but the sex urge has remained. Similarly, there is no evidence that the survival or victory urge has suffered from the sophistication or abstraction of society. Neither has the biological urge toward a belief in "god," or, in some, the urge toward leadership or self-gratification been suppressed by the abstraction of societies into "democracies" or welfare states.

In other words, the basics still apply, even if we have forgotten them.

Because of the changes which accompany the growth of human numbers and the steps we have taken to ensure that nature can support them, we continue to see changes in family, clan, and state affiliations. But the urge to have such affiliations has not changed. Even when the frameworks change, the old survival skills still apply.

One of the immediate lessons of all of this is that, particularly in times of change or crisis, leaders need to be generalists: people who are comfortable understanding, and working with, a wide range of knowledge and disciplines. And yet, because of the long period of stability and "peace" which the modern world has known, the path to wealth has been specialization. Great success has attended those who have rejected any understanding of the environmental context of life; they have grown rich by specializing in narrowly defined areas of, for example, law or computing sciences.

But, despite their wealth and community standing, these are not skills which make leaders.

So in planning the "gift of victory" which we must give ourselves, we must consider that context and balance are everything, and that our present way of doing business in modern societies ignores the changing context and is out of balance in terms of dangerous dependencies on the continued existence of the status quo. We are totally dependent on our ability to have unfettered access to foreign resources and manufactured goods, and on the freedom of the seas and airways. And yet such "unfettered access" is a historically rare occurrence, and is by no means guaranteed for the long term.

Significantly, in this regard, we do not see, for example, the major oil companies moving swiftly toward creating new forms of energy. They have too much invested in the infrastructure of oil. But capital moves more rapidly, which is why we see that the new energy sectors are being funded by venture capitalists. Thus, a new economic sector will arise and many of the older energy companies will either adapt or die over the coming decades or century. Many old trades and economic sectors have disappeared or become less powerful over history: the salt traders, the letterpress printers and typographers, the lace traders; the list goes on.

To become free of foreign energy suppliers, then, we must turn to, and control, new forms of energy. To become capable of securing our defense we must constantly adapt. Indeed, it was the Japanese attack on Pearl Harbor in 1941 which finally broke the unwillingness of many in the U.S. Navy to dispense with outdated battleships and move to aircraft carriers. We are reluctant to change unless forced to do so, and we have much of our capital and sense of self tied up in things we have built. So it is in societies which have "excess capital"—often the product of the "service economy" base—which have the ability to bypass the old investments and structures, and to build the new.

The danger comes when "service economies" become so preoccupied with themselves that they forget to invest in modernizing the fundamentals of the provision of energy, abundant water, agriculture, and manufactured goods. We have begun to create a new global hierarchy, which has yet to define itself in social terms in many ways, and we now need to understand how it must work.

I earlier cited what the late shah of Iran told me: that he feared the "unholy alliance of red [communist] and black [religious extremists]." We now need to think in terms, inside every modern economy, of a "holy alliance" of blue and white (blue collar, in the old parlance, and white collar). That would indeed be a rich part of the victory gift to oneself.

None of this is easy. It is why we must venerate and encourage strength and courage.

Strength and Courage: The Hallmarks of Victory

TWENTY-FIVE

No victory was ever created or sustained by weakness.

O
ne of the great classic movies, the 1959 comedy *The Mouse That Roared*, depicted a troubled and backward little duchy, Grand Fenwick, declaring war on the United States with the motive of being defeated and then being rebuilt—à la the Marshall Plan—with U.S. aid. The film had a quirky logic to it. But significantly, only a few years ago, it prompted North Korean leader Kim Jong-Il to consider whether the proposition of the movie had some merit. He dispatched a team of emissaries to meet in Europe with a trusted old European politician to ask whether, if North Korea began a war with the United States, it could end its strategic impasse and find riches.

The European politician—as I was told by a colleague in the room when the meeting occurred—hastily assured the legation from Pyongyang that declaring nuclear war against the United States was extremely inadvisable, and would lead to unimaginable and negative consequences for all involved. The thought by Dear Leader Kim Jong-Il that such a concept might have merit certainly demonstrated his lack of sound understanding of the outside world. But more important, it betrayed his fear that North Korea faced a threat which could not be met by its forces.

This fear, based on irrational perceptions of imminent invasion by the United States, caused North Korea (and Iran) to adopt "poison pill" defenses: They declared their nuclear weapons capabilities in order to avoid the fate of Saddam Hussein in Iraq. The Iranian and North Korean perception was that Saddam had lost to the United States because he did not have his nuclear deterrent in place. As a result, Iran and North Korea have skewed their national defenses and their place in the global economy by embarking on major nuclear weapons and ballistic missile programs.

By so doing, they have distorted and damaged their chances for victory. They have sacrificed the development of balanced economies and comprehensive, long-term defenses in order to meet short-term fears. Their nuclear weapons programs, in fact, express not their strength, but their weakness.

There are two imperatives which underlie victory: First, victory is collective, and second, victory demands strength. To these attributes, as we have already seen, the characteristics of wisdom, decisiveness, and willpower must be added, but weakness and cowardliness in a society can erode and undermine even the wisdom and decisiveness of its leaders. And while there are those with apparently innate courage and strength, these are attributes which can be chosen, nurtured, and used with skill, both individually and societally. But these virtues can also be abandoned and forgotten.

VICTORY IS COLLECTIVE: Like religion, victory dwells not only within individuals, but in the spaces between people, providing the link, binding them together in common purpose. Single accomplishment cannot parallel communal accomplishment, but each makes the other possible.

For victory to be collective, or for collective strength to achieve or sustain victory, there must be common understanding. This implies, even demands, common language and common imagery. With very few exceptions (Switzerland, perhaps), a society of diverse languages is effectively an empire with one group dominating the others. Thus when a society with a single public language allows, even encourages, parts of its population to fragment into separate language groups—without the dominance of a single lingua franca—then it is, knowingly or not, surrendering its grasp on victory. From the standpoint of building enduring good for a society, this coddling of separatism within a society is weakness, and may spell eventual doom for the victory of that nation-state. This is not to deny pride in cultural origins—or the need for nurturing immigrant languages—within societies' various communities. These add richness and flexibility to a society. But the deliberate avoidance of ensuring universal communication in a single, unambiguous voice in a society is a mark of appeasement and decline.

VICTORY DEMANDS STRENGTH: To abdicate strength is to abdicate victory. But the strength of victory is balanced. Great economic strength achieved in the absence of one's own military strength has, axiomatically, been achieved under the umbrella of someone else's military strength. Even in peacetime, economic strength which is not married to military strength ultimately declines, often rapidly. Economic strength which is sustained under the umbrella of a greater power can never equal the strength of the greater power, to which victory truly belongs. Equally, great military power attained without the accompaniment of economic power will never equal the strength and enduring victory of the balanced power.

The economic strength of Britain, France, and the Netherlands at the start of the twenty-first century was the residual wealth of historical military strength, albeit now sustained by alliances. The economic strength of Germany and Japan at the start of the twenty-first century also had a link to the sense of national purpose generated by earlier military strength, but it was enabled, in its modern (post–World War II) form by dependence on the military umbrella of the alliance with the United States. Full reassertion of victory by any of these powers would demand independent strategic action, which is possible only by renewed military credibility. Germany has essentially rejected this path. Japan is attempting to rebuild its military quietly and with delicate regard for its strategic environment.

And both economic and military strength will atrophy without intellectual strength in the society and in leadership. The evolution of society has been from instinct-driven physical strength—to achieve dominance over territory and mating—to the acquisition of material well-being, to the acquisition of the means to best manage these resources.

This implies dynamism. While the temptation is to believe that victory, once achieved, can be sustained as the status quo, such a belief is illusory. There is no such thing as a static victory. "Static victory" is wasting victory. All victory is dynamic, and no aspect of victory's dynamism can be neglected. Therefore it is imperative that the economic, military, technological, sociological, and philosophical systems of society be advanced uniformly and in harmony.

A leader who pursues economic strength but ignores, despises, or misuses military and geosocial strengths is guilty of short-term greed and is not a victory-oriented leader. A leader who focuses solely on military strength is doomed to see victory lost within a single generation. He will be like Ozymandias, preoccupied with his own power, but failing to sustain it as victory.

Within this soup of history, then, it is easier to observe the end of victory than its commencement. For when victory first becomes apparent it is usually already into its adolescence. The origins of victory occur in the dim recesses of societal formation, and all things build upon that.

If we take the case of Singapore's unquestioned present victory—within the framework of a trading world protected by greater powers—we can see that its emergence occurred with independence from Britain in 1960. But that emergence would not have been possible but for three things: the historical culture and character of its forming peoples, mostly of Chinese, Indian, and Malay origin, shaped by British colonialism; the geographic placement of the island state at a crossroads of trade; and the galvanizing strength and vision of Prime Minister Lee Kuan Yew. Prime Minister Lee transformed the other two attributes into victory through absolute personal strength, courage, and vision, whereas, in similar circumstances elsewhere, many others had failed. He also ensured a strenuous and unambiguous commitment to Singapore's national security and defense, within a framework of military, diplomatic, and intelligence capabilities which reach far beyond its limited shores.

WHO TODAY BUILDS STRENGTH?

Of the major powers in the world today, few consciously build their military strength as part of an overarching and balanced sense of mission. The United States, under Carter and Clinton, frittered away defenses. It was rebuilt under Reagan and George W. Bush. China now consistently also builds its defenses with great zeal within the framework of a national mission. India also does, but with less consistency than China in some respects. And Russia consciously uses its gradually rebuilding economic strength to preserve command of its military capability. Such formerly great military powers as France, Germany, and Britain are just marking time, buying new systems to replace old ones, but lacking a sense of strategic purpose.

The disproportionate commitment of Iran, North Korea, and Syria, for example, to military strength is out of balance, and is more a reflection of fear than of positive planning for a future victory. It is the imbalanced commitment to military spending which is most dangerous, both to the societies which are imbalanced and to their neighbors. Handing power to a weak person or giving guns to frightened people are the analogies in everyday life.

The most difficult combination to achieve, however, is strength and courage. There is no doubt that, if a clear threat of great magnitude arose today, the people of the United Kingdom or Germany would have the courage to respond to it. But would they have the strength? Strength is not achieved overnight; it is part of the careful construction process of victory.

The strength and courage of a society can, however, be easily diminished. Determining our path toward victory is all the more difficult in times of great upheaval, such as we now face. We must look at how the ambitions of individuals can undermine the victory of society.

My Country, Right or Wrong . . .

TWENTY-SIX

An enemy can on no account be ignored, and while an enemy's motive must be understood, it can never be given greater respect than the defense of one's own victory.

U.S. Navy Commissioner Commodore Stephen Decatur, speaking in April 1816 after the final defeat by the Navy and Marine Corps of the Barbary pirates, made his famous toast: "Our country! In her intercourse with foreign nations, may she always be in the right; but our country, right or wrong." Few would want their country to be morally on the wrong side of a major issue, but even if it was, how many would wish to take issue on the matter in such a way and at such a time as to weaken the country's chances of survival or sustained victory?

U.S. congressman John Murtha (Democrat, Pennsylvania) on November 17, 2005, called for U.S. troops to be withdrawn immediately from their combat mission in Iraq. A former Marine, he subsequently said that he would not, if he was young, enlist in the U.S. armed services. U.S. troops were, meanwhile, at the height of their campaign to address the hydra-headed Iraqi insurgency, sponsored by a variety of groups, but principally by the government of Iran.

Murtha clearly did not represent the majority views of

the Congress, or of the United States government, but his comments (and the debate which surrounded them), and those of his colleague, ultraleftist congresswoman Nancy Pelosi (Democrat, California) and some other dissidents, gained international attention. Murtha's and Pelosi's comments, however, provided great sustenance and motivation to jihadists fighting to defeat and drive out the U.S. forces in Iraq and to topple the elected Iraqi government.

Jihadists involved in the fighting against the United States and the Iraqi Government specifically cited the Murtha-Pelosi comments as proof that the jihadists had, essentially, already defeated the United States, and gave them heart to push ahead with their war. Murtha and Pelosi had given greater priority to the cause of the enemies of the United States than to the interests of the United States itself, and they did so in order to gain domestic political advantage within the United States.

Another U.S. congresswoman, Jean Schmidt (Republican, Ohio), cited on the floor of Congress a U.S. Marine who had written to her that the Marines did not "cut and run," which was taken as a hint that Murtha was motivated by cowardice. She later said that in citing the Marine in the debate on Murtha's motion, she had not intended a personal slur against the congressman, who had served thirty-seven years in the military and fought in Korea and Vietnam. Indeed, it was *not* cowardice which was the motivation for Murtha's comments, but—whether accidentally or not—Murtha had placed personal and party power above the good of the country.

Treason—defined by the *American Heritage Dictionary* as "isolation of allegiance toward one's country or sovereign, especially the betrayal of one's country by waging war against it or by consciously and purposely acting to aid its enemies"—also requires courage. However, society views treason as possibly the most unforgivable of betrayals. Certainly, in the case of Murtha and Pelosi, their behavior was not consciously motivated by treason, but occasioned merely by greed—the hope of gaining political advantage over the elected leadership of their country—and thoughtlessness. Nonetheless, they had placed the interests of the enemies of their country above the interests of their own country.

Americans look back with some justification at the actions of Revolutionary War general Benedict Arnold, who, in 1780, at the height of the war, attempted to betray the colonists' cause. Without achieving his promise to the British of delivering the American garrison at West Point, he nonetheless defected, and became a British brigadier general. Significantly, General Arnold was not a coward; he proved an audacious commander in the service of both the American and British causes. Nor was he unique in switching sides during that confused period, bearing in mind that the Revolutionary War had erupted not specifically to seek independence, but to seek redress and attention by London to the colonists' complaints.

Nonetheless, the name "Benedict Arnold" has the same connotation of contempt which the name Quisling was to arouse during and after World War II. Vidkun Quisling, a Norwegian fascist and a major in the Norwegian Army at the time of the fall of Norway to the Germans, was made, by the Germans, minister president of Norway from February 1942 until the end of World War II, the period that the elected social democratic cabinet of Johan Nygaardsvold was exiled in London. Quisling was executed after World War II, following the defeat of the Germans.

Significantly, the cases of Arnold and Quisling were substantially different from each other. Arnold betrayed his fellow colonists for personal reward; Quisling attempted to retain Norwegian control of his country when the Germans invaded, albeit by cooperating with the Germans.

Nonetheless, to apply the term "a Benedict Arnold" or "a Quisling" to someone is to evoke the emotions of absolute contempt. Such is the depth of feeling which society has for those who betray their "sacred loyalty" to country and people. Adultery, by and large, is forgiven in modern society—and has historically been an accepted practice by many societies at various times—and yet this is, in some senses, a betrayal at a very personal level. Still it fails to evoke the same emotions as treachery at a societal level.

But how is treason to be described in the current period of globalization, when sovereignty and national identity appear to be less clearly defined than, say, even in 1950? What would have been treasonous behavior at the height of World War II is regarded with but passing interest in the West in the early twenty-first century. Have standards changed? Has human nature changed with regard to its feelings about group loyalty? Certainly, human nature remains unchanged. But the standards of measurement of behavior have indeed been suspended as the world passes through its "Age of Transformation," with—as we have discussed—the flattening of hierarchical structures. This temporary lateralizing of hierarchy embodies the delegitimizing of traditional leadership structures, which implies that loyalty to the *ancien régime* is no longer required.

At the bottom of all of this is the fact that the West— the modern world, including China and Russia—is undergoing as profound a revolution as the developing world. Both "revolutions" come under the rubric of globalization, but each world reacts in different ways. Hierarchical structure is more rapidly reasserted in much of the developing world because it lacks the wealth and complexity to cushion its decisions and perspectives. In the West, however, the revolution literally creates the wealth upon which it feeds: Globalization generates enormous wealth, which is spreading rapidly to modernize more and more societies.

But great and widely dispersed wealth also complicates the process of the reassertion of hierarchies within the societies. In short, wealth and globalization have—because of the implicit criticism the phenomenon generates of traditional structures—made it more difficult to define what, in fact, constitutes our society. And if we can no longer starkly define who we are as a society, then how can we define treason, loyalty, and our overall objectives—our grand strategy?

We spoke in Chapter Twelve on "The Care and Feeding of Enemies," but no greater task exists—or any greater duty—than the "care and feeding" of one's own self and one's own kin and society. It is only through success in this that all other things become feasible. It is the essence of survival, procreation, and the basis of the ability to achieve victory. We have also discussed—in Chapters Twenty-three and Twenty-four—that victory cannot be given by one state to another (or one individual to another) and that victory is the gift which one gives to oneself. It follows, then, that one's own victory is of primary importance to sustain.

Globalization will not be overturned; it is a natural expansion of human capabilities. And the spread of wealth should continue to be encouraged. Both phenomena, interrelated, hold the keys to the ability of the human race to overcome disease and to feed and care for the growing human population. Even the nineteenth-century methods of agriculture and distribution could not feed the world population as it is today, and human numbers continue to grow.

Much of the answer, then, lies in giving equal attention to the need for identity security; the understanding and definition of who we are as societies. In other words, what, then, becomes of critical concern is to ensure that there is a clear definition of what constitutes one's own society and sovereign entity. That, in turn, requires a reassertion of a structural hierarchy which can sustain a national purpose, and such a hierarchy is unlikely to be lateral. That does not deny democracy—the role of each individual in accepting and assigning responsibility within society. On the contrary, it demands a greater sense of an articulated democracy.

The present "revolution" has, in fact, *denied* the essence of true democracy. It created what Plato feared most: mob rule. The current breakdown in the prestige of traditional hierarchy has separated much of society from its leaders, and authority and power is viewed, in a sense, laterally. Societies in the West go through the motions of democratically "assigning" power to leaders, through elections, but then disallows them the authority to act. In other words, society has overturned the balance of democracy and has, because of the independence which wealth and modern technology gives to the individual, assigned far greater power to individual responsibility than to leaders. That would be well and good if individuals then fulfilled the requirement—previously assigned to leaders—to serve the common weal.

Let me repeat something I said in Chapter Seventeen: "It is when insecurity or greed, each a short-term expression of ignorance (and a reflection of Plato's definition of the 'appetite' or desire aspect of societal personality), motivates individual and mob action through emotional appeal that laws or constitutions are trammeled, misused, or forgotten, and humanity rushes from the path of progress to the self-destructive path of the lemming."

What has happened, then, with the populist assault on traditional leadership and icons of hierarchy is not that individuals are taking a greater burden of responsibility for the welfare of their society. Rather, having removed the ability of the old structures to work, they have replaced them with, essentially, the leadership of the mob—that is to say, with no leadership at all. Little wonder, then, that the jihadist movements watch the Western media and petty politicians sniping, attacking, and destroying their elected (or monarchical) leaders and believe that the West's guard is down, and that it cannot respond to attack.

Part of the natural response of societies which are in the process of revolution is that, eventually, the pendulum swings back, usually with a vengeance, creating new, rigid hierarchies and great "political correctness." Even the laissez-faire models of society in Western Europe and the United States before each of the two world wars succumbed rapidly, when conflict erupted, into a discipline and conformity—a conservatism—which snuffed out the ages of petty and personal indulgence. Today, globalization and wealth have given momentum to self-indulgence in the West, at the same time that the threats to the cohesion and security of Western societies have risen.

So the fundamental of giving priority to the defense of one's own victory remains as it has always been. The real question, however, has become whether we can decide who we are. This is no longer a question of merely understanding one's country of origin, or family history. One of the most significant strategic factors of the globalization process has been that, today, more and more people are *deciding* who they are; who they *choose* to be.

Nationalism was once a matter largely predetermined by the birthplace of an individual, along with the cultural, linguistic, and ethnic background into which the person was born. The Roman Empire introduced the concept of making Roman citizens of some members of its subject nations, but it was the creation of the United States which essentially began a process of creating a new nation-state to which people came with the object of becoming citizens of that new entity. The period of European exploration, particularly from the fifteenth century onward, not only created colonies out of existing nations of peoples, it also created totally new nation-states, such as the United States, Canada, Australia, New Zealand, Brazil, Argentina, and Chile, which specifically attracted migrant populations.

Today, with globalization's movement of capital, goods, ideas, and—most significantly—people, it is people who are choosing where they wish to place their loyalties, as they would choose a football team to support. Most important, the acceleration of this trend means that some people may choose to live in, and even become citizens of, several countries over the course of their lives. This is only part of the equation, however. A still larger segment of modern society, while it may not choose to take the step of migration, nonetheless feels part of a global community, free to identify selectively with different cultures, leaders, and ideologies.

All of this places an overriding strategic priority on governments—which of necessity are geopolitically oriented—to devise "population strategies" to account for the accelerated and uncontrollable movement of populations across their borders, either physically or intellectually. It also becomes important for governments not only to devise methods to retain the services and loyalty of the most productive members of their societies, but also to attract immigrants who can, ideally, become an enduring part of the long-term victory of the nation-state.

Population strategies, which governments traditionally avoid considering due to political sensitivities, must also encompass methods to prevent people who might be unproductive, counterproductive, or disaffected from the mainstream of the society from entering, and becoming part of the state.

People, like investment capital, will increasingly vote with their feet, and this makes the creation of population strategies urgent for states. And the phenomenon is mirrored in how corporations structure themselves as societies. Arguably, indeed, the phenomenon we have seen develop over the past half-century with corporate "population strategies"—with the movement of workers from company to company, career to career—has now found its way into the nation-state complex.

All of this begs the question of whether national loyalties can be sustained over generations, or whether the emotional commitment to the nation-state must be won and reshaped continually. Clearly, the geographical shape of the nation-state endures (but may be modified by treaty, conquest, or division), along with its structures and infrastructures. Its population, while essentially centered on the geopolitical entity, is the fluid dynamic. How can social hierarchies, then, be built and sustained around the geopolitical unit? That is the ultimate challenge for governments and the essence of sovereignty in the twenty-first century.

The infinite variety of factors makes it clear that victory is achieved through an artful balancing of constantly changing priorities. It is the sum of all strengths.

THE SUM OF ALL STRENGTHS

TWENTY-SEVEN

Victory that depends solely on a single element—whether strength of force, religion or belief, wealth, culture, or intellect—will fail.

S hocking truths began to emerge when the Soviet Union and the myth of communism collapsed in 1990. It was then that it was learned, for example, that Stalin had—even by the estimates of his successor leaders—killed at least 60 million of his own people, excluding the number of Soviet citizens who died in World War II. (Mao Zedong, in the People's Republic of China, had liquidated some 60 million Chinese during the Cultural Revolution's militant phase from 1966 to 1969.)

But one startling set of statistics showed that at the time of its collapse, the gross domestic product (GDP) of the USSR—a state then of some 290 million people, more populous than the United States—was approximately equivalent to that of the Netherlands, with a population of only 16 million. Moreover, more than 80 percent of that Soviet GDP was related to military activities.

The coincidence of the collapse of the USSR, the size and use of its economy, and the systematic suppression of the Soviet population was symptomatic of a society (or a leadership) out of balance with the necessities of victory. The entity of the communist USSR, it turned out, was one seventy-year-long gamble for a single triumph—defeat of the West—which it hoped to transform into victory. But it was clear that its preoccupation with the gamble itself had derailed or curtailed any thinking about how the wished-for triumph against the West could be translated into victory.

This state, predicated upon "historical determinism," had failed to heed the lesson of history, that victory is achieved only through balance.

How many of us as individuals gamble our future, and the future of our descendants, on the hope of a lottery win—even when we don't buy tickets—or the "assurance" that the safety net of social security will underwrite our later years? As we discussed in an earlier chapter, former Argentine military leader Lieutenant General Leopoldo Galtieri gambled his leadership in a single toss of the dice: an invasion of the Falkland Islands.

But the Soviet leaders were not unique in gambling an entire empire on the use of military power (at home and abroad) to solve their problems. The Chinese communist leaders, until the death of Mao Zedong in 1976, did the same thing, and China only emerged as a comprehensive power *after* Mao's tenets were abandoned. The Iranian clerical leadership today places all its faith and focus on a military solution; again, at home as well as abroad. This "single-strand" dependency in physical actions can be carried remarkably far when supported by determined will (in God, or the pseudo-god of ideology). But when faith dies, so does will.

The jihadist Islamists base their hopes for victory solely on faith-generating will. They have none of the other essential ingredients for victory, not even the military-industrial capability of the Soviets or Iran. Certainly they lack the complex, balanced, sustaining infrastructure of victory. Much of their sustaining will, even, is based on the credibility they derive from Western "respect" which their demands receive, and from the tribute which their black-mail of decent and moderate Muslim societies achieves. So the jihadists must transform or fail, and even if the West capitulates to them, their inability to master the necessity for balance will cause them to ultimately fail.

But how often do we see our chance for success skew away from its designed path when we become fixated upon a single solution to life and victory?

Overdependence on a single anything is a recipe for problems: a single source of critical widgets for a production line, a single source of oil, even a massive dependence on a single commodity—oil—to power an economy. Balance in all things is critical to victory, as it is in the harmony and satisfaction of life. And it is *that* innate understanding, rather than just concern over the finite quantities of available oil in the world, which powers the search for alternative forms of energy. Let us return to that theme in a moment, but first revisit the comprehensive importance of balance.

THE BALANCE OF VICTORY

It is easier to define victory than to devise the formulas for its achievement. Victory is the sustained survival, growth, and dominance of a society through history, theoretically forever. This embraces economic wealth; it embraces the dominance of the society's beliefs, language, and culture; it embraces the strength of the society's structural framework to permit the best possible means of teaming with nature to ensure security of food, health, shelter, and energy; and it embraces the defense of these things—all within a balance appropriate to the challenge of the times.

Victory depends on physical warfare and the ability to wage war as essential ingredients. But, poorly used, warfare can end or waste victory. Solely relied upon, war and the threat of war may give the illusion that victory is imminent, but it will never, under such circumstances, arise. But societies which do rely solely on war or the threat of war can disrupt the victory of others and can on no account be ignored. The ability of such societies to harm others—while doing no good to themselves—is such that any delay in dealing with them merely increases the damage they can do to victorious societies.

Victory depends on "God" in the sense that victorious societies require an ethic based on the cohesive, communal spirit. This spirit forms the basis of all the major religions. And yet, solely relied on, religion merely allows societies to wither in the face of other forces.

Victory depends, too, on leadership appropriate to the time, which we will discuss again in our final maxim.

Sun-tzu talked of the harmony—the balance—of all the elements of heaven and earth. We now know that such harmony engages the mind, heart, and soul of all individuals, operating within frameworks which provide the motivations, disciplines, and freedoms appropriate to the great variations in human aspiration and individuals' need for the survival of their bloodline and their beliefs. Victory, then, is in the grasp of, and is the responsibility of, all individuals—individuals acting consciously in concert, ideally with an appreciation of the need for a multiplicity of often competitive viewpoints and strengths within the society to enable it to apply the appropriate facet to each challenge.

The Art of Victory lies in the achievement of the balance which makes success achievable and enduring. It is not for the faint of heart, nor for those without vision, but there is, as Clemenceau said, no irreparable defeat except for the cause that is abandoned.

But let us return to the question of energy, because it is at the center of the question of balance in modern societies.

THE END OF U.S. ENERGY DOMINANCE?
OR JUST THE TWILIGHT OF FOSSIL FUELS?

The West, in 1973, was dependent not only on a single fuel—oil—for automotive power and for much of its electrical power generation, but to a large degree on a single supplier bloc: the Organization of Petroleum Exporting Countries (OPEC). At that time, the extent of oil expenditures as a percentage of U.S. and Western GDPs was significantly higher than it became by the early twenty-first century. Today, OPEC no longer dominates the supply of oil to the major consumer nations of the world, and certainly does not dominate the supply of gas. And today, oil as an economic factor within Western GDPs is far smaller than it was in 1973, when OPEC imposed its depression-inducing embargo on oil exports.

But despite the fact that the consumer nations won the strategic battle with the supplier states, the West continues to be obsessed, justifiably, with the security of oil supplies, particularly the supplies from the Arabian Peninsula and Iran. It is undoubtedly true that a significant extent of the U.S. concern over the stability of Saudi Arabia, the war in Iraq, and the State Department's clear desire to seek compliant leaders in Central Asia is about oil. It is, to be sure, about other things as well, but oil plays a major part.

And to a great extent this is an idée fixe, a mental fixation based upon backward-looking and reactive judgments. Inevitably, as well, it is bound to fail, just as King Canute demonstrated to his courtiers the foolishness of their claims that he could compel the tides not to rise.

So, as we see the finite lives of humans, organizations, companies, societies, and states, so, too, do we see the passing viability, primacy, or favor of technologies and certain commodities deemed at some stage to be essential for life or supremacy. Remember societies sustained by peat as fuel, or others made wealthy and powerful through the manufacture of lace. And if we look at the question of balance from a global perspective, so must we see that the world itself cannot exist with just a single superpower. Inevitably, the world must seek balance.

Not only, then, is the brief age of the sole superpower ending, so, too, is the age of U.S. dominance of the global oil markets before it even achieved the pinnacle of success it had sought. But no matter. Oil will not be the great and overwhelming currency in fifty years that it is now, or was in 1973, unless Western decline occurs and we remain in this backward age of oil-fired internal combustion.

But there will be a few years, a hiatus, before that new and more diverse energy world appears. In the meantime, a quiet momentum is building to steer oil pipelines in various parts of the world away from U.S. influence. This has brought some formerly adversarial states into discreet, tentative cooperation in building patterns of pipelines across formerly hostile borders. This is beginning a hesitant sort of peace which diplomacy and coercion had until now failed to do. But this is a delicate process, and not to the taste of all players, including, in some instances, the United States. So beneath the surface of a number of international disputes in the coming decade will be the question not just of oil, but of pipelines.

While this process continues—with attendant small wars, contrived "color revolutions" against elected governments, and the like—new energy processes will take increasing percentages of the energy market. The results will change the degree of dependency on oil imports by the United States. It will reduce the total reliance on petroleum as the basis for automotive fuel, and the total reliance on oil, gas, coal, and old-style nuclear power for electrical power generation. And, given the massive investment which the oil majors and the support industries have in infrastructure, ships, and terminals, the change will be resisted strenuously—and to the detriment of the West's security—by some.

We have constantly touched, in this book, on the question of the transformation of energy technologies, and it is one of the central themes of the emerging age. There is no alternative to this technological development, even if abundant new oil were to be discovered (and there is still plenty available in various places and forms for some time to come). If human populations are to continue their rate of increase, and if the standard of living of these great populations is to continue to rise (as it must if societal collapse is not to occur), then more viable forms of power must be found. Oil, as we noted, is already of less significance as a proportion of Western GDPs than it was in 1973. But new technologies will reduce this proportion even further, allowing monies to be spent on other necessities and luxuries. With this evolution in technology, too, an environment already overburdened because of the increasing human population can be relieved of some of its pressures.

But of equal importance in many ways is the fact that the employment of agriculturally farmed biomass to create liquid fuel (ethanol) can, within a decade if we chose to make it so, eliminate the dependence of the United States, Japan, Australia, and the like on imported oil. Ethanol can be produced cost-effectively now (which was not the case when oil was so cheap) and blended with oil for automotive and power plant fuel. Clearly, other technologies are also on the march—the new, safer nuclear power forms; hydrogen fuel cells; and so on.

Think, though, of the impact on U.S. foreign and strategic policy if the dependence on imported oil was not the cause of imbalance which it is today. To be sure, Egypt, Saudi Arabia, and Yemen would still be important because of their geographical position alongside the Red Sea–Suez sea lane, but the vital importance of the Middle East would decline. So, too, would the relative economic significance of Saudi Arabia, which remains burdened with an economy focused on that single theme: oil.

And think, too, of the rise of the wealth of the U.S. agricultural states, which would create the biomass. The process of achieving balance in energy would serve also to balance the political spectrum in the United States. And the rise of biomass as a central core of fuel for motive power would once again transform nations which are strong in agriculture into masters of their own fate.

It is time, after all, to bring the question of energy back into balance in our matrix of priorities.

If victory is about context and a balance of factors, then it can only be achieved by teamwork among individuals, societies, and nature.

THE TEAMWORK OF LEADER AND SOCIETY

TWENTY-EIGHT

Victory is beyond the power of any individual,
and yet is absolutely dependent on the strength
of the individual leader.

F ew people outside the Balkans remember Ante Pavelić,
a right-wing terrorist and assassin who suddenly
emerged in 1941 to become leader of the "Independent State of Croatia." He did not last long. His state was
created on April 10, 1941, by nazi Germany, and disappeared with the collapse of the Third Reich in 1945.
Pavelić was smuggled out of his short-lived and blood-
stained country to Argentina, where he served as a security
advisor to President Juan Perón. He died in Argentina long
after his country itself had died. When Croatia was re-
established as a sovereign state in 1991—even though it
adopted many of the same fascist icons as Pavelić—it was
with the recognition that modern Croatian society would
have to address the whole question of legitimacy and internal hierarchical validity which Pavelić failed to master.

If we have learned anything throughout human history
it is that everything is achieved because of the cooperation,
mutual need, and balanced tension between individuals
and societies—even between man and nature. For one society to ensure its prosperity—to achieve victory—in competition with another, the balance and tension between

leadership and society must be particularly finely tuned. When the balance between societies and leaders fails, nations fail.

Look at the nations which have risen and fallen in a single generation—not just the "Independent State of Croatia," but even the USSR and Yugoslavia, both states which lasted about seven decades, approximately the life expectancy of the average man. And look at the corporations which have done the same. Indeed, most U.S. start-up corporations fail within the first seven years; the average life of a corporation in Western Europe is only a dozen years. In many instances, they have had powerful leaders, but leaders who failed to create a bond with their societies in order to establish a lasting pattern of devolved responsibilities and leadership succession.

Much of the increasing "shortness of life" of corporations—as with nation-states and other societal bodies—has to do with the acceleration of all forms of social activity because of technology, the growth of urbanization and globalization, and the like. We have known since the 1960s that this was happening, but it is, nonetheless, significant to note the pace of change. The *Times* of London, on November 17, 2005, citing a 2005 study of corporate life expectancy in European economies, found that it had declined from forty-five to eighteen years in Germany; thirteen to nine years in France; and ten to four years in Great Britain.

Victory—whether societal or corporate—depends on leadership which is appropriate to the time. Good leadership is not always aggressive, but it must always strive to take action appropriate to the circumstances. This means that the compact between the instruments of society and the instruments of leadership must always be dynamic, in the sense that they can allow for the appropriate degree of strength, symbolism, and unity to face the needs of the day. Great consolidations of societal strength through scientific progress and mercantile gain are most often achieved in times of extreme competition when there is also a galvanized and often extreme sense of identity, but not necessarily under such extremities as might force a constraint of thinking or free action within societies, as the lessons of the Gutenberg revolution demonstrated.

An impoverished society, battered by history and deprived of power, can find its opening to victory through the epiphany of a single leader, whose vision may lay the foundations for future generations. Societies which have historically created and built wealth require less vision through which to sustain themselves, but, if they lack leadership for any protracted period, they can be rapidly undone by lack of vision. Leadership is the indispensable eye of victory, for all other vital aspects require the orchestration which only leadership can set in motion.

Societies, to survive, reject rulers, if they can, when those rulers do not have the collective survival at heart, or are heading down the wrong path in pursuing it. The Art of Victory lies in harmonizing leadership and society within the context of other societies. Most people are innately aware of the maxim cited by the T'ai Kung in the eleventh–twelfth century B.C.E.: "Fortune and misfortune lie with the ruler, not with the seasons of heaven." In more modern, complex societies, leaders who fail the society can often be removed by mechanisms such as elections. In societies which even today lack working mechanisms such as elections, leaders can for a time avoid removal by suppression of society, and inevitably in those societies it is the leader's failure to sustain a national victory which causes his downfall, rather than any spontaneous rising of the population against his tyranny.

Even in societies with election mechanisms, leaders and aspirants for leadership often manage to avoid rejection by effectively (if not consciously) treating their societies as enemies to be beguiled by the manipulation of imagery. Control of imagery has, in "democratic" societies, replaced the crude instruments of physical oppression. But when the victory of the society is challenged externally by a competing power, incapable leaders are often exposed for their weaknesses, and rejected.

Victory depends on every aspect of society; it is an interdependent phenomenon. The sinews of victory, therefore, are visceral and psychological, for there is no victory merely with the application of military force; no victory merely because of great leadership; no guarantee of continued victory merely because of great economic strength at a certain period; no guarantee of victory because of the piety of a society's citizens.

Victory is beyond the grasp of an individual. Even personal victory in a single human life depends upon the balance of strengths of an interdependent society. How much more complex, then, must it be to achieve and sustain victory for a society within the multigenerational, multidimensional continuum? And yet if all citizens are part of the victory of a society, it is critical that they all be made aware of their role in it, for the societies which have had the greatest success are those in which appropriate, timely contributions have come from members who have responded to the challenge unbidden and not motivated solely by thoughts of personal gain.

HIERARCHIES ARE TEAMWORK, AND THEY WILL CREATE OUR FUTURE LEADERS

One of the most instructive aspects of our current situation, with its flattening of hierarchical lines caused by globalization, computerization, new channels of mass communication, and rising wealth, is that every man is a king, answerable to no one, placing no one above himself. Who, then, can lead when no one will assign the function of unfettered leadership to another?

The answer is that new hierarchical structures *will* develop, because they are innate to nature. Where they do not, societies will collapse, and other societies will replace or absorb them. Therein—for those societies which eschew leadership—lies the loss of victory, or the failure to achieve it. This was the true cause of the collapse of the former Federal Socialist Republic of Yugoslavia: Upon the death of Tito, leadership devolved onto a collective presidency and a rotating leadership. That, at least, was a conscious effort to *assign* leadership in the absence of a leader acceptable to all the country's communal groups, but it was bound to failure.

What we are seeing in today's "flattened hierarchical society" is that a large element of society in most countries wants the fruits of victory without accepting the necessity for leadership. The very *mediums* of the new flattened social structure have gained stature by becoming the vehicles to criticize and destroy the old hierarchical structures. Marshall McLuhan once said that "the medium is the message." He was correct. It has become so. The media, once designed to *convey* messages (news and the information which indicates and confirms the structure of society), has become the instrument of power. As with collective leadership, this is a recipe for the frustration of unity and the destruction of national purpose.

And yet "freedom of the press" is meant to equate to democracy, with the ability of society to formulate and express its will to the leadership, and vice-versa. But what has happened is that it has, in fact, usurped the leadership, ceased to become the vehicle of communication between leaders and led, and has become a voice of advocacy. This is part of the process of revolutionary change on which we are now embarked, and merely reflects the leavening of the hierarchy. It does, however, leave society essentially separated from the leaders its citizens have chosen. Ultimately, then, the situation will change, either organically or by *diktat*, if those mostly Western societies are to survive as effective and victorious units.

Indeed, the major change which we already see in this regard is the greater lengths to which leaders must now go to indirectly bend the media to their message. Leaders must create images which the media cannot ignore. The process, then, becomes indirect and open to misinterpretation, and society is robbed of the clear communication it needs with and from its elected leaders. Little wonder, then, that most people find either the media or the political leadership untrustworthy. Leaders are forced to send messages, essentially with the indirectness of Javanese *wayang kulit* (shadow puppets); the media is using advocacy to shape the political debate.

It is significant that major threats, or crises, tend to dampen quarrels and cause people to rally around their kinsmen. Ayatollah Khomeini used just such a technique in 1982 when the querulous Iranian people were about to overthrow him; he diverted them by engaging in war with Iraq. President Bill Clinton used the same technique in the 1990s, creating a "national security emergency" by conjuring up—literally out of thin air and fabricated or distorted intelligence—a war against the Serbs in order to divert attention from the inquiries of the Cox Committee in Congress. The media and public followed the Pied Piper without a question. What this shows is that greater, rather than less, image manipulation will be used to govern electorates going forward. If it is not used, endless carping will merely weaken societies to the point of strategic vulnerability. And if it is used, the fabric of democracy will inevitably be cut and shaped according to professional manipulation.

All of this raises the question of what type of leadership will be necessary to successfully navigate the United States—and the West generally—through the growing chaos?

A NEW FORM OF SOCIETY AND SOVEREIGNTY

What we are seeing, then, is that a new form of society is emerging, and with it the need for leaders to understand the modalities of more fluid concepts of what determines the state, or the social framework. The old, static forms of sovereignty—and some of the mechanisms and rituals of governance of nation-states—are giving way to this new social construct. Populations, capital, ideas, concepts of identity, loyalties, and much more are now all mobile, transnational, and subject to change or constant redefinition.

Yet we can only live in one place at a time; geography does not change. Individuals cannot fulfill the functions of a society, and vice-versa. So it would be a mistake to think that everything we have built, layer upon layer since mankind emerged, will suddenly be irrelevant or changed in its fundamentals. On the contrary, it is the *context* which has given the appearance of change, so a knowledge of the building blocks of this context is critical.

Abandoning fundamentals in the belief that "super-industrialism"—or whatever we wish to call our new societal framework—is a *totally* new construct would be like deliberately discarding a map when entering a strange and complex landscape. Loyalties and group identities (such as nationalism and love of our familiar natural surroundings) will still exist, for example, simply because these provide the mechanisms by which we determine our horizons. It is *this* mosaic which, regardless of the pace of technological change, or the fashions of politics or dress, or the pressure of increasing population density, enables us to survive as a species. To survive, we still must reproduce; not only reproduce, but also nurture the welfare of our descendants.

This impels us, genetically, then, to pursue the goal of victory, even if we must periodically—as we must now—review what constitutes "the state." After all, the modalities of republicanism have scarcely changed in three thousand years. Neither have the rules of the mob. Nor the need for society to assign leadership.

The Age of Global Transformation has given us the opportunity to re-evaluate what history has given us and how we can shape our future. We have entered an Age of Opportunity.

EPILOGUE

The Art of Victory in the Age of Opportunity

R ough winds of our post–Nuclear Winter still shake the boughs of civilization, and Summer's abundant charms and calm are not yet near upon us. Global society's framework has been battered by the events of this current stormy era. Battered, but not destroyed. Humanity's jewels still glitter. Victory—the storehouse of these gems of wisdom, wealth, security, opportunity, culture—remains loose-grasped in the hands of what was once called "the West." It also now lies within sight and reach of all humanity.

"The West" itself has become a new and more amorphous entity, the "modern world" or "post-Western society," embracing more and more of humanity. And the more that post-Western civilization embraces formerly hostile peoples within its frame, the more its greater society is enriched. To achieve this, the framework of sovereignty and national hierarchical structures was leveled by the waves of technologies and human interaction after the Cold War. These waves first flooded the old impediments in the East, removing governments, hierarchies, values, and beliefs. They then began to erode the coastline of the West, leaving structures such as governments intact, but washing away centuries of social hierarchical construction. Everywhere, the constraints which gave us all our place and options in life were removed, or weakened, by the global revolution, and the way cleared for all individuals and societies throughout the world to achieve or rebuild victory.

The Age of Global Transformation thus begins to give way to the Age of Opportunity.

In reaching the Epilogue of *The Art of Victory* we have also begun the Prologue of our new era. We have looked back over the life of humanity during the past few thousands of years and then into some aspects of our future. Our context has changed and promises still further change. But the unbroken thread of human development continues to provide the foundation of what we do, and how we cope.

But transformation is a chaotic business, involving—as we have seen—the destruction of many old pillars of our lives. Change brings uncertainty, and uncertainty generates fear. Fear itself generates hostility and strong reactions. But we will see, gradually, new certainties arise in our social structures and national frameworks. We will see, surprisingly, that many of the familiar landmarks and icons have survived, some reburnished and refreshingly adaptable to our future.

We have already been washed over by the tides of change, and have emerged fresh, strong, and with the assets to rebuild the world better than before. Our assets are the twin and inseparable tools of wisdom and its creation, technology. Both have been built in an accretion of layers since man first walked upright.

Dismiss the belief that "modern technology" has dispensed with all the old ways. "Modern technology" has its origin in the primal steps of mankind, going back perhaps one hundred millennia into history and prehistory. Buried within our capacity to undertake today, for example, engineering at a molecular level is the original development of the human skill to coordinate the use of thumb and forefinger and thus to be able to strike rock against wood to create a spear. And physical tools cannot be separated from the intellectual and emotional tools we have developed over this timeframe. Yet we see people grasping modern manufactured products, the deep origins of which they do not understand, and thinking such physical possession makes them powerful. Or others, wallowing in the richness of inexplicable financial wealth, believing that their wealth has made them wise.

How could we forget what has built the present victory of the modern world? Generations of stability—or of any form of constancy, including constant war—cause lessons of other times, other situations, to disappear into myth. Long Summers of tranquility and wealth allow the searing lessons of the past to slip away, and, when crisis comes, few understand what the adrenaline demands of us.

Within post-Western civilization we see the old, core Western societies—North America and Western Europe— caught in the increasing vortex of technological and social change, and failing to see the need to reassert the long-held victory of their societies. We see the new members of post-Western civilization, the memories still fresh of the collapse of their states and values, keen to grasp victory.

Outside post-Western civilization we see the recognition that many societies have yet to achieve victory, but know that they must strive for it. Out of frustration and fear, there are large elements within these societies who believe that they must at least remove the security and wealth of victory from the undeserving of the West, who seem not to value it. Those who covet the West's wealth and victory, or would destroy it rather than seek their own victory, are right: Many in the West *do* fail to value, or to be prepared to defend, the victory their forebears constructed.

So there are still wars *within* post-Western civilization to define the future of societies which have been created through an amalgam of Judeo-Christian, Hindu, Buddhist, Confucian, Muslim, and other religious-intellectual beliefs. And there is war *within* Islam for command of the future of the Muslim *ummah*. The raging storms within modernism and Islam are separate turmoils.

The clashes now underway between extreme elements of Islam and post-Western civilization are, in many respects, peripheral and incidental; they serve as *diversions* to the societies of each bloc, distracting each from the business of defining the new world.

And in all societies we define that new world using the tools with which mankind has always defined its place in nature: the fundamental principles of human organization achieved through leadership, beliefs, communication, competition, and security. We had forgotten these fundamentals, to a large extent, or failed to restate them in relation to our modern context.

The major trends which we see emerging—from the growth of China and India to the use of space, and the changes in energy technologies and dependencies—are all coming into perspective. There will be many variations in these trends, and newer, unexpected trends as well. Our concepts of sovereignty will change, and with it will change economic modalities and opportunities. We have seen change before, as we discussed at the beginning of this book, and it will come in faster and more comprehensive waves.

It is the innate knowledge of who we are—as individuals and as members of societies—which will enable us to cope with the change and maintain our identity and direction during the present and anticipated period of societal restructuring. Rudyard Kipling put it all on a personal level when he said, *"If you can keep your head when all about you / Are losing theirs . . . Yours is the Earth and everything that's in it, And—which is more—you'll be a Man my son!"*

The Art of Victory entails the employment of the embedded laws of nature and human experience to meet challenges to the survival and progress of the species. The knowledge, pride, and delight in the experiences and great achievements of our forebears do not, when we understand the beauty of the flowering of humanity, leave us yearning for the past, but for the future. The maxims by which mankind has achieved its position in nature are the keys of human learning to open for us the doors to the future of our choosing.

BIBLIOGRAPHY

The following are some of the seminal works referenced in this book, although the author acknowledges the impact of many additional sources of input.

Akaev, Askar. *Kyrgyz Statehood and the National Epos "Manas."* English-language edition, New York: Global Scholarly Publications, 2003.

———. *Looking to the Future With Optimism; Reflections on Foreign Policy and the Universe.* New York: Global Scholarly Publications, 2004.

Bloodworth, Dennis, and Ching Ping. *The Chinese Machiavelli: 3,000 Years of Chinese Statecraft.* New York: Farrar, Straus & Giroux, 1976.

Bobbitt, Philip. *The Shield of Achilles: War, Peace, and the Course of History.* New York: Alfred A. Knopf, 2002.

Bodansky, Yossef. *Bin Laden, The Man Who Declared War on America.* Roseville, Calif.: Forum/Prima, 1999.

———. *The High Cost of Peace: How Washington's Middle East Policy Left America Vulnerable to Terrorism.* Roseville, Calif.: Forum/Prima, 2002.

———. *The Secret History of the Iraq War.* New York: Regan Books division of HarperCollins, 2004.

Canetti, Elias. *Crowds & Power.* New York: Continuum, 1981. Originally published by Claassen Verlag, Hamburg, in 1960 as *Masse und Macht.*

Clausewitz, Carl von. *On War.* Berlin, 1832. Also the translation published under the title *War, Politics and Power,* translated and edited by Edward M. Collins, Col., USAF, and published in 1964 by Regnery Gateway, Chicago. This includes *On War,* and a translation by Stefan Possony of Clausewitz's *I Believe and Profess.*

Clemenceau, Georges. *Demosthenes*. Translation by Charles Miner Thomson. Cambridge, Mass.: Houghton Mifflin, 1926.

Copley, Brian Wallie Earl. *The Copley Family in England*. Perth, Western Australia: unpublished manuscript, 1991.

Copley, Gregory R. *Defense & Foreign Affairs Handbook on Egypt*. Washington, D.C.: International Media Corporation, 1995.

———. *Defense & Foreign Affairs Handbook*. Washington, D.C., and London: International Strategic Studies Association. Various editions, 1976–2006.

———. *Ethiopia Reaches Her Hand unto God: Imperial Ethiopia's Unique Symbols, Structures and Rôle in the Modern World*. Alexandria, Va.: International Strategic Studies Association, 1998.

Crozier, Brian. *A Theory of Conflict*. New York: Charles Scribner's Sons, 1974.

Gladwell, Malcolm. *The Tipping Point: How Little Things Can Make a Big Difference*. New York: Little Brown, 2000.

Hobbes, Thomas. *Leviathan*. New York: Norton, 1997. Originally published 1651.

Hoffer, Eric. *The True Believer: Thoughts on the Nature of Mass Movements*. New York: Perennial Library, Harper & Row, 1951.

Howard, Michael. *Clausewitz*. Oxford: Oxford University Press, 1983.

Kagan, Robert. *Of Paradise and Power*. New York: Alfred A. Knopf, 2003.

Kellas, James G. *The Politics of Nationalism and Ethnicity*. New York: St. Martin's Press, 1991 and 1998.

LeBon, Gustave. *The Crowd: A Study of the Popular Mind*. New York: Viking, 1960. Our edition, New York: Macmillan, 1896.

Liddell-Hart, Sir Basil H. *Strategy*. London: Faber & Faber, 1954 (revised in 1967). In the United States: Frederick A. Praeger, New York.

———. *Memoirs*, vols. I and II. London: Cassell, 1965.

Lorenz, Konrad. "Ritualized Fighting," in *The Natural History of Aggression*. London and New York: Academic Press, 1966.

Machiavelli, Niccolò. *The Prince*. The translation by George Bull, first published, London: Penguin, 1961.

————. *The Discourses*. London: Penguin, 1969.

Mackenzie, Compton. *Marathon & Salamis*. Edinburgh: Peter Davies, 1934.

Mahan, Alfred Thayer. *The Influence of Sea Power Upon History, 1660–1783*. Originally published in the United States in 1890. Twelfth edition, published by Little, Brown.

Malthus, Thomas Robert. *An Essay on the Principle of Population*. New York: Norton, 1976. Edition edited by Philip Appleman. Originally published 1798.

Man, John. *The Gutenberg Revolution*. London: Headline Book Publishing division of Hodder Headline, 2002.

Manfredi, Valerio Massimo. *The Last Legion* (fiction). London: Macmillan, 2003.

Milward, Alan S. *War, Economy and Society, 1939–1945*. Berkeley, Calif.: University of California Press, 1977.

Naisbitt, John, and Aburdene, Patricia. *Megatrends 2000*: Ten New Directions for the 1990s. New York: Avon Books, 1990.

O'Connell, Robert L. *Ride of the Second Horseman: The Birth and Death of War*. New York: Oxford University Press, 1995.

Olson, Steve. *Mapping Human History: Genes, Race, and Our Common Origins*. New York: Mariner/Houghton Mifflin, 2003.

Possony, Stefan T. *Lenin, The Compulsive Revolutionary*. U.S. edition, Henry Regnery Company, 1964. London: George Allen & Unwin, 1966.

————. "Organized Intelligence: the Problem of the French General Staff," in *Social Research*. New York: May 1941.

————. *Tomorrow's War: Its Planning, Management and Cost*. English edition, London: William Hodge, 1938.

————. various works, within *Defense & Foreign Affairs* publications, and separately.

Possony, Stefan T., and Pournelle, J. E. *The Strategy of Technology: Winning the Decisive War*. Cambridge, Mass.: University Press of Cambridge, 1970.

Sargant, William. *Battle for the Mind: A Physiology of Conversion and Brainwashing.* London: William Heinemann, 1957.

Sawyer, Ralph D. (translator). *The Seven Military Classics of Ancient China.* Boulder, Colo.: Westview Press, 1993.

Sumption, Jonathan: *The Albigensian Crusade.* London: Faber & Faber, 1978.

Sun-tzu. *The Art of War.* Particularly the 1910 edition, translated and with notes by Lionel Giles. Many publishers have produced this work; our copy printed anonymously in Taipei, undated. Also, New York: Barnes & Noble (Classic Series), 2004.

Taft, Robert A. *A Foreign Policy for Americans.* New York: Doubleday, 1951.

Taylor, A. J. P. *Bismarck, the Man and the Statesman.* New York: Vintage Books division of Alfred A. Knopf, 1955.

Toffler, Alvin. *Future Shock.* New York: Random House, 1970.

Waltz, Kenneth N. *Man, the State and War: A Theoretical Analysis.* New York: Columbia University Press, 1959 and 2002.

Watson, Peter. *War on the Mind: The Military Uses and Abuses of Psychology.* New York: Basic Books, 1978.

Weatherford, Jack. *Genghis Khan and the Making of the Modern World.* New York: Crown Publishers division of Random House, 2004.

ACKNOWLEDGMENTS

I t is true and right that success should have a thousand parents while failure remains an orphan. Any success in the development of thoughts and concepts stems from the accretion of ideas contributed by a diverse array of minds. Failure is the result of the individual being unable to properly assimilate and develop those contributions. So it can be said that any success which this work has in developing and conveying new and provocative ideas is directly the result of many years of discussion with friends and acquaintances, and any failure in this regard is my own.

As this text is the result of decades of listening to accounts of other people's experiences, there are too many individuals to acknowledge and thank properly. Many people, I am sure, influenced my thinking without my being fully aware of it. But there are some whose outstanding wisdom and perception were invaluable to shaping this study. Among them, principally, are my father, Brian Wallie Earl Copley, a man of such fine intellectual balance that I still marvel each day at his lessons; Dr. Stefan Thomas Possony, one of whose great contemporaries called him "the greatest strategic philosopher of the twentieth century," although his work was even wider-reaching than that, and who for more than twenty years guided me, taught me, reprimanded me, and inspired me. And then Maxwell Newton, one of the greatest political economists of the twentieth century, and yet still little-known, whom I had the pleasure of knowing as a friend and colleague for several decades. And Miles Copeland, Sr., a U.S. intelligence officer whose perceptiveness and wit made him an oddity in his profession. All of these great teachers are now gone, and I can only hope to make their thoughts live on with this work.

Among those who continue to inspire and provoke I must especially thank Dr. Assad Homayoun, a great strategic thinker, diplomat, Iranian nationalist, colleague, and close friend of many decades. In addition to his great strategic insight, it was Assad who kept bringing books and philosophies to my attention. If there is any justice for the world, and particularly for the Iranian people, this great man—a statesman without his state—will one day help lead his country back to the greatness which history has shown the Persian civilization can give to mankind.

Another of my closest friends who contributed to the development of this book was Yossef Bodansky, a strategist, analyst, historian, provocateur, and relentless researcher who is unique in his field (as well as being an outstanding colleague, a close friend, and a U.S. national treasure in his role as an author and former director of the U.S. House of Representatives Task Force on Terrorism & Unconventional Warfare). It is difficult to go a day without the intellectual stimulus and support I receive from Bodansky and Homayoun; history will acknowledge them.

As well, I must thank my old friend, General Alexander M. Haig, Jr., for taking the time to read early drafts of the manuscript and offering valuable suggestions. Alexander Haig is one of the few modern statesmen to have grasped the great concepts of strategy and history; he was too often, like the teacher we shared, Stefan Possony, surrounded by short-term thinkers, who failed to give broader and more selfless leaders the room or scope to achieve all that could have been achieved.

There have also been friends with whom I have worked for many years and whose actions and philosophies I was able to study. Among these are such outstanding individuals as my great friend Lieutenant General Aliyu Mohammed, the national security adviser to the president of Nigeria (and former army commander); Sir Charles Court, former premier of Western Australia, who—had circumstances been different—could have been the greatest prime minister in Australian history, but nonetheless contributed enormously to Australian and international progress, apart from his role as friend to both my parents and me; and my friend and inspiration President Dr. Askar Akaev, the founding president of the Kyrgyz Republic and Father of the Kyrgyz Nation, for highlighting the importance of cultural identity and passion in leadership. So many great people have inspired, assisted, and befriended me in my quest of the past half-century: Field Marshal Mohammed Abdelhalim Abu Ghazala, the former defense minister of Egypt and Egypt's great soldier-statesman; Elkana Galli, onetime journalist and former political adviser to Israeli prime minister David Ben Gurion; Kim Beazley, the former defense minister and deputy prime minister (and currently opposition leader) in Australia and, indeed, one of the best defense ministers in Australia's history (and certainly one who understood history and strategy like no other); the late shah of Iran, who, although forgotten by history since 1979, was a greater strategic intellect than most of his peers on the world stage; Vice Admiral Ko Tun-hwa, the former vice minister of defense of Taiwan and a great strategist; former Fijian prime minister (and soldier-statesman) Major General Sitiveni Rabuka; the late president of Pakistan, Mohammed Zia ul-Haq; the Right Honorable Sir Geoffrey Pattie, former british minister of defense; and the late Viscount Younger, British prime minister Margaret Thatcher's secretary of state for defense. I am also grateful for the continued advice and friendship of Prince Ermias Sahle-Selassie Haile-Selassie, whose work with me on my Ethiopian book contributed so much to forming my beliefs on victory as it applied throughout the development of Ethiopian society.

I would like to pay special tribute, too, to Australia's outstanding head of state, the governor-general, Major General Michael Jeffery, the former commander and constant patron of the Australian Special Air Services Regiment, and currently patron of Future Directions International (FDI), Australia's center for strategic analysis. General Jeffery, a good and inspiring friend, has a great sense of what victory entails.

As well, I am happy to thank Geoffrey Hazzan, whose breadth of thinking and knowledge of history is always so welcome, and whose insightful comments during the preparation of this manuscript proved extremely helpful. His inspiring wife, Dr. Joan Vernikos-Hazzan, author and former director of life sciences at NASA, also provided great stimulation for this book.

Linda K. Bridges, one of the great editors of New York, used her incredible skills to make the original drafts of the academic version of *The Art of Victory* manuscript readable; she has the breadth of knowledge to debate the finer points of strategic, political, and social philosophy, and applied considerable thought to this project. Through her, I met the most redoubtable of literary agents, Alexander Hoyt, who proved both an inspiration and the great facilitator of the publication of this book. Through Alex Hoyt I was given the wonderful opportunity to work with Simon & Schuster's Threshold Editions' editor-in-chief Mary Matalin, Pocket Books publisher Louise Burke, and editor Kevin Smith.

Other colleagues, such as former Royal Marine Bill Carr, and a number of others, also contributed considerably to my understanding of military strategy.

Of course, I leave a special place to acknowledge the vital contribution of my family, including my mother, Marjorie, and brother, Howard, for their strong roles in shaping my outlook and ability to debate issues. As was the case with my late father, they exemplify the qualities of loyalty and generous love. And I particularly acknowledge my wife, companion, and colleague of three decades, Pamela, whose fierce loyalty inspires me to be the best that I can be, and without whom nothing is possible for me.

INDEX

terrorism and, 138–39, 141–42, 151
India, 31, 45, 68, 101, 113–15, 251, 269, 279
individuals
belief systems and, 86, 87, 90
cooperation and, 83, 299–300
democracy and, 201–3, 205–6, 207
focus on entrepreneur and, 71
interdependence of, 216, 302
responsibility and, 202, 205–6, 259–64, 286, 294
sense of victory within, 39–40
Iran
ballistic missiles of, 12
belief systems and, 92–93
challenge of, 78–79
China and, 228
geopolitical power and, 76–77, 116, 117, 232–33, 234
Islamist jihadists and, 44
military strength of, 280, 292
national defenses of, 276
oil and, 101–2, 227, 295
terrorism and, 149
warfare and, 68–69, 81–82
Iraq, 82, 263–64
Iraq War, 111–12, 215, 234, 263–64, 295
Islamist jihadists, 15, 43–44, 58–59, 90–92, 132, 233–34, 257, 269, 282, 287, 292–93
Israel, 56, 81, 92, 142, 227

Japan, 38, 57, 65–66, 103, 115, 118, 125–26, 256, 297

Khomeini, Ayatollah Ruhollah, 82, 174, 189, 194–95, 304

leadership
attainment of, 174
challenges and, 113
clarity of, 62
crowd leadership, 199–200
democracy and, 192, 198, 201–3, 208, 286
elemental type of, 57
emotional/objective functions of, 99
enhancement of, 100
generalist nature of, 272
heroic, 198–99
history and, 183
incremental path to, 96, 110
leader/led relationship, 200, 209, 211–14, 216
legitimacy of, 88, 181, 182, 194, 284
need for victory and, 53
passion of, 191–95
perceptions of, 197–209
planning and, 167–68
power positions and, 176, 206
primal qualities of, 108
process-driven, 112
psychological strategy and, 121, 123
society and, 213, 299–304
strategic leadership, 186–89
strengths of, 249, 294, 299–306
terrorism and, 141
transition in, 37, 51, 199, 212–13, 300
true leader, 183–89
warfare and, 68
LeBon, Gustave, 74, 81, 88, 192, 199–200, 213
legitimacy, 88, 173–82, 194, 284
loyalty, 215–23, 225–28, 284, 288–89, 305

Printed in the United States
By Bookmasters